S. D. BURMAN
The World of His Music

S. D. BURMAN
The World of His Music

Khagesh Dev Burman

*Translated from the Bengali by the author
and* S. K. Ray Chaudhuri

RUPA

Published by
Rupa Publications India Pvt. Ltd 2013
7/16, Ansari Road, Daryaganj
New Delhi 110002

Sales centres:
Allahabad Bengaluru Chennai
Hyderabad Jaipur Kathmandu
Kolkata Mumbai

Copyright © Khagesh Dev Burman 2013

Pages 289-91 are an extension of the copyright page.

All rights reserved.
No part of this publication may be reproduced, transmitted, or stored in a retrieval system, in any form or by any means, electronic, mechanical, photocopying, recording or otherwise, without the prior permission of the publisher.

ISBN: 978-81-291-2063-2

10 9 8 7 6 5 4 3 2 1

The moral right of the author has been asserted.

Typeset in Lapidary333BT 12/15.5

Printed by Replika Press Pvt. Ltd, Haryana

This book is sold subject to the condition that it shall not, by way of trade or otherwise, be lent, resold, hired out, or otherwise circulated, without the publisher's prior consent, in any form of binding or cover other than that in which it is published.

Dedicated to the memory of
Sangeetacharya Kumar Sachindra Chandra Dev Burman
with love and respect

Contents

Preface   ix

1. The Background   1
2. Comilla: 1906-24   11
3. Calcutta: 1925-31   26
4. Calcutta: 1932-44   43
5. Bombay: 1944-75   73

Epilogue   205

Appendix I: Chronology of Life   217
Appendix II: List of Songs of S. D. Burman as Singer   226
Appendix III: List of Songs of S. D. Burman as Music Director   236
               (Bengali Films)
Appendix IV: List of Songs of S. D. Burman as Music Director   245
               (Hindi Films)

Acknowledgements   289

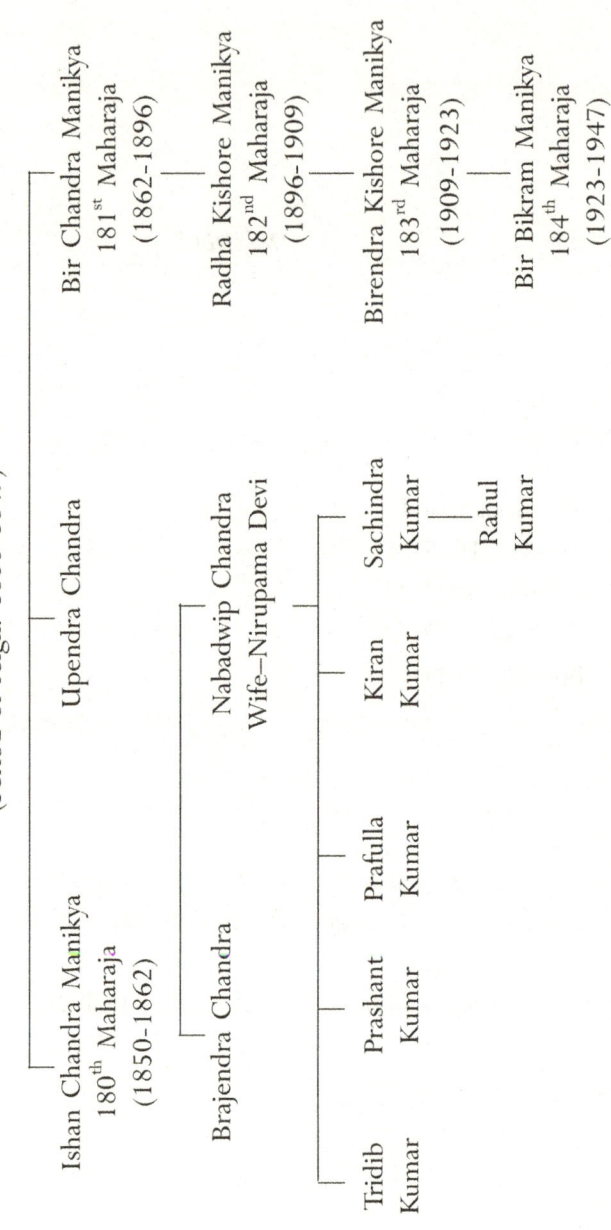

Preface

Music was the leitmotif of Sangeetacharya Kumar Sachin Dev Burman's world. All aspects of his life were tuned to the world of music he created. What I have attempted in this book is an analysis of his multifaceted musical talent and its contribution, and in the process, I have cast a look at how music shaped his life. I am not a connoisseur of music and in my attempt to discuss Sachin-karta's music, depending solely upon my sense of hearing, I may have missed many a finer point and made many mistakes. I beg the indulgence of experts for the same.

This book is the first attempt at a chronological analysis of the master's music in the English language.

Sachin-karta's music is like the elixir of life. It sends a delightful shiver through the body and mind. It resonates with the flavour of life and raises a storm in the deep recesses of the hearts of listeners. The irresistible strains of the flute—dakatiar banshi (dacoit's flute)—captivate one's heart.

The novelty of his songs creates an unparalleled sensation amongst one and all, high and low. Sachin-karta presented ragas through folk music and folk music through ragas, without distorting them, to bring about a delectable harmony of rural and urban sounds. What set his music apart was his style. It is easy to comprehend but impossible to imitate, full of the aroma of rain-sprinkled earth. His music is soaked with a sweetness which attracts everyone, induces one and all to shed all inhibition and sing; music which can never die.

Many of Sachin's contemporary musicians have been forgotten. What is it about his music that keeps people spellbound even today? The answer is life. Like flowers falling to the ground from a tree in full bloom, his music rains on the senses, curing listeners of afflictions and sorrows, and filling them with an inner joy. Like Rabindra Sangeet, Sachin's music is clearly discernible. It has its own tradition.

It has been my long-standing desire to write a book on Sachin-karta. What I have attempted in this book is to bring out the unity in his life and music. This account of the maestro's life is based on exhaustive research into his oeuvre and I hope I have been able to document the history of the man and his life in music well.

Sachin Dev Burman wrote his autobiography *Sargamer Nikhad* in 1970 which was published in the Bengali journal *Desh*. For close to forty years, this has remained unnoticed. In order to satisfy the longing of his many admirers, I have quoted extensively from *Sargamer Nikhad* in this book.

I gratefully acknowledge the contribution of Debashish Mukhopadhyay, Sanjoy Sengupta, Ujjal Nandi and *Screen*. It will not be enough to say that the book has benefitted from their inputs. If it indeed becomes a collector's item, it is in no small measure due to the sheer volume of data they provided. Merely conveying my thanks will only be demeaning their contribution.

Sumita Dev Burman has been a source of constant encouragement. It is meaningless to convey my gratitude to one who has tolerated me, my entire personality all along, with whatever good or bad it contains.

All my efforts will be considered a success only if readers accept this book with love.

Khagesh Dev Burman
Kolkata

1
The Background

S. D. Burman was not born with the royal insignia. It came to him through providence which in its own whimsical way also deprived him of it. There are a few fortunate ones who are born to royalty. At the same time, some are not apparently destined to ascend the throne. There are examples galore of this in the royal dynasty of Tripura. The throne should rightfully have come to Sachin's father, Nabadwip Chandra Bahadur. But by a cruel twist of fate, he not only lost his throne but was also exiled to British-controlled Comilla, the headquarters of Chakla Roshanabad, a zamindari of the royal family of Tripura. The man who became king was Sachin's uncle, Bikramaditya Maharaja Bir Chandra Manikya. After Bir Chandra, the crown adorned the head of his son Radha Kishore.

Nabadwip Chandra's misfortune cast a deep shadow on the life of his son Sachin Chandra too. In order to understand certain traits of his personality and character, it is essential to know this side of the story of the royal family. The contrast in Sachin's manner in Tripura and Comilla—barefoot but endowed with the gift of the gab in Comilla but quiet and reserved in Tripura—shows two aspects of his personality and above all the development of his creative talent. This was the outcome of the internal feud in the royal family. Acharya Dineshchandra Sen has written in his *Brihat Banga*, 'Of all the princely states in India, the Tripura dynasties are the oldest. In no other dynasty can we find the chronology of 184 kings starting from the ancient times.'

Tripura was ruled continuously (barring a few years under Shamser Ghazi) by 184 generations of kings from AD 590 to AD 1949 (Tripura Era 1359). The annals of the Tripura kings describe them as Chandravanshi Kshatriyas. They are said to have descended from the Pandavas. In that case, the Tripura kingdom was founded much before AD 590. The kingdom of Tripura was not limited to its present area of 4,116 square miles. It extended to vast tracts of Assam, Arakan and Bengal. Even at the time of the Partition in 1947, East Bengal's Chakla Roshanabad was acknowledged as the zamindari of the king of Tripura, even though it was British-occupied territory.

Nabadwip Chandra's misfortune resulted from the dispute over the control of this property at Chakla Roshanabad. This zamindari encompassed a total land area of 395,631 acres, divided into four parts—Southern Division (79,502 acres with its headquarters at Feni), Central Division (146,186 acres with its headquarters at Comilla), Northern Division (140,943 acres with its headquarters at Mogra) and Sylhet Division (29,000 acres with its headquarters at Laharpur). Records show that the British government accepted the rights of the Tripura maharaja but not his sovereignty. Sheer negligence on the part of both the Tripura government and the Congress government at the provincial levelled Hindu-majority Chakla Roshanabad to become part of Pakistan in 1947.

In order to understand Sachin's world of music, it is imperative to understand why someone destined to be born at the Ujjayanta Palace in Agartala was born at Comilla, the cultural centre of Chakla Roshanabad. It can be said without a trace of doubt that had he not been born at Comilla, there would have been no Sangeetacharya Sachin Dev Burman. At best, we would have had a powerful bureaucrat with expertise in music.

The history of the royal family of Tripura records that after the death of Maharaja Krishna Kishore Manikya in 1849, Ishan Chandra Manikya, the 180th king in the royal lineage, ascended the throne in 1850. At the time of the coronation itself, Ishan Chandra, deviating from the custom of declaring sons as princes, proclaimed his brother Upendra Chandra as prince and gave the title of barthakur (eldest prince) to his son Brajendra Chandra. A series of unusual incidents occurred within about two years of Ishan Chandra's coronation—a revolt by his subjects, an attack on the Dewanbari (the finance minister's house), a conspiracy to dethrone and kill the king and the death of Prince Upendra Chandra. The palace turned into a hotbed of intrigues. Immediately after his coronation, Ishan Chandra had started building a palace at Agartala and was planning to shift the capital there (earlier the capital was at Puran Agartala or Old Agartala). But as luck would have it, the king suffered a severe paralytic stroke in 1861 and was rendered completely immobile.

His father Krishna Kishore had left behind a debt of eleven lakh rupees. The treasury was empty. In his autobiography, *Abarjaner Jhuri*, Nabadwip Chandra has detailed the king's financial plight thus:

> The other day, father completed his daily worship and was explaining the need for a few small amounts of expenditure to a court employee amounting to a few paisas. The man

hesitated and submitted that even those few paisas were not available in the treasury. (*Abarjaner Jhuri*)

In this troubled condition of the state, Maharaja Ishan Chandra, in spite of the insistence of his inner circle of advisors, did not risk the lives of his children by proclaiming Brajendra Chandra prince and Nabadwip Chandra barthakur. He decided to maintain the status quo till he got well.

But he never recovered. Ishan Chandra passed away on 1 August 1862, a day after shifting into the new palace at Agartala. But misfortune never comes alone. In Nabadwip Chandra's words:

> I woke up early in the morning to a din and bustle in the palace and cries of sorrow. Dada [Brajendra Chandra] had been suffering from cholera and was no more. The sudden death of father the same day delayed the shraddh ceremony. After the inauspicious period [of the father's death] passed, I had to perform the shraddh ceremony of both father and brother. (*Abarjaner Jhuri*)

After the death of Prince Upendra Chandra and Barthakur Brajendra Chandra, the throne was legitimately due to Nabadwip Chandra, who was a child at that time. What came in the way was the robekari (a royal proclamation issued and notified for general information of the subjects throughout the state) dated 31 July 1862, a day prior to Ishan Chandra's death. In this order, Ishan Chandra had proclaimed brother Bir Chandra as prince, Brajendra Chandra as barthakur and Nabadwip Chandra as karta.

Bir Chandra's stepbrothers, Kumar Chakradhwaj and Kumar Neelakrishna, declared this order a forgery and filed a petition in the civil court for establishing their rights over the zamindari of Chakla Roshanabad. In the absence of proper evidence and witnesses, the order could not be established as forged and the high court declared Bir Chandra the maharaja of Tripura. The privy council upheld the high court order and Bir Chandra ascended the throne.

In his famous book *Rajmala ba Tripurar Itihas*, Kailash Chandra Singha has called the robekari a document of deceit and conspiracy. He has made many allegations against Maharaja Bir Chandra Manikya, none of which would be proved true in later years. Nabadwip Chandra himself never alleged any mental or physical torture at the hands of Bir Chandra in his autobiography. Besides, it may be noted that immediately upon coronation, Ishan Chandra appointed his brother Upendra Chandra prince. As such, as per rules, after the death of Ishan Chandra, Upendra Chandra would have become the king had he been alive. Thus the appointment of Bir Chandra as prince was in keeping with the initial order of Ishan Chandra. There is also nothing wrong in Bir Chandra appointing his son Radha Kishore prince. It is not a measure of his weakness resulting from blind love for his son but merely the way royal succession functions.

Nabadwip Chandra became the first karta in the Tripura royal family through his father's robekari. Since then, all rajkumars have been designated kartas. Till date, the male descendants are known as karta and the female descendants' husbands are known as thakur in the royal family of Tripura. Prior to this contentious robekari, everybody used to be known as thakur. Even in Ishan Chandra's robekari, son Brajendra Chandra and brother Bir Chandra have been mentioned as thakurs. The title of karta was created by this very robekari. And this is how Kumar Sachin Dev Burman became Sachin-karta.

Let us now visualize his uncle, Maharaja Bir Chandra, through the eyes of Nabadwip Chandra. It is undeniable that he had accepted the ascension of his uncle to the throne. What he could not accept was the declaration of his cousin Radha Kishore as prince. There was a hope, however subdued, that noble-hearted Bir Chandra would nominate him as the successor to the throne. But that did not come about. Nabadwip Chandra's last hopes were dashed in September 1870, when Bir Chandra appointed his son Radha Kishore prince. Nabadwip Chandra wrote:

> About a year later, on 27 Phalgun 1279 (Tripura Era), Lord Ulick Browne, commissioner of Chattagram, in his capacity as the representative of the British government, confirmed the ascension to the throne of Tripura by Maharaja Bir Chandra Manikya[…] As a sequel to this, a deep schism developed between uncle and me. The estrangement was so severe and intense that after a few months, in the month of Ashadh (June-July) 1280 (Tripura Era), I left the kingdom of Tripura with my mother. (*Abarjaner Jhuri*)

Beset with financial hardships, Nabadwip Chandra filed a suit in AD 1874 seeking declaration of Ishan Chandra's robekari as forged, claiming inheritance to the throne and rights over Chakla Roshanabad, besides a regular maintenance allowance. The order dated 25 February 1875, in Suit No. 35-1874, *Rajkumar Nabadwip Deb* v. *Maharaja Bir Chandra Manikya, Radha Kishore Thakur and 11 ors.*, in the Court of F. C. Vowel Esq., judge, Tripura, laid down the following:

1. Nabadwip Chandra could have claimed the throne had he been appointed prince or barthakur under orders of Ishan Chandra Manikya.
2. As Maharaja Bir Chandra is the de jure maharaja, it is well within his right to nominate his legitimate son as the prince.

3. The robekari could not be proved false by the plaintiff. Besides, the plaintiff has himself informed the commissioner of Chattagram in his own submission that the defendant was declared prince by the plaintiff's father. Even the plaintiff's mother and other witnesses had accepted the fact of the defendant having been nominated prince in the earlier suit filed by Neelakrishna.
4. The property at Chakla Roshanabad is accepted as the zamindari of the de jure king of Tripura. Nobody else can claim any right over the same.
5. During the pendency of the suit by Neelakrishna, Bir Chandra was functioning as the de facto king. Based on the judgment of the privy council dated 15 March 1869, Bir Chandra Manikya became the de jure king on 9 March 1870, with the approval of the British government.

The high court's verdict read—'The king of Tripura is a sovereign king. This court does not have the jurisdiction to deliberate on such a suit against him.'

The suit was filed in the British court because Chakla Roshanabad was in British territory and the case was also related to ownership of the same. Judge Mr Vowel read his verdict as under:

> Should the plaintiff be entitled to a decree for the Lands in British territory, the Raja defendant may say to him, 'Very well, you take the zamindaris and I will keep the Raj. You cannot enforce your decree against me as far as the possession of the throne is concerned and the lands comprising independent Tipperah and I do not intend to give them up.' The Raja might very well say this and of course, our court could not interfere in any way. The determination of the question of title to the throne would,

so far as this court is concerned be only an incidental one, affecting the rights to the lands in British territory only, and which part of the decree I am of the opinion, this court would have full power to enforce. The Raja, I consider in every way a subject of British India in regard to these lands. (*Abarjaner Jhuri*)

Despite the unfavourable court order, the intercession of the ex-chief secretary of the Bengal government, Mr Peacock, led to the grant of a monthly allowance of ₹525 to Kumar Nabadwip Chandra by Maharaja Bir Chandra. The palatial haveli at Chartha in Comilla and a part of the jagir also came to Nabadwip Chandra as a favour from the maharaja and he never had to face any financial hardship. But he never set foot in Agartala during the reign of cousin Radha Kishore. However, he could not resist nephew Maharaja Birendra Kishore Manikya's appeal. He adorned the mantle of the premier in 1909 and remained so till his death in 1931.

Even during the lawsuits, Nabadwip Chandra asserted in the court that Maharaja Bir Chandra had maintained him well as his guardian. He had an abiding respect for his uncle. It will not be unfair to say that Bir Chandra was the first modern thinker among all Tripura kings. He had an artistic bent of mind and was well conversant with Urdu, Sanskrit and Bengali. He had great proficiency in music and poetry, as revealed in the lyrics he wrote and songs he composed. His work, both with the camera and on canvas, was almost unparalleled. His court was adorned by scholars and ustads like Jadu Bhatta, Qasim Ali Khan, Nisar Hussein, Qalandar Baksh, Kehsab Mitra, Panchanan Mitra, Bholanath Basu, Kshetra Mitra and many others. Above all else, he was the first to recognize Rabindranath Tagore as Bengal's greatest poet. In Rabindranath's own words:

Bhagnahriday was published in 1881. One fine morning Minister Radharaman Ghosh of Tripura visited Jorasanko. He said that Maharaj Bir Chandra had recognized me as 'shreshthakobi' [great poet]. I was young at the time with not many writings to my credit. Most of the readers used to ridicule them as juvenile. Whatever fame I acquired in later life, it was he who marked its beginning through his congratulatory message. One who is at the peak can easily see things not seen by others. Similarly, Bir Chandra also clearly saw in me what was not clear till then. (*Rabindranath 'O Tripura*)

It was Bir Chandra who first tried to modernize Tripura. In his autobiography, Nabadwip Chandra has paid glowing tributes to his uncle. In the light of the fact that he does not denigrate his uncle even once in his autobiography, on the contrary speaking highly of him, it stands to reason that Kailash Chandra Singha's tirade against Bir Chandra owed itself more to personal malice.

It must be mentioned that Nabadwip Chandra was himself a talented person and thus could and did appreciate talent. The following statement made by him about his uncle is testimony to his large-heartedness and devotion to truth:

> On the death of father, his younger brother and next king of Tripura, Bir Chandra Manikya, became our guardian. He was a man of culture with a heartfelt desire for higher knowledge and education. It was during his reign that the new light of Western education entered the kingdom of Tripura. His excessive zeal for new-age education used to be debated in every household. After father's demise he arranged for our English education. (*Abarjaner Jhuri*)

Bir Chandra also taught Nabadwip Chandra how to write poetry. It is necessary to mention Nabadwip Chandra's attitude towards his uncle despite being entitled to believe that he had been deprived of the throne of Tripura by his uncle's act of anointing his son as prince. The two families would be united in future primarily because of the respect each had for the other.

But tales of deprivation are difficult to forget and forgive even if the hand of friendship is extended later. Traces of resentment remain. Sachin-karta's behaviour at times showed signs of this. But that is a later story.

2
Comilla
1906-24

Deprived of his rightful due, the kingship of Tripura, Nabadwip Chandra repaired to Chartha, Comilla, where he had a palatial building constructed with funds provided by Bir Chandra Manikya. It was here that Sachin Dev Burman was born on 1 October 1906. And though Nabadwip Chandra could not become king, there is more than a little consolation in the fact that he will forever be remembered as the father of Sachin-karta, the king of kings in the world of music.

Sachin was the youngest of nine siblings, five brothers and four sisters. His father Nabadwip Chandra was a man of the arts, an expert painter and sculptor and a skilled sitar player possessing an excellent voice that could mesmerize listeners. His mother, Nirupama Devi, hailed from the royal family of Manipur and was steeped in the artistic ambience of Manipuri music, songs and dances. The love for the arts extended to Sachin's siblings too; his sister Tilottama was endowed with a melodious voice while his chhorda (youngest of the elder brothers), Kirankumar, in Sachin's words, was one whose '...mind was always occupied by the fine arts. He had an extremely sweet voice capable of rendering a delectable mix of khatki, murki, taan and laya. He was also a painter and sculptor.'

The synergy of the two cultural streams of his parental lineage, coupled with the mysticism of folk songs, local village songs and bhatiyali (a musical form primarily sung by boatmen) which was nurtured by the indulgent climate of East Bengal and Tripura, had a deep influence on Sachin's life. In this ambience lay the foundation of his style of music too. Besides inheriting music in his genes, so to speak, he also inherited it from his land, Tripura, which at that time was an altar of music, its holy seat. In Sachin's own words:

> There is a saying about Tripura that in its palace, the king, the queen, the princes and the princesses and even the servants and maids, everyone sings. No one born there is devoid of musical talent. In its paddy fields the ploughman ploughs and sings, the boatman cannot steer his boat in the rivers without singing, the fisherman throws his net with a song on his lips, the weaver working on his looms weaves his own music and labourers find solace in singing in the midst of their toils. This prevalence of music in all aspects of its life is God-given. I am a son of that soil of Tripura. Perhaps that is why I spent my entire life on songs and songs alone—music is my first love. (*Sargamer Nikhad*)

Members of the royal family were connoisseurs of Bengali art and culture. Tripura's horizons echoed with music which flowed through the veins of its natives. The royal family could not envisage life without music. For ages, the inner courts of Tripura reverberated with discourses on music, drama, poetry, painting, literature and culture. The kings of the Manikya dynasty were not only patrons of art and culture, many of them were successful artists in their own right. Sachin, however, broke free of palace culture and royal traditions to create a separate tradition through the folk music of rural Bengal, hitherto considered as belonging to the lower strata of society.

Nabadwip Chandra's palace, his outhouse and inner courts stood on a sprawling sixty acres, a short distance away from Dharmasagar (the tank dug by Maharaja Dharma Manikya) and Nanuadighi (the tank named after Dharma Manikya's wife, Nanua Devi). A large tank adorned the front and two the rear. In the courtyard was a tennis court where Sachin learned the game. An abundance of fish in the tanks aroused in him a love for fishing. Breathing the fresh air of Dharmasagar, Nanuadighi and Ranidighi, Sachin revelled in the joys and sorrows of the common folk around him, imbibing the spirit of their music, learning to let go of his princely antecedents. In Agartala, he would probably have carried the air of a prince donned a mask; as it were. At Comilla, he could be the chhoto-karta, the junior master, Sachin, or even Dalimkumar.

Amongst all his names, Dalimkumar was Sachin's favourite. It was the custom in the Tripura royal family to appoint individual nurses (Dai-ma) for each child. In a sense these were wet nurses, breastfeeding the princes and princesses along with their own children. Sachin's nurse was called Robir-ma (it was the usual practice to call maids and nurses after one of their children's names, so Robir-ma would mean that Sachin's nurse had a child by the name of Robi). She was very fond of Sachin and brought him up with great care and affection. She named him Dalimkumar because of his fair complexion. Sachin remembered the name and the person associated with it fondly all his life.

The ambience in and around the household played a large part in helping Sachin emerge as a sangeetacharya, a master of music. It was a daily routine for the entire family to sit together for prayers and sing devotional songs. Nabadwip Chandra used to organize musical soirees at home which were attended by all his children. The house used to resonate with music day in and day out with brothers Kirankumar, Prafullakumar and sister Tilottama giving free rein to their voices or Nabadwip Chandra himself playing Raag Darbari Kanara on the sitar in the dead of the night.

As he grew older, Sachin got so immersed in musical notations and scales that he started losing interest in studies. He was not alone in this pursuit of music. His servants Madhab and Anwar became his accomplices in his playing truant from books. It is said that a song is not born till your ears are ready. It was Madhab and Anwar who opened his senses, alerted his ears to folk music. He immortalized the unlettered, rustic Madhab and Anwar thus:

> Madhab's recital of the Ramayana in a modulated voice in his plain and simple style would intoxicate me. He was no master at singing but what effortless ease he brought to the art! Anwar's bhatiyali renditions with the accompaniment of a dotara (a two-stringed instrument) would bring my grammar studies at night to an end. Next day I would be scolded by my teacher at school. But again at night I would keep aside my grammar and mathematics and lose myself in the words and tune of Anwar's bhatiyali. (*Sargamer Nikhad*)

Apart from such informal lessons, Sachin had already had his initiation in music from his father. He has acknowledged his contribution thus:

> Under his [father's] influence, I could gain a bit of his multifaceted talent in fine arts and craft. I am built in the mould of my father. His lessons laid the foundations of my music. His teachings helped me develop whatever little knowledge I have of the art of music. (*Sargamer Nikhad*)

But pursuit of music alone wouldn't do. He had to receive formal education. He was admitted to Kumar Boarding at Agartala. But within a year, his father brought him back and got him admitted to Yusuf School in Comilla. He did so because children from the royal family were indulged and pampered in Kumar Boarding, with no provisions for punishment even if they neglected their studies and committed other offences. A great lover of books and highly committed to the pursuit of knowledge, Nabadwip Chandra knew the value of education. He believed that without proper education one can never acquire moral excellence and virtue. He realized that his son would never have a proper upbringing in Kumar Boarding.

Sachin-karta himself felt suffocated in the atmosphere of Kumar Boarding. It was against his temperament to affect artificial gravity and don the sullen and glum appearance that princes were expected to assume. More importantly, his pursuit of music came to a standstill at Kumar Boarding. He heaved a sigh of relief on his return to Comilla where he would resume his music lessons from his father.

From a very early age, folk music's rural roots, its liveliness, its melancholia and spontaneity deeply attracted Sachin. This led him to roam around in the riverine expanse of rural Bengal and, like a honeybee collecting and storing honey, build his collection of tunes and music. In later years, this would earn him recognition as a composer.

The common people of rural Bengal have, in their own extraordinary way, sown the seeds of their sorrows and joys in their own rustic tunes, in their mystic colloquialism. The prince immersed himself in the deep recesses of the then ignored folk songs and music. These proved to be the uncut gems he later polished and presented to the world.

Sachin's elder brothers Prafulla and Prashanta had their early education in Santiniketan and continued with their studies in St. Paul's School, Darjeeling. Chhorda Kirankumar also joined them in due course. Only the sisters and Sachin stayed at home. Sachin clamoured to join St. Paul's but father Nabadwip Chandra wouldn't send him away. He was the apple of his father's eye and after the short-lived experiment at Kumar Boarding, he wouldn't let Sachin out of his sight. Just as well. How else would Sachin have roamed the woodlands and the marshes, journeyed up rivers and streams, walked around the towns and villages and marketplaces building up his repertoire of folk music? If he had moved away from Comilla, how would he have unravelled the secrets of folk music, its structure, its philosophy, the cadences and intricacies of its various forms—baul, murshidiya, fakiri, darbeshi, kirtan, agamani, bijaya, maharamer jari, nilpujar gaan, manasar bhasan, jhumar, bhatiyali and so on? Who would have sung the song of the cowherd grazing his cattle on the meadows, '*Nitey elam bhai Kanai, sajai de ma gocharaney jai*'? Who would have composed '*Subal, bol bol bol chai, keman aachhe Kamalini Rai?*' or the tragic '*Ki kari ami ki kari, bol re Subal, bol dada*' or '*Kalsape danshila amaaye*'. All which became memorable successes in Bengali music in later years? Who would have, like Bhagirath, brought so many streams of folk music to the doorsteps of each household of Bengal?

At that time Shyamacharan Datta was an established singer of dhrupad and khayal. He was willing to teach Sachin but the latter opted for the discipleship of his father. He stayed back in Comilla and completed his schooling there. He gave his first public performance on the occasion of Saraswati Puja when he was a student of Class V, singing songs that he had learnt from his father. So impressive was his performance that his headmaster could not help writing a letter of praise to Nabadwip Chandra. Sachin reminisces about his schooldays:

> Adjacent to the school was our playground with a large banyan tree beside it. Under the tree we used to have our regular music sessions during the tiffin break. In the open, beside Dharmasagar tank, I used to sing Anwar's songs. What a pleasure it was—singing those earthy songs, those rural tunes day after day, in nature's company, under the canopy of large trees, undaunted by the seasons, come sun or rain, storm or cloud, summer or winter. Alas! That pleasure is lost forever. City dwellers will never be able to appreciate it. In plain and simple words, Anwar's songs would vividly describe a philosophy of life, the union of Radha and Krishna. What a pleasant aftertaste it would leave—difficult to describe in words. (*Sargamer Nikhad*)

In *Sargamer Nikhad*, Sachin-karta has alluded to an incident of his childhood to explain the charm of Anwar's songs. Sachin and his friends were once detained by a station master for travelling without tickets. One of the friends, Mohit, knew about the weakness of the station master's mother towards dhapkirtan, a variety of the devotional kirtan, attended with slow dance movements. On Mohit's advice, Sachin started singing. His voice reached the mother's ears. In no time at all, the station master released the boys at her insistence. Apocryphal though it may seem, the incident cannot be dismissed off-hand. Indeed, if anything, it is a proof of the affective quality of the folk songs Sachin grew up with.

In 1920, at the age of fourteen, Sachin passed his matriculation examination and timidly expressed his desire to pursue higher studies in Calcutta. His father overruled him and Sachin joined Victoria College, Comilla. Two years later, he passed his Intermediate of Arts and brought up the matter of going to Calcutta once again. But his father told him, 'In two years you will have to go to Calcutta for your MA. Stay with me for these two years.' Sachin deferred to his father's wish.

Again, this proved immensely beneficial for the flowering of Sachin's musical talents. A grown-up boy now, he was no longer subject to strict restrictions. He was at liberty to roam around anywhere he pleased and for as long as he wanted to—he no longer had to return home by nightfall. Thus began Sachin's quest for musical jewels. The neighbouring Nawab's mansion hosted concerts by famous singers, musicians and dancers every night. Sachin would sneak away from home night after night to enjoy the musical soirees. The dulcet strains of thumris had Sachin riveted, particularly the songs of Radha's separation from Krishna enacted by Muslim dancers. This would later prove a boon when Sachin set about learning the rudiments of composing a pure thumri from Amiyanath Sanyal.

Despite hailing from the royal family, he had no qualms about mingling with common folk in search of inspiration. He roamed from village to village, imbibing lessons in rare musical forms—songs soaked in rusticity but eternal in their liveliness—from the farmer and the boatman, the beggar and the baul, the fakir and the servant. Each one would fill his beggar's bowl with their music. His father, given his own love for music, never objected to Sachin's nomadic existence in search of the elixir of folk music. Later, Sachin would hone the tunes that he collected during this phase and embellish them in his inimitable style with his own words and tunes, giving them a new identity altogether. In his own words:

I started my BA course. I could feel the transition from adolescence to youth. I used to roam around in the countryside. At times I would float around in a boat on a river. I even bunked classes, and spent my vacations in the company of farmers, fishermen, bauls, bhatiyali singers, Vaishnava mendicants and gajan troupes [...], singing with them, learning from them, listening to them, smoking their hookah.

There is hardly any village in that part of East Bengal that I did not set foot on. It was there that I built my capital—my present stock of tunes. I have been hoarding this treasure since then and even now I can feel the taste of those days in every pore of my being. The treasures through which I am now serving the cause of music have their origins in my memories of those days.

I have composed all kinds of music. But it is folk music that truly satisfies the thirst of the soul. I grew up in the company of sons of the soil. That is why their simple, rustic tunes find an echo in my compositions. Their music lies in the kingdom of my imagination. It rises on its own, rings within me on its own, and finds life in my voice automatically. It needs no effort on my part. The music is part of my bloodstream. (*Sargamer Nikhad*)

Another source of musical training came in the form of the royal court of Tripura. King Birendra Kishore Manikya had invited Nabadwip Chandra to join his court as prime minister in 1909. This gave the young Sachin unrestricted access to Tripura's royal darbar, one of the greatest centres of music at the time. Famous vocalists and instrumentalists were regularly invited to the court to perform and Sachin, who visited his father at Agartala during the summer and puja vacations, had his first lessons in classical music from these stalwarts.

Nabadwip Chandra's house in Agartala, with its beautiful ambience, influenced young Sachin's love for music. The royal palace had two lakes with crystal-clear water, Krishnasagar and Radhasagar, named after the divine couple and the ghat of Durgabari, with its steps leading into the water, stood right in front. Rows of sirish, kusum and krishnachuda trees lined Shakuntala Road and wove shadowy patterns on the walls of the palace. The breeze playing amongst their leaves would bring the music of the trees to him. Two paths of reddish murram stretched before the house and any traffic on these would make a soft sound as if it were the murrams murmuring. All this and more he garnered for his harvest of a musical murmur. Ankur Deb Burman, Kirankumar's son and Sachin's nephew, described the house thus:

> A pucca house where Rabindrabhavan stands today [...] it was a rectangular house with a veranda facing south, a wide courtyard in front and a drawing room with thatched roof for guests to sit in. The famous singer K. C. Dey also gave musical performances here. To the west were flowering trees of nagkeshar, and a solitary alcove in the shade of mango and jackfruit trees. To the south-east corner was a large lake along which grew bhant flowers and on its east bank stood bamboo groves—a special type of bamboo from which flutes used to be made. ('Maramigo Tomarai', *Kumar Sachin Deb Burman Centenary Book*)

Speaking of flutes, it needs to be mentioned that Kumar Sachin more or less started his journey in the world of music with a flute. This was no ordinary flute but what is known as a Tippera flute, one made of the slender Tripura bamboo, and one that is

Tripura's own, special treasure. And Sachin made it his very own instrument right from childhood. He would be seen, flute in hand, in the midst of Vaishnav assemblies, in kirtan performances, in a baul's hut, in the dargah of a fakir or dervish or in the company of boatmen on the Gomti River. He would sit on the desolate bank of Comilla's Ranidighi or under the bakul tree in the Nawab's compound, alone at night, playing his flute, often right through the night. In Agartala too, sitting on the steps of the Durgabari, feet immersed in water, his practice sessions would last the whole night. Older residents of Agartala, who have had the good fortune of listening to Sachin indulge in his nocturnal affair with the flute, often talked of its mystic tunes which would even arouse the king and queen asleep in the inner chambers of the palace. The haunting tunes of the flute in the dead of night would convey the message far and wide: Sachin-karta was in town.

Sachin would never forget these trysts with the flute—the first love of his childhood and adolescence. In fact, it is a love he has immortalized in his songs. There is hardly any song in Sachin's repertoire which does not have a flute interlude or in which he has not used the flute. Not only did he use it extensively while composing a song, even the lyrics for a number of his Bengali songs have the word 'banshi' in its first line. Some of the more well known of these songs include '*Banshi shuney aar kaj nai*', '*O-oh banshi Allar dohai*', '*Baje na banshi go*', '*Sei je din guli banshi bajanor din guli*', '*Tui ki shyamer banshi re*', '*Ashomoye bajao banshi*', '*Banshi aaj kende koy*', '*Aamari jibone shune banshi toba*', etc., all of which evoke the mesmerizing qualities of the flute.

The cultural ambience of Comilla in those days played an important role in the development of Sachin's musical faculties. Comilla was then the nerve centre of music and drama in the area, boasting of a number of institutions and personalities who furthered the cause of music and culture. Organizations like Suralok of Thakurpara, the drama troupe Sabuj Sangha of Kandirpar, the Great Vernal Theatre Party, the Young Men's Club, etc., were able to create a robust and lively climate of art and culture. Maharaja Bir Bikram founded a large number of cultural establishments in Comilla, including the Town Hall, the Bir Chandra Milanayatan Kendra Theatre Hall and a library. Surprisingly, the king showed no such initiative in his capital town Agartala. Perhaps this was because Agartala did not have middle-class intellectuals in such large numbers as in Comilla.

Sachin's friends and contemporaries who rose to name and fame in their later life were all musically and artistically inclined. These included Surasagar Himangshu Dutta, lyricist Ajay Bhattacharya, Mohini Chaudhuri, famous dhrupad singer Souren Das, Sudhin Das and film-maker Sushil Majumdar, among others, all of whom would assemble at Suralok for their music practice and outings. In fact, Himangshu Dutta, Ajay Bhattacharya and Sachin Dev Burman were often referred to as the three musketeers. The three came together in Comilla and later created waves in Calcutta briefly, before the untimely deaths of Dutta and Bhattacharya robbed the music world of two shining jewels.

Well-known Bengali music expert Rajeshwar Mitra has spoken of Himangshu Dutta as an extraordinary composer and one with a keen intellect who freed the Bengali song of its association with dancing girls and other vulgar trappings and established it in the cultured society of respectable artists. Born in the same year as Sachin, Ajay Bhattacharya was a talented lyricist who, in his brief life, composed over two thousand songs. The combination of Dutta's music, Bhattacharya's lyrics and Sachin's voice revolutionized Bengali music. Unfortunately for music lovers, Dutta and Bhattacharya died young, the former at the age of thirty-six and the latter when he was only thirty-seven. Sachin, who sang as many as forty-one songs written by Bhattacharya, lamented at the latter's death: 'Whose song shall I sing now?'

The company of such greats inspired Sachin to explore the close relationship between folk and classical music which can be seen in his various efforts to bring about a fusion of the two in his songs. The Young Men's Club, which Sachin frequented, was another rendezvous of musicians, lyricists, poets and litterateurs, including Tagore's favourite, Professor Sudhir Sen, and the poet Kazi Nazrul Islam, who would became a close friend and associate of Sachin.

Nazrul lived at Churulia, Bardhaman, but visited Comilla quite often where he used to stay on the west bank of Talpukur. The songs and poems he composed those days often had references to Talpukur, Ranidighi, Dharmasagar, etc., in Comilla. Sachin and Nazrul would often be seen together at Kandirpar or around Talpukur, Sachin playing his flute or giving free rein to his voice. It was Sachin, in fact, who introduced Nazrul to the glory of Bengal's folk songs. They would often meet at the Young Men's Club where they would punctuate the animated conversation with impromptu duets. Curious onlookers would assemble to listen to them. Nazrul also sang in the haveli of the Dev Burmans and its stone walls bear the inscription: *In this building (the palace of Maharajkumar Nabadwip Chandra Dev Burman Bahadur), the poet Nazrul Islam used to have musical performances with Kumar Sachin Dev Burman.*

There is no doubt that Nazrul's advent in Comilla inspired Sachin's experimentation with music and had a salutary effect on his music, elevating it to a different level. Later, in Calcutta, this association developed into a deep friendship. Despite this, it may come as a surprise that Sachin sang only four songs written and composed by Nazrul: '*Kuhu kuhu koelia*', '*Chokh gelo chokh gelo*',

'*Meghla nishi bhore*' and '*Padmar dheu re*'. This may be because, though close friends, they were very different as people. Sachin preferred singing songs he composed himself. Though he did sing a few songs for which Himangshu Dutta and others composed the music, he was never comfortable singing songs set in tune by someone else as far as his Bengali songs were concerned. Likewise, Nazrul not only wrote songs, he also composed his own music, never quite relishing the idea of someone else doing it. In fact, it is difficult to recognize the above mentioned four songs of Nazrul which Sachin sang as Nazrulgeeti, deviating as they do from the thumri and khayal styles that characterize, rendered them in a heady mix of the classical and the folk instead.

Though Nazrul may not have objected to the spin Sachin gave to his songs, and it did not affect their friendship in any way, the fact remains that these are the only songs of Nazrul which Sachin had recorded. There is one Nazrul song which Sachin loved to sing often—'*Arunakanti ke go jogi bhikari*'—connoisseurs of Hindi film songs will recall this as the composition '*Poochho na kaise maine rain bitaai*' from the film *Meri Soorat Teri Aankhein* years later. Sachin, however, never recorded the song and only sang it at musical soirees when the audience clamoured for a Nazrul song from him.

It can be said without hesitation that his years in Comilla played an important role in the evolution of the genius of Sachin Dev Burman. But for his trysts with the folk music of the area, his wanderings in search of various musical forms and his interaction and involvement with the cultural renaissance taking place in Comilla at the time, the world would probably have been denied the incredible talent of the singer and composer.

In 1924, Sachin passed his BA from Victoria College. Now he was to join the university for his MA. Calcutta beckoned him. Sachin wanted to shine like the sun in the musical firmament.

This time he would not be denied. His father too realized that the time had come for the young man to follow his own path, free of the fetters of familial obligations, in a place which could offer greater opportunities than Comilla ever could. Nabadwip Chandra's only condition now was that Sachin would not undertake the initial journey alone. He wanted to ensure that Sachin got accommodation in the Tripura Palace while in Calcutta and did not have to face undue hardship in settling down in a big city. And who could ensure this better than Nabadwip Chandra himself—the top-ranking minister of Tripura.

Thus, Nabadwip Chandra accompanied Sachin to Calcutta. He made all arrangements for Sachin's comfort in the huge Tripura Palace on Ballygunge Circular Road and then got him admitted to Calcutta University to pursue an MA in English. This was the first time that Sachin would stay away from his father. He would now have to find his own world away from his father's protective care. Asking Sachin repeatedly to write to him in case of any difficulty, an anxious father returned to Agartala.

Ujjayanta Palace, Agartala

Part of S. D. Burman's House at Comilla

Nabadwip Chandra Bahadur—
S. D. Burman's Father

A Young S. D. Burman

S. D. Burman and Meera Dev Burman

Creating Music Together—S. D. Burman and Meera Dev Burman

The Parampara Continues: S. D. Burman Practising Music with Son, R. D. Burman

A Proud Father—S. D. Burman with Son, R. D. Burman

3
Calcutta
1925-31

Calcutta, the city of dreams, the cultural seat of India, the nerve centre of music, literature, art, theatre and cinema was also, in the early part of the twentieth century, one of the the premiere cities of India. Talented artists from all over the country went there in search of recognition. Inevitably, therefore, Sachin too was attracted to Calcutta for he knew that only Calcutta could bring him the recognition he craved. Besides, he wanted to learn the various styles of music and attain proficiency in them. Music, he knew, was a vast, boundless ocean. He had to immerse himself in that ocean. It was not possible to discover new depths sitting on its shores. Now, reaching Calcutta, he was one step closer to his dream. But who would quench his thirst for music? Would his separation from his family lead to success?

Modernization was the key word in the world of Bengali music of the era. Five famous personalities can be credited with bringing in a modern touch to Bengali music—Dwijendralal Ray, Rajanikanta

Sen, Atulprasad Sen, Rabindranath Tagore and Kazi Nazrul Islam. Experts in working their way through intricate ragas and creating a new harmony from them, they can be regarded as the founders of what came to be known as 'adhunik geeti' or modern songs. They ushered in a new kind of style which expertly blended three diverse streams of music—Western, Hindustani and Carnatic. Each one of them had his own distinctive style and brought in a new yet natural feel to his music. Creativity, style and appealing tunes came together in the work of these artists to generate a renaissance in the world of Bengali music. Sachin would draw on these influences to create his own style fusing the diverse forms of classical, folk and modern songs.

Initially, Sachin felt lonely in Calcutta as he didn't have any friends there. The soil which he had worshipped back in Comilla, and in praise of which he was inspired to compose songs, seemed alien to him once he began to live in Calcutta. The pomp and splendour of the city made him uncomfortable. He missed the proximity to nature he enjoyed in Comilla—the cooing of birds, the joys of splashing about in a pond, the kirtan at the break of dawn, the bhatiyali songs of the boatmen and the company of dervishes, fakirs and Vaishnavas. Life in the city became a tired routine of going to the university, attending classes, visits to the library and then back to the Tripura Palace.

He soon realized that this was not why he had come to the city. Though he had come to Calcutta on the pretext of higher education, it was music that he really loved. He wrote in his memoirs, 'Even as a student of Comilla College, I had a strong desire to listen to the music of and to learn from ustads of Hindustani music in Calcutta.' Since it was impossible to ride in two boats simultaneously, he chose music over studies. When one has the mind of a baul, when one's heart hums like a bee, when one has plunged into the ocean of music, it is impossible to be bound to bookish learning. So Sachin gave up his post-graduate degree and became a disciple of the famous singer Krishna Chandra Dey. At that time K. C. Dey was at the pinnacle of fame and glory. His full, rich baritone had enthralled music lovers of the era. Some of his songs like *'Chhuiona chhuiona bondhu oikhane thako'* from the film *Chandidas* had become a rage. Besides, he was the cynosure of the Bengali stage. He created a sensation on stage by singing D. L. Ray's *'Oi mahasindhur opar hotay'* in the character of a beggar in the play *Chandragupta*. Even classical songs conveyed an irresistible distress of the soul when he sang them. It was not only the correctness of the tunes he sang but the way he sang them that touched the listener's heart. It was emotion over and above skill. This is what appealed to Sachin, who had discovered the pain and grief of the innermost soul in the native, earthy songs of rural Bengal. To him, music made no sense unless it was able to arouse the deepest emotion in the listener. K. C. Dey honed Sachin's musical skills further even as Sachin moulded his mentor's classical style with his own individuality. The influence of K. C. Dey on Sachin's music is undeniable.

Meanwhile, Nabadwip Chandra learned about Sachin giving up studies in favour of music. He rushed to Calcutta and got the truant student admitted to Law College, tempting him with trips abroad and a job in the royal court. But all of this was to no avail. Sachin remained dedicated to his passion. He forsook the foreign trips and the chance of occupying a senior position in Tripura administration in order to pursue his deep love for music. Supremely self-confident, Sachin preferred the uncertainty of a career in music to the certainty of comfort and stability in life. Eventually, the father had to give in to his son's singular love for music.

K. C. Dey had a busy schedule those days. He performed

regularly in musical soirees. Sachin used to attend all his performances. Besides, whenever Krishna Chandra attended musical performances by great classical singers, instrumentalists and baijees, he would take Sachin along. Incidentally, it was K. C. Dey who made Sachin give up one of his passions for the sake of music.

Sachin loved tennis and he was well-known as a player in Comilla. After coming to Calcutta this was a pastime he assiduously cultivated. Music and tennis went together. He became a member of the YMCA (Young Men's Christian Association) and surpassed the Anglo-Indians at the game. All the members gradually wanted to play with him. But trouble arose when he caught a severe cold once and went down with a hoarse voice, unable to sing for days. It was then that K. C. Dey told him he would have to choose one of the two, either music or tennis. Sachin had given up his studies for music; he gave up tennis too.

Though K. C. Dey was one of Sachin's greatest mentors, he did not limit himself to his discipleship alone. A strong believer in the diversity of music, he was unwilling to be tied down to any particular style. So, seeking K. C. Dey's permission, he started training under Ustad Badal Khan Saheb, who was K. C. Dey's guru. Ustad Badal Khan was revered as one of the greats and had ushered in epoch-making changes in the music scene. His disciples included maestros like Bhishmadeb Chattopadhyay, Girijashankar Chakrabarti, Zamiruddin Khan, Shailen Dasgupta, Sachindranath Das, and many more. K. C. Dey's deep baritone and Badal Khan's dulcet voice had an abiding influence on Sachin.

The years 1925-30 were the formative years of Sachin's pursuit of music. He acquired a measure of name and fame by singing folk songs of East Bengal on the radio and at musical functions. With his nasal voice accentuating the inherent mournfulness of folk songs, he was beginning to develop his own distinctive style and manner. There was an earthy feel to his renditions which captivated listeners.

During this period, he used to visit Agartala and Comilla twice a year, during the Manipuri Raas festival or the autumn festival and the Holi festival. During Holi, the entire state of Tripura would be immersed in songs and music. These festivities in Tripura inspired India's poet laureate Rabindranath Tagore to introduce the Basanta Utsab or spring festival in Santiniketan.

New songs would be composed at this time. Troupes would go around the town singing these songs and the songs would spread from person to person till Holi became as much a time for music as of colour. Inspired by the revelries, Sachin often composed the music for these songs. With the kartas and the thakurs of the royal family in tow, he would sing Holi songs as he made his way through the alleyways of Agartala, like a minstrel, immersing everybody in music and colour. In the evening, after the day's revelries were over, he would overwhelm the group with his songs composed in new ragas and raginis.

A deep friendship had developed between Tagore and Sachin's father ever since Tagore's first visit to Agartala. In fact, Tagore visited Agartala as many as three times in the year 1905. Over the next twenty years, the poet was a regular visitor to Agartala and on his last visit in February 1925, he even stayed at Nabadwip Chandra's house for a few days. During this visit he raised the issue of Sachin not singing his songs. Though Sachin did not sing Rabindra Sangeet—he believed his voice was not suited for it—he was well aware of the great depths of the songs.

Sachin revered Tagore as the first person to teach artistes that music is the manifestation of emotions through an amalgamation of poetry, style, tune, rhythm and tempo. It was Himangshu Dutta who introduced Sachin to the cadences of Rabindra Sangeet, incorporating its structure and blending it with classical music to create raga-based semi-classical songs. Sachin's appreciation of Rabindra Sangeet and its inner meaning went a long way in enabling him to become a successful music composer and singer. In later years, particularly in the Hindi film songs he composed, Sachin often reproduced the strains of Rabindra Sangeet.

Sachin Dev's trips to Agartala continued till 1946, reducing in frequency after his father's death in 1931, and ceasing altogether in 1946 when he visited Agartala for the last time to attend the last rites of his elder brother Prafulla. Nabadwip Chandra was the prime minister of Tripura, next in protocol to the king himself. It is thus that Sachin developed the dual personality I have mentioned earlier. Dictates of royalty would make the elders caution him to maintain his individuality and distance from the masses right from his childhood. But as his father had neither pride nor prejudice, Sachin stayed humble and unassuming, at least while he stayed in Comilla. Since this was not to the liking of many in the royal family, Sachin had to undergo a personality change in Agartala, where he had to behave, perforce, like a prince. The man of the soil who used to roam the countryside, frolicking in the rivers and streams at Comilla, put on a princely mask at Agartala. In the words of music connoisseur and historian Sharangadeb, who followed Sachin's early life closely: '[He] used to maintain his individuality [in Agartala]. There he was Kumar Sachin Dev Burman, the son of Nabadwip Bahadur. Mixing with the masses was not at all possible for him.' ('Sachin Karta', *Prantik,* 2006) He had to maintain the decorum that his father's position called for. Had Sachin grown up in Agartala, we would probably have lost the indomitable child in pursuit of the treasure of folk music.

Sachin's visits to Agartala would be occasions for organizing musical soirees. The general public would assemble in the char-chala (four-thatched) drawing room attracted by rural Bengal's bhatiyali tunes. At times, Sachin would invite beggars and Vaishnavas in order to listen to their songs. If he liked a particular song, he would write down its words. One such person from whom Sachin learned many songs was Saheb Ali, a mason by profession. Saheb Ali performed only at the homes of connoisseurs, who, in lieu of his performances, used to give him what was called 'sidha', the gift of uncooked food items. Sachin even recorded one of Saheb Ali's songs '*Manodukkhe morirey subal sakha, brajer kishori radha bine*'.

It was on such visits that Sachin brought renowned artists from Calcutta to perform in his hometown. On one such visit, he presented his guru K. C. Dey not only to the royal court of Tripura but also to the general public in Comilla. Eyewitness Narayan Chaudhuri, who had the opportunity of seeing Sachin from close quarters, remembers the excitement surrounding the staging of Natyacharya Sisir Bhaduri's drama *Sita* in Comilla Town Hall. Many famous actors of the town—Brahmananda Nag (Jubilee Nag) the pleader, Sushil Majumdar (later the famous film director), Ajay Bhattacharya and others—acted in the play. However, what had the entire town of Comilla agog was the news that K. C. Dey himself—the singer who had captivated the entire city of Calcutta as Baitalik in *Sita*, singing the songs '*Katha kao, katha kao*', '*Andhakarer antarete ashrubadal jhare*', '*Jay Sitapati sundaratanu*'—was expected to come from Calcutta to take part in the play. The very possibility sent a ripple of excitement through the town. Narayan Chaudhuri recalls: 'The credit for bringing Krishna Chandra to Comilla should go entirely to Sachin Dev. It was on his invitation that the great singer came to Comilla.' Narayan Chaudhuri was also a witness to the rehearsals: 'I saw Sachin during the rehearsals. He would not utter a word, never say anything. All along he remained a silent spectator, an obedient disciple to his guru.' Narayan Chaudhuri has other memories of Sachin, when the latter was no longer a mute spectator but the very centre of attraction during a musical soiree:

> The function was organized at the house of the famous advocate and mass leader of Comilla, Kamini Kumar Datta. [...] Sachin Dev Burman and Himangshu Dutta were the main performers. I still remember, Sachin Dev first sang Nazrul's famous ghazal *'Chheyona sunayana, ar chheyona nayana paney'*. With the very first song he brought the house down. What a mesmeric voice it was! Impossible to describe! Even today, after all these years, whenever I recount the pleasant memory of that day and the song, I feel a shiver run down my spine. Sachin Dev sang a few more songs that day whose details [sic] I cannot remember but I will never forget the lingering resonance of *'Cheyona sunayana'* in Bageshri and Pilu raginis, sung in his melodious voice. Later, I listened to the same song in other artists' voices many times over, heard it on gramophone records, but the joy and thrill of that first audience made light the joy of all subsequent hearings. ('Kanther Jadukar Sachin Dev Burman', *Prantik,* Jan-Feb 2006)

On another occasion, Sachin brought Ustad Badal Khan during the autumn festival to the princely court. Stalwarts like Inayat Khan the sitar player, Munna Khan the famous shehnai player, Alakananda the danseuse and Baba Alauddin Khan used to participate in such programmes. It is said that Sachin was greatly annoyed at the inadequate monetary honorarium offered to Ustad Badal Khan, which he thought was too paltry to befit the status of a princely court.

Sachin was a frequent visitor to the houses of music maestros

Maharajkumar Mahendra-karta and Maharajkumar Bimal-karta, who were his uncles and used to live adjacent to his own house in Agartala. Another close friend at Agartala was Narendra Chandra Dev Burman alias Naru Thakur who had just returned from Santiniketan after completing his studies in Rabindra Sangeet. Naru Thakur took great pains in getting Sachin's songs recorded with Hindustan Musical Products. Pulin Thakur, who was six to seven years younger than Sachin, held a degree of Sangeet Bisharad from Bhatkhande Music Institute of Lucknow. Sachin learned the music of the Lucknow gharana from him.

At Agartala, Sachin would impart music lessons to people like Ramakanta Deb, Nripen Shil, Rabi Nag and others. Nag eventually wrote a memoir describing his relationship with Sachin. Sachin advised Rabi Nag to follow the style of the ghazal queen Akhtari Bai and Abdul Karim Khan. He also directed Rabi to collect Tripura's and rural Bengal's folk songs. Rabi Nag reminisces:

> Moonlit nights were Karta's favourite. I remember one such night when we walked from Jagannath Badi Road to Shakuntala Road. I was holding his hand. Karta was telling stories: 'It was a full-moon night. Every bit of the earth sparkled in silvery moonlight. The boat was drifting as if aimlessly…' I used to listen to him enchanted. So many dreams used to float before my eyes. All of a sudden, he started humming—'*Na amare shashi cheyo na*'. He was humming and gazing at the sky with steadfast eyes, as if enjoying the beauty of the full moon. What passion! What sweetness in the depth of his voice! Karta seemed to be sinking into the unfathomable depth of the ocean of music. The song ended after some time but its sweet tremor lasted as if for eternity.

However, there seems to be some discrepancy in Rabi Nag's story. When Sachin visited Agartala for the last time in 1946, Rabi Nag was in the prime of his youth. In the memoirs, Rabi mentions walking, holding Sachin's hand, which means he must be talking of the period between 1926-35 when Sachin was a regular visitor to Agartala. The song 'Na amare shashi cheyo na' was written by Sachin's wife Meera Dev Burman in 1972. Sachin recorded it (Cassette No. 45 N-834596) in September that year.

The reminiscences of a few of his acquaintances in Tripura provide glimpses of Sachin's style. In the words of essayist and photographer Robin Sengupta, who remembers a song session from sometime around 1942-43:

> I used to accompany the seniors from our house at the central neighbourhood to the tank at Durgabari to swim. On one such occasion, there was a small crowd in the long tin-shed verandah of Nabadwip Chandra Dev Burman or Prafulla-karta's house. Someone was singing a song. Curious, I walked towards the verandah. I could behold the majestic figure of a tall, slim young man with a fair complexion accompanied by four or five people. He was wearing a dhoti and panjabi. He went on singing one song after another to the accompaniment of a harmonium. I came to know later that this was Sachin-karta. By his side was today's music maestro Rabi Nag on the tanpura and on tabla were Ramakanta Deb and Nripen Shil. Was it true or was I dreaming? I could not believe my eyes. Was I looking at the person whose words, whose songs had developed a close relationship with rural Bengal right from his childhood? Karta would stop intermittently and ask, 'Hey, how do you all like it? Don't you want to listen

to a few more?' We used to reply, 'Karta Maharaj, please sing the *Taj Mahal* song.' 'Oh, the love song! Well, then. Rabi, hold the proper tune.' Seated next to Karta with his milky-white feet was his son Pancham (Rahul Dev Burman), at that time around three or four years old. ('Dakley Kokil Roj Bihaney'—*Prantik,* Jan-Feb 2006)

In his article 'Sachin Karta' (*Prantik*, Jan-Feb 2006) Sharangadeb wrote about the life in those days at Agartala:

> Life was easy those days. Sachin-karta used to walk around the town. He was a replica of his father—slim, fair, delicately built. His dhoti smartly tucked behind, he used to keep his shirt sleeves folded. He wore slippers with rounded snout-like fronts. I often saw him walk from his house to the football ground of Umakanta Academy whenever he was nominated as referee in any major football match. I always got the feeling that he was reserved and talked very little. People in Agartala looked up to him. Whenever he visited Agartala, he used to sing in select gatherings. Given an opportunity we would go and listen. He did not have a deep voice but what was extraordinary was his style, his artistry, the melody he conjured. He could carry off the most difficult tunes with effortless ease.

Sachin's nephew Ankur Dev Burman remembers Sachin's fetish for discipline with regard to matters connected with music and how it affected the household when his uncle came calling:

> I heard my mother say that whenever Sachin Dev Burman visited Agartala, everybody at home would be busy bustling about trying to maintain discipline in matters related to his music practice, his dietary prescriptions and prohibitions,

ensuring that the drinking water was clean, and so on. I have heard, even in the Thakur Boarding in Comilla, his rehearsals created some sort of disturbance to the residents. But under no circumstances would he desist from his practice. ('Maramigo Tomarai' *Kumar Sachin Deb Burman Centenary Book*)

Another eyewitness, Prabir Deb, who was only ten at the time, remembers:

> Once, when I was just ten or twelve years old, uncle [Ramakanta Deb, the tabla player] made me accompany Karta on tabla. That day's memory still remains indelible. He sang in kaharba and at the end asked me to note down a new symbolic sound (bol) of tabla in kaharba—*tadhi gedhi nara ke ne, tadhi gedhi nara ghe ne*. I still remember those words. ('Maramigo Tomarai' *Kumar Sachin Deb Burman Centenary Book*)

During 1925-30, there was hardly any music expert in Calcutta with whom Sachin did not come in contact. Obsessed as he was with music, Sachin enjoyed the company of many maestros and specialists in search for his own metier. Music researcher Kalyanbandhu Bhattacharya has written:

> Sachin Dev's inclination was towards specialization. With absolute dedication and diligence he mastered Krishna Chandra's extraordinary knowledge of tempo (laya), his expertise with dadra and his skill. Its influence could be seen in his later creations. Sachin assimilated his unique style of creating music from his other guru Bhishmadeb Chattopadhyay, synthesized it with the ardour of folk music, and developed his own style which was absolutely 'Sachindevian'. ('Sachin Kantha', *Desh*)

Sachin changed gurus frequently but never abandoned any. Shyamlal Kshetri, a famous harmonium player and thumri specialist of the era, was one such guru. Realizing Sachin's ardent desire to learn classical songs and his deep devotion and respect for music, Shyamlal had no reservations in taking the young man under his wing and acquainting him with new frontiers of music. Sachin mastered the Benares-style thumri and the manner of creating the thumri's 'bol'. Shyamlal Kshetri was a respected name in the music world. There was hardly any artist in Calcutta and its adjoining areas who had not performed at his house or in musical functions organized by him. His disciples had the good fortune of listening to famous vocal and instrumental artists and professional baijis. At one such function, Sachin was introduced to Dhurjatiprasad Mukhopadhyay. Dhurjatiprasad developed a liking for Sachin instantly. Connoisseur that he was, Dhurjatiprasad saw the immense possibilities in the young man on hearing him sing. Sachin has often spoken of him as one of the masters who encouraged his search for music.

It was through Shyamlal Kshetri that Sachin came to know Atulprasad Sen, poet, lyricist and singer and the legendary musician and singer Girijashankar Chakrabarti. He also came in touch with Sudhirendra Sanyal and Hemendra Kumar Ray, publicity secretary of New Theatres and editor of the journal *Nachghar*. These contacts would stand him in good stead in the years to come. Talent cannot express itself in a hostile or unfavourable ambience. If the environment is favourable, if one's friends and acquaintances are also fellow-travellers in a similar quest, talent finds a way to express itself. As Sachin Dev has himself acknowledged:

> It is difficult to put in words the extent of encouragement that I received from Krishna Chandra Dey, Hemen Ray, Sudhirendra and Dhurjati-da during the years 1925-30.

But for their encouragement and support, I might not have been able to advance as much as I did. With their inspiration I fully dedicated myself to the worship of music. (*Sargamer Nikhad*)

In the meantime, Sachin also started training under Guru Badal Khan's favourite disciple, Bhishmadeb Chattopadhyay, who was in fact younger than Sachin. In effect, Sachin accepted a co-disciple as his guru. Bhishmadeb has said:

> He has always respected me as his guru. In many cases I have seen that once established, many people do not feel like remembering their gurus. But Sachin was an exception. Till his last days he recognized me as his guru. (*Sargamer Nikhad*)

Thanks to these associations, the initial suffocation that Sachin had felt in Calcutta was no longer there. There was hardly a musical function in Calcutta those days that he did not attend. His heart now overflowing with the magic of music, the feeling of loneliness was gone. Many of his old friends from Comilla like Himangshu Dutta, Sushil Majumdar, Subodh Purakayastha and others, come to Calcutta in search of a living. Thus began a lifelong love affair with the great city. How deeply Sachin loved Calcutta is revealed by his lament for the city from the coast of the Arabian Sea. In his heart of hearts he never wanted to go to Bombay and would not have left Calcutta had he got due opportunities as a music director there.

There was another reason for the extraordinary attachment he felt with Calcutta, his love for football. Calcutta has always been the Mecca of Indian football and Sachin loved the city even more on that count. He himself was quite adept at the game and used to play as centre forward. Nothing could keep him away from the football ground if there was a match between East Bengal and Mohan Bagan. A diehard supporter of East Bengal, he would stop eating if the team lost a match, weep copious tears in anger and sorrow, and it would take days for him to get back to his jovial mood.

Even as Sachin settled down in Calcutta, overcoming his initial feeling of alienation, catastrophe struck in the form of the death of his father. Nabadwip Chandra passed away quite suddenly in September 1931 (S. D. Burman's own memoir, *Sargamer Nikhad*, mentions the year as 1930). It naturally left Sachin devastated. As he recalled years later: 'I felt absolutely helpless. It took me a long time to come to terms with the terrible reality.'

Since Nabadwip Chandra was the prime minister of Tripura at the time of his death, Maharaj Bir Bikram requested Sachin to take charge of the ministry of education. His elder brothers were already employed in senior positions in the Tripura administration. The position was his for the asking. Since his monthly stipend too had stopped now that his father was no more, it would have been prudent and wise to accept the king's offer and go back to Tripura. But to his eternal credit, even in such a situation, he did not lose sight of his ambition. Music remained his foremost love and he decided that hardships in the path of music were more welcome than opting for ease and plenty without music. Faced with the harsh realities of life for the first time, he decided he would try and manage on his own.

He realized that Tripura Palace was a costly place to live in, quite beyond his means under his straitened circumstances. Therefore, he rented a room on Palit Street. The scion of a royal family, he started providing tuitions in music to earn his living. Apart from teaching, he would spend his days honing his skills in music. During this time of hardship he received a call from the stage. Hemendra Kumar Ray initiated him into theatre. Sachin directed the music for Sachindranath Sengupta's plays *Satitirtha* and *Janani* which had nine songs each. Hemendra Ray himself was the lyricist for all but one of these eighteen songs. Dramatist Sachindranath reminisces: 'I shall be eternally grateful to Sachin Dev Burman for composing the music for these songs. The magical touch he imparted to these songs took the plays to a new level.' It was the result of his contact with the stage that Sachin could, in his musical life spread over nearly six decades, impart a dramatic note to his songs. His experiments and experience with music in theatre paid off in later years. In *Satitirtha,* we find an early incarnation of his famous song '*Ami takdum takdum bajai*' in '*Ar kato gan gaibo balo*'. Again in '*Kon bagane rasik oli*' we find the bhatiyali strains of his latter-day hit '*Ore sujan naiya*'. Besides, he gave glimpses of his versatility with songs like '*Nabaghana shyam nabin nirad*' and the Tagore-inspired '*Chokher jale bhijiye dilam galar beler mala*'.

Augmenting his income from music tuitions, there was also the remuneration he received from singing for the radio—a princely sum of ten rupees a session. He sang for the first time in Indian Broadcasting Co. (Radio station of Garstin Place, Dalhousie, Calcutta) in 1927. In his memoirs, S. D. Burman mentions it as the Indian State Broadcasting Company. It was during one such session at the radio station that he was introduced to music composer Rai Chand Boral who said this about the meeting:

> I was speechless hearing him sing the first time I did. To tell the truth, I was astonished at the diversity of his tunes. Sachin Dev Burman brought as much diversity in the field of folk songs as Begum Akhtar had done in the field of Hindi ghazals and dadra. I became a fan right

from the beginning. When he used to sing a folk song in his inimitable style I felt as if I was travelling in the countryside. I could smell the soil, hear the roar of the river in spate.

4
Calcutta
1932-44

The year was 1930 and Sachin was not even twenty-five years old. For a composer like Rai Chand Boral to heap such praise on so young a talent meant that Sachin's rise was inevitable. However, this rise to glory was not easy. The path to success was strewn with innumerable obstacles.

In those years, His Master's Voice (HMV) was the most famous record company with a monopolistic position as a recording company. Artists had no other option but HMV if they wanted to record albums of their work and to be accepted by HMV was an honour almost every artist coveted. Sachin was no exception. However, shocking as it may seem, he failed his audition test. Sachin was informed that his nasal voice was not fit for recording, that the market would not accept it. Interestingly enough, the same fate befell the singing sensation of the 1930s, K. L. Saigal. Sachin was shattered.

It won't be improper to assume that the root cause of Sachin being rejected was a lack of patronage. Rajeshwar Mitra has written:

In later years, Sachin drifted away from K. C. Dey. The reason was perhaps that his guru did not help him in publicizing his potential. This lack of patronage was also behind his rejection in HMV at the first instance. ('Sachin Karta', *Prantik,* 2006)

The world of music has always been competitive. Cut-throat competition marks the music scene even today and Sachin was no stranger to competition during his time. Sachin personally knew the movers and shakers, the pioneers of the industry at the time, whether film directors, music directors, famous actors and actresses, stage performers and connoisseurs. But nobody lent a helping hand when it came to recording his songs. The same indifference would later result in his departure from Calcutta. But despite HMV's refusal, Sachin would not be denied his rightful glory. At around the same time as HMV rejected Sachin, one Chandicharan Saha had brought a new recording machine from Germany and founded a new company, Hindustan Musical Products. He was on the lookout for artists. Chandi-babu had a passing acquaintance with Narendra Dev Burman or Naru Thakur and had mentioned his new company to him. Sachin had already narrated his tale of woe to his friend Naru Thakur who then went to Chandi-babu. Chandicharan Saha was initially hesitant about accepting an artist rejected by a behemoth like HMV. After all, he was a businessman. But on Naru Thakur's request and in spite of his personal reluctance, he signed on Sachin. And this opened the gates of Chandi-babu's fortune. Later, he gratefully recounted this episode as a gift from God. Hindustan Musical Products' publicity brochure of the record (dated September 1932) which had two of Sachin's songs mentioned:

Kumar Sachin Dev Burman, Esq. is not new to the world of music even though he may be new to the world of recordings. You will appreciate the musical skill he has acquired at this young age once you listen to the two songs in Hindustan records. Perhaps it is enough to say that he is the best of all the disciples of the famous singer Krishna Chandra Dey. The lyrics are unparalleled. Equally matchless is his melodious voice. One hearing will be enough to acknowledge that this record is one of the greatest gifts to the world of the gramophone.

News of this record, once released, spread like wildfire. It became a major success story. One side of the record had the song 'Dakle kokil roj bihane', written by Hemendra Ray and rendered by Sachin in the manner of a folk song. The other side contained 'E pathe aj esho priyo', cast in the classical-based khambaj thumri style. Shailen Ray was the lyricist. Sachin composed the music for both the songs. They were drastically different in genres, one a folk song and the other a classical number. With this, a new star rose on the musical horizon of the country. Sachin Dev Burman never looked back after this. The experience of recording his songs and of listening to them floored the artist himself who confessed with childlike innocence: 'I was listening to my own voice. Initially, it was a thrilling experience for me.'

Before long, news of the record travelled to Agartala and created a sensation in Sachin's home state. However, it was also a cause for some heartburn in the royal quarters. This was the first time a prince had crossed the boundaries of the royal palace and offered his music to the public. Hitherto, singing by princes was limited to the inner courts. Maharaja Bir Bikram himself had recorded his sitar and flute recitals, but despite repeated requests by the gramophone company, had never agreed to release these in the market on a commercial basis. The royalty was offended by what it considered demeaning behaviour on the part of Sachin. The masses of Tripura, on the other hand, were not perturbed. On the contrary, they were elated. A son of Tripura had stormed Bengal. Jyotish Dev Burman, elder brother of Naru Thakur, a relative and friend of Sachin-karta, remembers the heady feeling of those days:

> Sometime after his first record was released he came with it to his family home in Agartala after a sojourn in Comilla. It was during the reign of Maharaja Bir Bikram. A little away was Thakur Boarding. People assembled at Karta's residence to listen to the songs. Everybody was immersed in joy and merriment. A record by a son of Tripura was a matter of no mean importance. Suddenly I ran away with the record. Karta shouted, 'Hey, this is the only copy. It can't be replaced if broken.' I replied, 'I won't break it, I won't. This is my treasure.' (*Gomati*, Govt. of Tripura, 2005)

In spite of the popularity of his first record, Sachin had to face disappointment soon after. In 1933, he sang for the first time for the film *Yahudi Ki Ladki*, which had music by Pankaj Mullick. This should have been his first film song, but thanks to the internal machinations that characterized the industry at that time, as much as it probably does today, it did not materialize. The song was recorded afresh by Pahari Sanyal.

If Sachin felt disappointed with the turn of events, he made light of it and in February 1933 released two more records. The songs '*Bondhu elo modhu ratey*' and '*Tumi toh bondhu jano*' were written by Ajay Bhattacharya and were set to music by Himangshu Dutta. Both are classical numbers, in khayal, and brought him recognition as a singer of classical-based songs. In songs of this kind, the stress is more on the raga and not on words. Sachin, however, took great delight in the way he articulated the words of a song. It was this that set him apart, made his music unique. He made an art of bringing out the essence of each word he sang, creating a perfect marriage of words and music. The tune for '*Tumi toh bondhu jano*' was borrowed from the song '*Kis kis ada se tuney, jalwe dikha ke mara*' by Mohammad Hussain (Khusru Mian), an unknown ghazal singer of Comilla. Sachin got Himangshu Dutta to hone it a bit. But in Sachin's voice it acquired a life of its own, as if the soul of a ghazal had been breathed into the flesh of khayal. Connoisseurs have pointed out how in the lines '*Marute basa baandhi*'—particularly the way he enunciates the word 'baandhi'—the tune is stretched that extra bit and then fades ever so slowly, its resonance seemingly never-ending. More than vocal music, it sounds like the strain of a tanpura.

Another record was released in July 1933, with lyrics by Hemendra Kumar Ray and music by Sachin himself. It had the heart-rending songs '*O kalo megh bolte paro*' and '*Ei kananer phul niye*', which effortlessly conveyed, through Sachin's mellifluous rendition, the sense of dark clouds hanging over a heart heavy with longing. It remains a popular number even to this day. The other song '*Ei kananer phul niye*' is semi-classical, compact, shorn of frills, sweet and has a delightfully sharp asperity to it. It can be enjoyed by everyone.

By this time, Sachin had begun to make a name for himself even outside Bengal. In 1934, he was invited to the All India Music Conference organized by Allahabad University. It provided him the opportunity to perform before many famous vocalists and musicians from all over the country and he took up the challenge. Though Sachin had not sung Hindi songs till then, he was undaunted. With great passion, he sang the heart-rending classical number

'Jadi dakhina paban asiya phire go dware'. The music, composed by Himangshu Dutta, was further embellished by Bhishmadeb Chattopadhyay. The song was already a mix of raga Jaunpuri and shuddh gandhar and, the addition of two dhaivat by Bhishmadeb Chattopadhyay gave it a new dimension. Sachin's rendition, in a style approximating khayal, created a sensation and was warmly applauded by the audience which included Ustad Karim Khan who blessed the young singer and later became quite close to Sachin. For the first time in his life, people sought Sachin out for autographs. The organizers, connoisseurs as they were, showed their appreciation by inviting him for the next three conferences. Sachin himself had fond memories of the conference:

> I still remember, it was at this conference that I gave an autograph for the first time in my life. It is difficult to explain what I felt after signing the autograph book. The audience in this conference included Sir Tejbahadur Sapru, Dr Kailash Nath Katju, Smt Vijaya Lakshmi Pandit and others. Dr Katju presented me with a medallion. (*Sargamer Nikhad*)

After the conference, Sachin toured the United Provinces and Bihar and true to his inquisitive nature when it came to music collected many folk songs of these regions.

In 1934, four more records of Sachin were released in March, May, August and October, which included the songs '*Swapana na bhange jadi*', '*Aji rate ke*', '*Jadi dakhina paban*', '*Alochhaya dola*', '*Jhulane jhulichhe Shyam Rai*', '*Raibo na ar ujan ghare*', '*Praner prabhu rahe prane*' and '*Manodukkhe marirey Subal*'. Barring '*Jadi dakhina paban*', Sachin composed the music for all the songs. Of these, singer-composer Kabir Suman (Suman Chattopadhyay) has singled out '*Alochhaya dola*', in raga Bahar, for special mention in his article:

At the fag end of *'Alochhaya dola'* there is a sharp stroke of melody in descent. Its pure (shuddha) seventh is doubled in median. This is followed by two notes per measure for the next five measures returning to the first note of the natural major C. It gives an idea of the artist's expertise in Hindustani classical music.

The other songs also deserve equal attention. *'Swapna na bhange jadi'* (an original creation of mixed Bhimpalasri and Dadra) and *'Aji rate ke'* are raga-based and are tuned in long strain. The rendition leaves a never-ending resonance. *'Raibo na ar ujan ghare'* is a pure and simple folk song with sharp deviation in rhythm. The song *'Praner prabhu rahe prane'* is a product of experimentation by S. D. Burman. This song is a combination of bhajan, kirtan and folk music. The piteous tone reflects one's desire for union with the lord of 'prana' (soul). *'Jhulane jhulichhe Shyam Rai'* is a raga-based devotional song. The most touching song is *'Manodukkhe marirey subal'*. The names of the lyricist and composer are not mentioned. S. D. Burman heard this song from Saheb Ali at Agartala. This type of song is generally sung in dhap yatra depicting estrangement of Krishna and Radha from each other. Krishna's grief is beautifully brought out by Sachin in the way he sings *'Brajeshwari rai kishori anniya dey amare'* reminds us of another folk song of East Bengal—*'Aami bandhur premaguney pora shai go'*. With slight changes to the original tune, SD made this song special.

Finally came his first song in a film. The year was 1935, the film was *Sanjher Pradeep* and the song was *'Oray sujan naiya kon ba kanyar deshe jaore chander dinga baiya.'* He not only sang the song in his characteristic manner but also composed its music in the style of bhatiyali. The film became a hit on the strength of these songs alone as the audience were carried away by their lilting strains.

The other song of the film *'Nishithey jaiyo phulabane'* is, in a word, unparalleled and remains popular even today. Along with singing, Sachin also acted in films at that time. In *Selima* (1935), directed by Madhu Bose, he was seen in the role of a beggar. Madhu Bose has drawn a loving portrait of those times in his autobiography *Amar Jiban*:

> A famous music director acted in a minor role in *Selima*. I was looking for someone to cast in the role of a beggar. This music director had just made a name as a singer and used to teach music to Sadhana (the director's wife). One day I broached the topic with him: 'There is a small role of a beggar. You needn't do much; just sit and sing a song, nothing else.' He was startled and said, 'What! How dare I act in a film? You know my family. If I act in a film they are sure to ostracize me. I sing, I record my songs and that's enough for my family to whisper about and scorn me.' I said, 'I'll give you such a make-up with beard and moustache that nobody will recognize you.' He agreed at last after a lot of persuasion. He sang the song well. Today he is a well-known music director—Kumar Sachin Dev Burman.

In 1935, Sachin debuted as a music director with the film *Sudurer Priya*. The film flopped but his songs *'Tumi ni aamar bandhu'* and *'Bandhu banshi dao more'* were hits. *'Bandhu banshi dao more'* is more rhythmic than *'Tumi ni aamar'*. Both are theka-based folk songs with mesmerizing tunes.

That year Sachin recorded eight songs. Though each of them gained unparalleled popularity, *'Nishithe jaiyo phulabane'* from *Sanjher Pradeep* was by far the most popular of all. Surely, one must possess that special something that reaches out and steals the heart—a gift of mellifluous melody. This song is so captivating that one is inclined to say: 'Only he can sing flowers to sleep.' Nothing much about his meend (glide from one note to another), taan or gamak (ornamentation in performance of Indian classical music but the way he presented this song laced with small intricacies sweeps the listener off the feet.

Sachin got the poet Jasimuddin to change a few lines of the original song penned by Sheikh Bhanu, thereby shaping a Sufi composition into a love song. But the overall effect was no less stunning than the original as Sachin's tune and rendering brought alive the bees humming in moonlight, the flowery bower and the note of caution requesting the bee to steal in softly so that the beloved's sleep is not disturbed. While the tune is redolent of romance, there is something about the composition which makes it almost dreamlike. It is almost as if the music has put the words in motion.

True, his voice was not as strong as that of dhrupad and khayal singers, but he had something which is invaluable to a music lover—the power to present songs in a simple yet sophisticated manner and capture the heart of the audience. Once Sachin said: 'I fused folk and classical music to develop a style of composition which was different from others.' He developed a style of rendition, or gayaki of his own. Karta's greatest contribution in the realm of modern Bengali music is the expression of poetry through music. The lyrical beauty of a song, delivered in his inimitable style, along the lines of raga or a folk song, continue to remain unparalleled in Bengali music. Sachin Dev Burman is revered almost as an institution.

Two of Sachin's songs based on traditional or Hindustani bandishes are *'Kanthey tomar dulbey boley'* and *'Ei mahua bane'*. The latter in particular highlights Sachin's extraordinary virtuosity as it almost appears that there is no instrumental accompaniment to the song. The tanpura is fixed at a single string. The tabla seems to be absent. The song was composed in raga Desh Misra but in its khayal overtures it has the feel of early-morning kirtans of rural Bengal. As a singer-composer, Sachin produced amazingly beautiful shades of the same colour, beautiful variations of the same raga paying due respect to its lyrical beauty, opening a new door to the appreciation of Hindustani classical music. These songs are not sung in public simply because it is impossible to reproduce those nuances—a twist, a turn, a phrase uttered in a broken voice—things which only the magical voice of Sachin Dev Burman could carry off with aplomb.

Besides this, there are the two agamani and bijaya songs—songs invoking goddess Durga during the Durga Puja—'*Swapana dekhechhe Girirani*' and '*Biday dao go moray*'. In one, the goddess is being welcomed home and in the other she is bid farewell. Sachin's voice carries all the nuances of both the joy of welcome and the pain of parting.

In 1935, Calcutta hosted the Bengal Music Conference. Rabindranath Tagore inaugurated the conference which was chaired by Maharaja Bir Bikram Manikya of Tripura. Many talented music maestros and instrumentalists participated. Sachin presented a thumri in the presence of a classical specialist like Ustad Fayyaz Khan who encouraged him. Their relationship developed further with time. Sachin never missed any performance of Fayyaz Khan in Calcutta. In later years, a number of Sachin's compositions reflected the influence of Fayyaz Khan.

Music, for which a prince had chosen to live like a commoner, the pursuit of which almost drove him to penury, now started bestowing her favours on her devotee. With recordings, radio programmes, musical soirees and tuitions, money was no longer a problem.

In 1936, Sachin shifted from the one-room accommodation in Palit Street to a two-room flat at 1A, Basanta Roy Road. There he founded his music school 'Suramandir'. His popularity drew students in droves. Initially, Sachin alone used to teach the students. In the evenings, musical performances were organized at the centre patronized by stalwarts like Bhishmadeb Chattopadhyay, Himangshu Dutta, Ajay Bhattacharya, Sudhirlal Chakrabarti, Suresh Chakrabarti, Haripada Ray, Sitarist Phani-babu and many others. The Saraswati Puja held every year was another occasion for soirees. Sachin, however, could not take care of this school for long. His other commitments left him with little time to devote to the school. Finding no other alternative, he had to hand over the responsibility of Suramandir to Suresh Chakrabarti, who bore this responsibility successfully for many years.

Sachin recorded three albums in 1936. There were six songs in these: *'Balo balo balo bondhu'*, *'Jagar sathi go mamo'*, *'Mamo mandiray ele kego'*, *'Natun phagun jobey'*, *'Tomari sathey soore'* and *'Paradeshey keno go'*. While the first two were classical-based ghazals, the others were classical compositions. As had become customary for Sachin now, he emphasized a word or two in a song, shortening or lengthening them, in a way that gave an altogether new spin to even a purely classical composition. In *'Natun phagun jobey'*, for example, his articulation of the word *'nache'* in the line *'tomare dharia nache'* presents a visual kaleidoscope of a dance. Again in *'Balo balo balo bondhu'*, the way he articulates *'balo'* seems to leave its resonance even after the song has ended.

'Jagar sathi go mamo' showcases Sachin Dev's nasal voice and fine workmanship of meend. Extra stress on some words of the ghazal has enhanced its beauty. *'Tomari sathey surey'* starts with the bandish of khayal and ends in resonance. In *'Pardeshey keno go'*, Sachin Dev's fine theka on *'rahiley'* and in *'elo je barasha nabo'*

eloquently welcomed 'barasha' with artistic tuning of the raga. *'Mamo mandirey eley kego'* is full of meend and juwary.

It is commonly believed that classical music is not for the consumption of general public, but SD's music remains for everyone. His music was much ahead of his times. Even after so many decades, his music still sounds young at heart. All the songs are refreshing and one is tempted to listen to them again and again.

It will not be out of context to mention here that Sachin's contemporary Bengali ustads used to present classical songs only in Hindi. The idea of presenting classical compositions in Bengali was unheard of. Even Bhishmadeb Chattopadhyay used to sing and teach in Hindi. Sachin not only rendered songs in Bengali, but successfully maintained the purity of ragas and raginis. His songs were essentially classical, yet had a style that was Sachin's own. In this context, Sachin himself has written:

> Sometime in the early 1930s I began to compose music for my songs and sing them myself [...] I started experimenting and composing music in my own individual style. Between 1930-36 I developed a style of my own, mixing folk songs and Indian classical, which was entirely different from those composed by others. (*Sargamer Nikhad*)

In 1937, Sachin composed the music for Sukumar Dasgupta's film *Rajgi* jointly with Bhishmadeb Chattopadhyay. He sang two songs set to his own music. He even acted in the film. Dressed as a potter working at his wheel, he rendered the song *'Saje nawal kishore, chander tilake'*. This bhajan in Kaharbataal was very popular with the audiences. The other song *'Ore bandhu re moner katha'* was also a big hit. Both the songs were recorded the next year.

Sachin often sang in films between 1932-38. In this context, he has mentioned:

Many of my friends used to say that even a single song in my voice would bring credit to a film. They even went to the extent of telling me that they would stop making films if I did not sing in their films. In the face of such love and affection I could not refuse them. But I used to lay down two conditions, which were always agreed to. First, I wanted to compose the music myself for the song to be sung by me (even if someone else was the music director) and second, no actor would lip-sync the song through playback. The songs had to be used as background prop to create a particular atmosphere. (*Sargamer Nikhad*)

Though it is true that his songs were inevitably played in the background in Hindi cinema, it needs to be mentioned that Sachin has unknowingly made some factual errors in his reminiscences above. Besides singing '*Chokh gelo chokh gelo*' with Nazrul's music in the film *Nandini*, he also sang '*Ke jeno kandichhe akash bhubanmay*' in the film *Nari*, the music for which was composed by R. C. Boral. Besides, Himangshu Dutta composed the music for the two songs sung by him in *Jibansangini*—'*Janama dukhini Sita*' and '*Banglar meye banglari tumi*'. Also, other actors did lip-sync to his songs in playback. '*Banshariya re*' in *Rajkumarer Nirbasan* and '*Janama dukhini Sita*' in *Jibansangini* were sung in playback. These are only illustrative examples. There are others too.

The year 1937 saw the release of five records with ten songs by Sachin (six Bengali and four Hindi) of which the following became immensely popular: '*Phuler baney thako bhramar*', '*Ke jabi chal Brindbane*', '*Jhanjhan jhanjhan manjira*', '*Pohalo rati jagiya*', and '*Gaurarup dekhia hoyechhi pagal*' and '*Pinjorer pakhir mato*'. Among the Hindi songs, '*Nayan morey darash bhikhari*', '*Ab mein sharana tumhari*' and '*Mere preetam pyare*' were bhajans. They were good compositions but not splendid.

Later, S. D. Burman set several bhajans to music in many Hindi film songs which proved to be intoxicating, accompanied by a flute. The other song *'Preet mein huye badnam'* is a well-composed ghazal. SD played with the word *'badnam'* in the khayal style.

While the first folk composition is redolent of the fragrance of the wet earth of rural Bengal, the other is a narration of the glory of Vrindavan. *'Pohalo rati jagiya'* is a classical song and *'Gourrup dekhia hoyechhi pagal'* is sung in adoration of Gouranga Mahaprabhu. *'Pinjorer pakhir mato'* depicts the rustic philosophy of rural thought in search of the self. *'Jhanjhan jhanjhan manjira'*, a Raga Natabehag composition set in teen taal, was patterned after Ustad Fayyaz Khan's khayal composition, *'Jhanjhan jhanjhan payelia'*; Sachin improvised it to create an original composition. He has spoken at length about this popular number:

> In 1950, I directed the music of *Buzdil*, a Hindi film directed by Shahid Latif, with Shailendra as lyricist. I remember the composition *'Jhanjhan jhanjhan payal baje'*, set in raga Natabehag. I first listened to this song in Ustad Fayyaz Khan's voice in 1935. The grace and beauty of his rendition overwhelmed me, the melody and rhythm that Khan Sahib created still rings in my ear. I used this song in *Buzdil*. The first line was the same. It was sung by Lata. It is difficult for a purely classical song to become popular in Hindi films. I maintained the classical raga in passing and introduced elements of a kirtan in it. It gained mass acceptance. (*Sargamer Nikhad*)

While Sachin was making rapid progress professionally, there were developments on the personal front too. One of Sachin's students at Suramandir was Meera Dhar, the granddaughter of the late Judge

Ray Bahadur Kamalnath Dasgupta. Meera had learnt classical music from Bhishmadeb Chattopadhyay and dance from Amita Sen (the youngest daughter of Pandit Kshitimohan Sen) of Santiniketan. Later she mastered thumri and kirtan under Dhirendrachandra Mitra and Rabindra Sangeet under Anadi Dastidar. In 1937, Meera was invited along with Sachin to the music conference at Allahabad. The duet sung by Meera and Sachin at the conference created a sensation.

It was not long before cupid struck. Since they shared a common love for music, this was not surprising. Soon enough, Sachin proposed marriage and Meera consented. On 10 February 1938, they tied the knot. His mother, the elder brothers, sisters-in-law and other relatives participated in the ceremony, but no one from the inner courts of Maharaja Bir Bikram showed up. Many others did not take kindly to this union. Even Bhishmadeb Chattopadhyay did not support this marriage between a guru and his disciple. Suresh Chakrabarti wrote:

> An orthodox trait of Bhishmadeb's pious character came to fore during Sachin-karta's marriage. Sachin's wife Meera Debi used to be trained under him prior to the marriage. She was Sachin-karta's disciple in the musical society of Dhaka and Calcutta. For a short while before her marriage she was also trained under Bhishmadeb, but was known to one and all as a pupil of Sachin. Bhishmadeb could not take this marriage with one's own student in the proper spirit. Many a time he mentioned this disapprovingly to me. (*Sudha Sagar Teerey*)

The reaction from the royal family was even worse. After the marriage, Sachin went to Agartala with his bride. He took her to the inner court. As per tradition, it is the queen-consort or any other queen who welcomes the bride. The wife of a karta had the status of a queen. But in this case, not only was no such custom observed, the ladies in the court deliberately insulted and neglected Meera Dev Burman. The royal family had never quite approved of a prince going around singing everywhere. His marriage to a non-kshatriya commoner only made matters worse. The behaviour of the ladies of the royal court deeply hurt the newly-weds. Sachin had forgotten the insult accompanying the loss of his kingdom. He would not forget or forgive this insult. Never in any of his future visits to Agartala would he cross the threshold of the royal court. In course of time, he even went on to sever all links with the royal family.

In 1938, Sachin Dev shifted to a flat on Hindustan Road. That year saw him record three albums. All the songs in these albums were hits. '*Saje nawal kishore*' and '*Ore bandhu re moner katha kaibar aage*' have been mentioned earlier. They were included in the film *Rajgi* (1937). '*Jago mamo saheli go*' in Kafi Bhairavi followed the style of '*Bhala mora mana bhanti murali bajai*' which he had learnt from Bhishmadeb. But it was patterned as a modern song based on classical tune avoiding the original keynote and musical scale. He sang it like a romantic number as if trying to rouse one's sweetheart from sleep—'*Jago mamo saheli go rajani pohay*'. Although '*Tumi je chhile more*' is a classical song, the jingle of cymbals in the style of kirtan is heard in the lines—'*Aajio phagune hashe banatal / Amar nayaney barasha utal*'. '*Prem jamunari parey*' (Kirana gharana, Bhaivari) and '*Tumi je giyachho bakula bichhano pathe*', though classical-based, cannot be classified as classical compositions since the style and mood of the songs are absolutely different. Despite their origins in classical ragas, there is none of the serious style or modulation of voice that generally accompanies classical compositions. These can probably be called classic-modern but would be best summed up as

'Sachindevian'. While *'Prem jamunari parey'* is patterned like a jhumar, the melody overwhelming one to the extent of bringing tears to one's eyes. *'Tumi je giyachho bakula bichhano pathe'* is a romantic song, which begins with the melodious strains of the sitar before the plaintive strains of the flute take over. The perfect confluence of words and music creates an image of the beloved passing through the bakul-strewn path, generating a feeling of remorse, lending an atmosphere of melancholy to the song.

Sachin Dev Burman is unparalleled in his capacity to create a sense of pathos in his music. He experimented relentlessly with the three streams of music—classical, folk and modern. The key to his music lay in his ability to cross the limits of the ragas to express feelings.

In 1939, the book *Surer Likhan* was published by D.M. Library. It contained notations for twenty-five of Sachin's songs. The book, dedicated to his father Nabadwip Chandra, is not available any more.

On 27 June 1939, Sachin and Meera became proud parents of a baby boy. Sachin named him Rahul. His pet name, the name by which he was referred to by near and dear ones, was Pancham, the fifth note of the musical octave.

That year Sachin came out with three records. The song *'Kandibo na phagun gele'* mesmerized the audience. This song once again demonstrated Sachin's expertise in taming sophisticated ragas and raginis and modernizing them. *'Aaj jhar layo'* in Charju ki Malhar which he had learnt from Bhishmadeb was suitably modified to another famous song *'Megh jhare jay'*. *'Champak jago jago'* is an example of lyrical grace in slow tempo. *'Chhilo madhavi raati go'* is a classical-romantic song. *'Aamar milan malati'* is a romantic song in Karta's broken voice and unique style.

Despite these successes Sachin was not satisfied. Reading his memoirs, one gets an idea of his state of mind at that point in time. It perhaps provides an explanation for his desire to leave Calcutta for Bombay. He wrote:

> I had an ardent desire to direct music in Bengali films but was not getting any opportunity. For a long time, I tried my luck at New Theatres and was encouraged by men in authority. But nothing came of it in the long run. I knew many of the famous directors in New Theatres those days, like Nitin Bose, my friend Hemchandra and Debaki Bose. They were all praises for my songs and compositions. The famous Pramathesh Barua and I used to play tennis together. Saigal and Pahari Sanyal were also my close friends. I often accompanied Saigal for musical performances outside Calcutta, particularly Ranchi. B. N. Sircar, the helmsman at New Theatres also knew about my music composition. I was also personally acquainted with him. In spite of all this, I got very few opportunities to compose music for Bengali films. I was somewhat offended at the neglect. I even started feeling that I was not being able to reach the public at large through my music. It's not that I didn't compose for any Bengali film—I remember two films, *Rajgi* and *Rajkumarer Nirbasan*—but I didn't find the satisfaction I was looking for. (*Sargamer Nikhad*)

It bears recall that so far Sachin had directed the music in only one film as solo composer, in *Sudurer Priya* in 1935. In *Rajgi* and *Rajkumarer Nirbasan* he was the joint music director with Bhishmadeb and Hariprasanna Das respectively. The publicity material of Kamala Talkies, however, clearly mentions that while Bhishmadeb Chattopadhyay and Hariprasanna Das were the music directors of the two films respectively, Sachin was the music composer, i.e. he composed the songs. The other two directed the background music only. From 1935 to 1971, Sachin directed the music in eighteen Bengali films, besides *Aradhana* (posthumous).

It was around this time that Sachin is said to have joined the Indian People's Theatre Association (IPTA). But the IPTA was founded in 1943 after the fourth session of the Progressive Writers Association (PWA) in Bombay. Sachin Dev most probably mistook PWA for IPTA. While depicting social problems afflicting the country, IPTA's dramas like *Banglar Dulal*, *Desher Dabi*, *Sangram*, *Shanti*, *Dui Purush*, *Natun Prabhat*, etc., sought to bring about social change. Sachin was an active member of the PWA during the late 1930s and became the president of the Bengali folk music division of IPTA at the very moment IPTA raised its voice demanding artistic freedom. His link with the group continued even after he shifted to Bombay. In his early days in Bombay, his was a permanent presence in all cultural programmes of IPTA. Many renowned musicians were associated with it in those days. Among them were Hemanga Biswas, Ravi Shankar, V. Balsara, Binoy Ray, Salil Chaudhuri, Bhupen Hazarika and others. Sachin wrote in this context:

> I was associated with IPTA's music section [what he means is perhaps the PWA] till 1939. The IPTA made me president of the branch of Bengali folk music. Many renowned singers from all over India were part of this committee. Listening to their songs and associating with representatives from other states helped me develop my knowledge of the regional music of our country. When I shifted to Bombay in 1944, I used to participate regularly in the musical performances of this society, particularly the

dance performances of the late Shanti Bardhan. Bardhan was a highly talented artist. I was charmed with his various experimentations. Thanks to my association with IPTA, I understood how diverse and rich Indian folk music is. (*Sargamer Nikhad*)

In 1939, Sachin Dev set the music for the film *Jakkher Dhan* with Dhiren Das as his assistant. The title page records: Music composers: Sachin Dev Barman [sic] and Dhiren Das. It seems that music director and music composer were synonymous in those days. Sachin did not lend his voice to any of these songs. The film boasts ten songs but none of them was a hit.

In 1940, Sachin worked as the joint music director with Hariprasanna in *Rajkumarer Nirbasan* and with Bhishmadeb Chattopadhyay in *Amar Giti*. In the former, he sang the famous tragic song set to his own tune '*Banshariyare, kothay shikhechho banshi bajano*'. The record came out in September 1941. He did not sing in *Amar Giti*.

Two records came out from Hindustan Musical Products in 1940. The songs included '*Premer samadhi tirey nemey elo*' (lyrics Shailen Ray, music Himangshu Dutta); '*Ami chhinu eka*' (lyrics Ajay Bhattacharya, music Sachin Dev Burman); '*Kuhu kuhu koelia*' and '*Meghla nishibhore*' (lyrics and music by Kazi Nazrul Islam). Records sold in volumes unprecedented in the history of gramophone records in the country. Sachin's popularity was at its zenith. Listeners realized that irrespective of the music composer, any song sung by Sachin Dev Burman had a characteristic cadence about it. It was no longer difficult to identify a Sachin song even if the music was set by others. He had mastered the art of harmonizing tune and rhythm which is the hallmark of any great artist.

The rhythm of a song is known as taal. Rhythm possesses the power of expression. The swing of various rhythms creates different tastes. Rhythm is used in symmetry with emotion. *'Premer samadhi tirey'* is one of those songs that have the power of rhythm. The song is a poetic beauty. It creates a vacuum in the heart. It palpitates with the sound *'hai, hai'*. The song is based on raga Darbari Kanada but sung by SD in a modern style. The modulation of voice in the song is unique. It is one of the greatest love songs.

Listening to *'Ami chhinu eka'* makes one feel like closing one's eyes and losing oneself in the lingering resonance of the song. Embellished in the style of a thumri, the song has an interesting background.

In a musical performance, Sachin was listed to perform after Saigal. Saigal had to sing a few more songs than scheduled on popular demand. He had to ignore further requests in order to keep his next appointment for which the organizers had already arrived. Almost at the gate, Saigal came to a sudden halt and stood like a statue. Sachin had started singing *'Ami chhinu eka'*. It had not been recorded as yet. Overwhelmed, Saigal sat down on a chair. He was dumbfounded. Was it not his song! It was he who had rendered the tune in Khambaj for the first time in *'Kaun bujhai Rama tapat mera man ki'*, a thumri. But in Sachin's voice, the intoxicating tune had been transformed completely. A feeling of solitude and loneliness filled the hearts of the audience. They were swept away on the waves of the anguish-laden melody—surpassing the tune, beyond the dictates of Khambaj—a mix of thumri and folk, which rose, reached a crescendo and then fell, only to rise again. Saigal sat mesmerized till the song ended. He came to senses at the cry of joy from the audience. Such was the magic of Sachin's style, the enchantment of his tune. In the words of Kabir Suman: 'Sachin-karta is unparalleled in the art of assimilation.' He could internalize the tune by any music composer and give it his own style.

Sachin even sang Nazrul's songs in his own style. It was he who suggested the main tune of '*Kuhu kuhu koelia*' to Nazrul. He had closely listened to Ustad Fayyaz Khan's song '*Na manungi, na manungi, na manungi*' in raga Khambaj. Restructuring the tune, he helped Nazrul create '*Kuhu kuhu koelia*'.

There is a story behind this song too, though its factual veracity is not clear. Nazrul had been struggling over the lyrics and tune for the song for quite some time. One day, he was at Aurora Studio in the Narkeldanga area of Calcutta. The dulcet voice of a distant cuckoo filled his heart with passion. Just then, Sachin entered with his elegant gait, humming to himself. Kazi Sahib said, 'Can you listen to the cuckoo?'

'I am listening to it. It's such a sweet note.'

'Try saying "kuhu, kuhu" once like the bird. Let me see if you can.'

'Tch! You must be joking.'

But Nazrul would not let go. Sachin shut his eyes and hummed '*kuhu kuhu kuhu kuhu*'. Nazrul got the words he was looking for. A memorable song was born.

The other side of the record contained the song '*Meghla nishi bhore*'. The choice of words and the music set in Sachin's style raised the two songs to a different level altogether. If one closes one's eyes and listens to the songs, one can almost visualize the Bengal countryside, the mud huts of rural Bengal, of thoughts forlorn and fugitive raising a storm in rivers, filling hearts with melancholy.

In 1941, Sachin directed the music for the film *Pratishodh*. He sang two songs in the film, '*Ore abodh neye*' and '*Ki maya laglo chokhe*' written by Premendra Mitra. That year, five of his records were released. Among these were two songs written by Munshi

Zakir Hussain. 'Prem ki pyari nishani' is the Hindi version of 'Premer samadhi tirey' and 'Chalo chalo prem ke saathi' is an SD trademark classical song. Others were the unforgettable 'Priyo ajo nay, ajo nay', 'Godhulir chhaya pathe', 'Chokh gelo, chokh gelo', and the famous 'Padmar dhew re, amar shunya hriday padma' apart from 'Banshuriyarey kothai shikhechho', 'Ki maya laglo chokhey' and 'Orey abodh neye'. As had become his forte by now, he freely traversed the distance between classical and folk, using raga-based music in folk tunes and amalgamating folk tunes in classical music, suitably altering both to match his own style that had the listeners asking for more. This was his individual speciality and he had an uncanny capacity for improvisation.

He had an instictive feel for the pulse of the people. The secret behind the popularity of his songs also lies in the way he articulated the words of a song. He had an intuitive understanding of which syllable or letter was to be emphasized in the tune for what effect. For example, in 'Godhulir chhaya pathey' emphasis was laid on the sound 'pa' and in 'Ami chini go' on 'go' in such a way that both the words created an unending meend of sitar-like jowari. In 'Priyo aajo noy', 'ka' of the word 'kandichhe' and 'hay' were unveiled in long bits and pieces to transform them into wailing. In 'Banshuriarey kothai shikhechho', Sachin delivered the song in a mystic voice twisting the words into a coil and then scattering them into the open windows of raga-ragini and folk music. He knew very well how melody can win over a heart. The aforesaid three songs are mere examples.

'Ki maya laglo chokhe' is a modern song without any touch of folk or classical music. 'Orey abodh neye' and 'Aamar ki holo' are a mixture of rural and urban culture. We get the essence of both folk and modern music in these songs.

The four Nazrul songs in Sachin Dev Burman's record were

specially written for him. Let us hear the story behind '*Chokh gelo, chokh gelo*' in Sachin's own words:

> Many people have listened to my song '*Chokh gelo, chokh gelo*'. The words are by Kazi-da. He composed it in four to five minutes, with music. I had requested Kazi-da, 'Please give me a song with a teasing tune in the style of a jhumar.' Kazi-da came up with the song almost immediately. (*Sargamer Nikhad*)

Those who have listened to this song know well that there is no orchestra in the background. Only the soft tune of a flute resembling the cooing of a cuckoo and the nightingale resonates in lieu of music. Also, it needs to be mentioned here that though the music was composed by Nazrul himself, Himangshu Dutta was the one who conducted the music.

Now let us come to one of the most famous songs of S. D. Burman, '*Padmar dhew re*'. Kazi Nazrul Islam is the lyricist and composer of this song. The song reflects the image of the river Padma. This song has everything! There is a tinge of an enchanting raga, bhatiyali's wailing slow measure, the bol of a thumri and the tomtom and cymbals of kirtan, all together in one song. The very thought of a lotus heart drifting down the stream of the Padma, dancing on the hood of its wave, if accompanied by a perfect tune, is bound to take the audience to a dreamland of its own. The song floods the shores of our heart with its thunderous waves.

Many of us are not aware that SD went to Bombay in 1941 to sing for the film *Taj Mahal*. This was his second solo playback song in Hindi films after *Selima*. Madhablal Master was the music director and the song was '*Prem ki pyari nishani*'.

In 1942, Sachin directed the music for the films *Milan* (directed by Jyotish Banerjee), *Abhayer Biye* (directed by Sushil Majumdar) and *Ashok* (directed by Ajay Bhattarcharya) independently. But the songs failed to click with the audience. He was invited by music director R. C. Boral to sing a song for the film *Nari* which released in the same year. Boral wrote in this context: 'The song attained extraordinary popularity. Everyone in the audience shed tears listening to "*Ke jena kandichhe akash bhuvanmay*".'

Even today, after so many years, one cannot but marvel at the extraordinary talent of the singer. His articulation of the words has prevented the song from getting dated even sixty years later. The other side of the record contained '*Bideshire udashire phire jao tumi*' from the film *Epar Opar*. He sang it at the request of the film's director, who was also his friend, though the music director was Binod Gangopadhyay. This particular song, though, was composed by Sachin himself. Sachin also recorded two songs written by Shailen Ray and scored by Himangshu Dutta for the 1942 film *Jibansangini*. These two songs—'*Janama dukhini Sita*' and '*Banglar meye banglari tumi*'—contributed in a big way towards the success of the film. In the film *Abhayer Biye*, he sang a Hindi song set to his own music, '*Aye dil-e-betaab use yaad kiye ja*'. In the same year he recorded the Hindi version of '*Nishithe jaiyo phulabane*'— '*Dhire se jana bagiyan mein*'. He also sang another Hindi song, '*Kaun nagariya jao re*'. He had experimented by mixing folk and modern styles in the song '*Kokilarey geo na gaan*'. The song that captivated every mind was '*Malaya chalo dhire*'. The words of the song implore the breeze to move slowly so as not to awaken Krishna who is sleeping. In Sachin's voice, you can make out the earnest request as he indulges in his trademark experimentation with the words of the song. He articulates the word '*malay*' as '*malay-a-a*', asking her to move '*dhi-i-i-re dhi-i-i-re*', expanding the syllables just that bit to convey the plaintive request. When he comes to the lines

'*Jagayo na, taare jagayo na*', it is as if he is on guard and a note of caution overshadows the pleading note of the previous line.

Thus whatever Sachin sang captivated listeners. But he did not have much success as a music director in Bengali films. Everybody wanted Sachin the singer but not the music composer. The reason for this is not difficult to seek. Every film song sung by him in his own music was enormously popular. But the audience never seemed to enjoy songs composed by him but sung by others. His unique style did not come across in others' voices. About ninety per cent of the songs sung by him were in his own tune and people enjoyed these. Bengali film songs sung by others under Sachin's music direction were no match to the film and non-film songs sung by him which attained phenomenal popularity immediately on release. In the case of Hindi films, however, barring a few initial years, exactly the opposite happened.

One reason for this failure was the inability of the playback singers of those days to rise to the demands of his tunes. Commentators Debashis Mukhopadhyay and Sanjoy Sengupta have relentlessly tried to catalogue the artistes who sang to Sachin's music. Though they could not find the names of all the singers they have listed the following—Bhabanicharan Das, Pramod Ganguli, Bimal Bhushan, Chhaya Debi, Shila Haldar, Ramala Debi, Girin Chakrabarti and Hemanta Mukhopadhyay. Barring the last two and Bimal Bhushan, posterity does not remember the rest.

Another reason was that Sachin was averse to the idea of some other actor lip-syncing to his voice in playback. The reason was simple. Sachin knew well that the timbre of his voice would not fit the voice of any of the actors in films; it would sound ludicrous. So his songs were either picturized on himself when he acted in a film or were played in the background. However, it is not that all songs composed by him and sung by others flopped. In 1943, a song in

Judgesaheber Natni, '*Baro nastami dustami kare chand re*', became hugely popular. Sung by Bimal Bhushan, this was probably an exception. Sachin left no stone unturned in his quest to become a music director. He roamed from one studio to another. He never fought shy of expressing his thoughts before friends and colleagues in the world of film and music. Still, the goddess of fortune did not smile on him. Nobody extended a helping hand. Of course, no one can be blamed for that. However, in a way, his failure to make it big in Bengali cinema was a blessing in disguise. Had he met with success in the few opportunities that came his way as music director, he would perhaps have continued in Bengali films and his music would probably have been limited to Bengal. His move to Bombay, prompted by his failure in Bengali films, would take his music to the rest of the country. Sachin remembers his initial interaction with film people in Bombay:

> Sardar Chandulal Shah was the first person who invited me to direct music for a film in Bombay. This was in 1942. Shah was the owner of the famous Ranjit Studio. I don't know why, but I did not quite relish the idea of leaving Calcutta for Bombay then. I was still hopeful of working in Bengali films in Calcutta. Chandulal felt sad about my not joining him then. When I met him later in Bombay he lamented my not coming earlier. (*Sargamer Nikhad*)

The year 1943 saw the release of three more records. Two memorable songs in these are '*Madhu Brindabane dole Radha*' (lyrics by Robin Majumdar) and the song from the film *Chhadmabeshi*, '*Bandar chharo jatrira sabe*' (an IPTA-inspired song written by Ajay Bhattacharya). The music of '*Madhu Brindabane*' was originally scored by Ustad Fayyaz Khan. '*Madhu Brindabane*' is a song from the Agra gharana. Sachin knew very well how to give prominence to some words in khayal to make them swing in a raga-ragini's coracle. In the sentences *'Doley Radha'* and *'Rangia ranga pade'*, he created a mystic ambience by stressing on the words *'doley'* and *'rangia'*. The other songs in these three records were—*'Katha dao, dao sara'*, *'Jabey aloker phool'*, *'Phire gechhi barey barey'* and *'Natun ushar sainik'*. *'Katha dao, dao sara'* is modern song sung in SD's trademark nasal tone. *'Jabey aloker phool'* is a romantic love song. *'Phire gechhi barey barey'* is a lovelorn song which epitomizes the mental agony of a frustrated lover. *'Natun usher sainik'* is inspired by IPTA.

Sachin was again invited to the Bengal Music Conference the same year. Maharaja Bir Bikram Manikya presided. Birendrakishore Raychaudhuri of Gauripur, Sangitacharya Girija Shankar Chakrabarti, Ustad Alauddin Khan and Thakur Anil Krishna Dev Burman also graced the occasion. Sachin had known Ustad Allauddin Khan from the time the latter was a regular performer at the court of Tripura. Anil Krishna Dev Burman of Ujirbari (the minister of state's house) was a top sitar and sarod artist. Both were Sachin's soulmates, so to say. He had often joined these two in entertaining the audience at Agartala. Even in this conference, Sachin enchanted the audience with his mesmeric voice.

This year, Sachin directed the music for the film *Jaj Shaheber Natnee*. The song *'Bado nastami dustami kode chandrey'* sung by Bimal Bhushan, set to music by S. D. Burman created an all-time record on the popularity charts for the first time.

In 1944, Sachin directed the music for three films—*Chhadmabeshi* (directed by Ajoy Biswas), *Matir Ghar* (directed by Hari Bhanja) and *Pratikar* (directed by Chhabi Biswas). Songs from these films did not create much of a sensation. The success of *Chhadmabeshi* and *Jajsaheber Natni*, released the previous year, brought some cheer to the otherwise melancholy Sachin. He was getting increasingly restless over his lack of progress as a music director in films. At this time, Bombay beckoned again. This time he could not resist the call. Shaking off all hesitation, he responded. As he has said:

> In 1944, Rai Bahadur Chunilal, the owner of Filmistan, and Sashadhar Mukherjee invited me to compose the music for one of their films. Initially I was hesitant. My friend Sushil Majumdar was also with Filmistan at that time. He repeatedly urged me to shift to Bombay and not give up the opportunity.
>
> Getting no response from the film world of Calcutta, I moved to Bombay in 1944 with not a little pain and hurt. In October, I shifted with my family to Bombay and joined Filmistan as a music director.
>
> Bombay appeared to be a neat and clean city. It was an ever-busy city and more cosmopolitan than Calcutta. I met some of my old acquaintances again in Bombay—singer Pannalal Ghosh, music director Anil Biswas, actor Pahari Sanyal, and instrumentalist Robin Chatterjee. Initially, I felt out of place. A land without the Ganga was a dry land; in the absence of a sense of leisure, the city was bereft of life's resonance. I started feeling lonely. Leaving behind the circle of talented friends and known surroundings in Calcutta, I felt melancholic in Bombay at the beginning.
> (*Sargamer Nikhad*)

It is easy to understand Sachin's mental condition at that time. He did not want to leave Calcutta. That very year he had conducted the music in three films, an indication of his growing demand. So it is possible that film directors were beginning to think of him as a music director. Yet Sachin responded to the call of an uncertain future and took the bold step of making Bombay his karmabhoomi, come what may.

Though he left Calcutta, the city remained a part of him all his life. His love for the city never wavered. Every winter he visited Calcutta. One reason for this was the abundance of fresh fish and green vegetables during winter. Besides, records of his Bengali songs used to be released during the pujas. Even after shifting to Bombay, the Calcutta chapter never came to an end.

Three of his records were released just before he left for Bombay. *'Kalsagarer maron dolay'* and *'Shyam rup dharia esechhe maron'* from the film *Matir Ghar* earned considerable popularity. *'Kal sagarer maron dolay'* is like a song of vivek (conscience) in yatra. SD sang it on a long measure with a classical flavour. But he gave a whole new turn to the song *'Shyam rup dharia esechhe maron'*. It was sung in a fast measure in theka taal. Sachin's articulation and voice modulation filled it with life and opened up a new horizon. *'Lalita marami sakhi'* depicts Radha's estrangement from Krishna. Another song that connoisseurs will remember is *'Pi ley pi ley Hari naam ka pyaala'*, a bhajan composed by Pandit Bhushan. *'Piya sang milan pyaasa'*, composed in the style of a jhumar, was the best song of the year, leaving listeners wondering about what they were going to lose with Sachin's shift to Bombay.

But Calcutta's loss was Bombay's gain. Sad though he was at having to leave Calcutta, Sachin realized that it was imperative for him to take that step if he wanted his talent to find better expression. With nothing but formidable confidence in his musical abilities, he set sail for the coast of the Arabian Sea, to Bombay.

5
Bombay
1944-75

As Sachin travelled from the Ganga to the Arabian Sea, he realized he would now have to hone his skills and learn to swim against the tide. The flow of a river may have brooked his inability to make it as a music director in Calcutta but the waves of the sea would not be indulgent of failure. Unlike Calcutta, where life had a languid rhythm of its own, people in Bombay were extremely serious about their profession. No one had the leisure of wasting time on idle talk. It is said that money floats in the Bombay air; it is up to you to be able to catch it.

The glitter of Bombay took Sachin's breath away. In the evening, the stretch from Nariman Point to Chowpatty appeared to put its pride of wealth on display with a diamond necklace around its neck. People of Bombay have aptly named it the 'queen's necklace'. However, Sachin was too preoccupied to enjoy the glamour the city had to offer. He had an important task at hand—to prove himself as a music director.

The competition in Bombay was formidable. It was the time when music directors like C. Ramchandra, Naushad, Sajjad Hussain, Anil Biswas, Shankar-Jaikishan, O. P. Nayyar and others were either making music or were knocking at the doors of Bombay's cinema world. It was the era when Naushad was busy introducing Hindustani classical music to films, O. P. Nayyar was experimenting with the rhythm of Western beats and trying to fuse it with Indian melody, Madan Mohan was on the lookout for a new musical horizon beyond the limits of thumri and ghazal, and Shankar-Jaikishan were deeply immersed in trying out everything from ragas to jazz. Sachin arrived at such a transitional juncture with his unlimited store of rustic folk music.

Even as he struggled to establish himself in Bombay, Calcutta kept drawing him to itself. Calcutta was his heart and soul. Bombay had for itself the musician and music director S. D. Burman but the singer in Sachin-karta belonged to Calcutta. Sachin continued visiting Calcutta annually and enriching its music. In 1945, three of his records were released. Three songs in these attained the pinnacle of popularity. The first, 'Rangila, ranglia, rangila re' was set to music in folk style. It has the surprise of a jhumar and the artistic trill of dhap yatra.

Bhatiyali becomes vivacious if sung in the seventh note but SD kept the seventh note under control. Instead, he arranged the tone between high and deep and between low and grave in an ornamental fashion. Let me quote singer-composer Kabir Suman (Suman Chattopadhyay) on the perfection Sachin achieved in rendering folks songs: 'Without perfection in the technique of folk music it is impossible to carry off the elongated *i-i-i* sound at the end of the line "*Tumi hoiyo kinar bandhu, ami gaanger pani*" in the song "*Rangila, rangila, rangila re*".'—(*Aajkaal*, 25 September 2005)

Further, take a look at the line '*Desh bideshey phirbo aami haiya paglarey*' where he pauses after singing '*Desh bideshey*' or '*haiya paglarey*'. The stress on these words introduced a swing in the rhythm of the song. Before '*Dubiye gelo bela*', the introduction of '*hay hay*' vividly creates the imagery of the setting sun. The other songs '*Tui ki shyamer banshi re*' and '*Priya rajanigandha baney*' too displayed Sachin's extraordinary skills in improvising both the music and words of a song to convey its mood so that even within the genre of folk songs, he never sounded repetitive. That is what appealed most to the lay listener.

The song '*Tui ki shyamer banshi re*' starts with the slow fusion of the meend of sitar and flute which do not overpower the voice. A question does not sound like an interrogation if asked on a low measure. The word 're' in the song '*Tui ki shyamer banshi re*' is drawn with a big thrust which is different from the 're' in '*Tora ke jash re*' so that the question hits the ear directly in its light-hearted tune. Sachin was very fond of tonal variations and that is why he used homonyms and same-sounding words wherever he could such as, '*kalar banshi*', '*khepar banshi*' in place of '*Shyamer banshi*'. He always tried to avoid repetition.

The wickedness of the flute is caught in the '*aa*' of the stanza '*Gharer bar karla banshi aamare*'. We are enchanted by his introduction of '*hay hay*' in the original lyrics of Jasimuddin Mollah which reflects his urge for improvisation and gives a new meaning to the song. Listen to '*Aage jadi jantam banshi chhariya jaba more (hay hay)*' or '*Banshi aamar maron bachon banshi aamar pran (hay hay)*' and you will discover how it has changed the whole taal.

The song '*Priya rajanigandha baney*' is a unique example of Karta's improvisation. At the beginning of the song, Sachin sang 'priya' in three different measures and then gave the formidable 'khatki trick' on '*Rajanigandha baney*'. He placed the word 'priya' in between the stanzas to enable the audience to appreciate the flavour of romance. The lifeline of the song is *'Dekha hobe priya, dekha hobe tabo saney, rajanigandha baney'*. *'Dhik dhik aamar e jiboney'* is a rhythmic folk song sung in fast measure. The other two songs are in Hindi *'Balam mujhse rooth ke'* and *'Mere jauban ki phulwari'*. The year 1945 also saw the release of another Bengali film which had music by Sachin Dev Burman—*Kalankini* directed by Jyotish Banerjee. Its songs, however, did not create much of a sensation.

The next year, in 1946, he visited Agartala for the last time, for the shraddh ceremony of his elder brother Prafulla. His nephew, Ankur Dev Burman, has written that in the memorial meeting for Prafulla-karta, Sachin sang *'Bhulaye amay dudin, sheshe ki hai bhulbe'* which was recorded and released the same year. It is difficult for me to say which of Sachin's songs is my personal favourite. But this one will be somewhere at the top of the list. The elegiac effect is so overwhelming that it is difficult to imagine such a beautiful merger of words and tunes in a song. Redolent with melancholy, this marks a high in Sachin's repertoire. Sachin has set this song to music going against all possibilities, so that it turns out to be an experience to hear if. Other composers would have given stress on *'bhu'* of *'bhulaye'* whereas he gave it on *'la'*, thereby making the syllable float a little. He displays a control over the tune, reins in his passion and delivers the song in such understated terms that the effect is shattering.

Even in other songs that he produced that year, there is a clear emphasis on remembrance, as if he was lamenting the passage of time. *'Ke amare pichhu dake'*, for example, invokes the feeling of someone from the past calling upon one's memories. The song became very popular. In the same year, he sang duets with his wife Meera Dev Burman—*'Gai jey papiya'* and *'Phool gendvaa na maro'*.

Both songs reflect Sachin's witty mood. Meera Dev Burman also sang '*Aj dol dila ke*' and '*Tum ho bade chitchor*' under S. D. Burman's guidance. The influence of Kazi Nazrul Islam can be traced in these songs. It is based on a Santhal tune in jhumar style.

An incident that year provides a glimpse of how the common people of East Bengal revered Sachin-karta. They used to address him as Hauli-karta (karta of the haveli). On his way back from Agartala, Sachin went to the fair of Karampur Dargah in a boat. A navigable river, pleasant breeze, a silver-coin moon in the sky, the boat floating smoothly downstream and the boatman started singing '*O re sujan naiya*'. Sachin looked at the boatman astonished. The boatman continued to sing, as if in a trance, forgetful of his surroundings. When the song ended, Sachin asked the boatman, 'Do you know whose song it is?'

'Of course, it is our karta's song,' he said.

'Do you know him? Have you met him?'

'No, I haven't. If I ever meet him, I will fall at his feet and say, "What a voice you have, Karta! It seems as if a koel resides in your throat." Long live karta.'

The true measure of a song's popularity lies in its ability to reach the common man. Only when the man on the street hums a song can it be said to have achieved its purpose. A boatman belonging to the Kutti community (a low-caste community of East Bengal, employed mostly as coachmen, boatmen, etc.,) comparing Sachin's voice to that of a koel—what more could a singer want!

Sachin introduced himself. The boatman fell at his feet. On the wavy waters of the Padma, in the flood of moonlight, karta started singing '*Padmar dhew re*'. The boat kept moving on its own, the boatman no longer on the stern, sitting as he was at the feet of his karta.

The year 1946 was the year of ordeal by fire for Sachin as a music director. While the Bengali film *Matrihara*, which had music by him, was released in Calcutta, he nervously awaited the response to Filmistan's *Shikari* in Bombay. Savak Vachha was the director and Ashok Kumar the hero in *Shikari*. The songs were written by the famous lyricist Pradeep. Ashok Kumar lent his voice to '*Dol rahi hai naiya meri*'. The other songs were sung by Paro, Ameer Bai and Shamshad Begum of which '*Duniya ne humein*' (sung by Ameer Bai), '*Har din hai naya*' (a duet by Ameer Bai and Ashok Kumar) and '*Rangeela rangeela*' (by Paro and chorus) are worthy of mention. The songs did not become very popular but they received good reviews in newspapers and journals. Though he was somewhat crestfallen at the lack of popular reaction, in a way it had a good effect on him. It made him even more determined to touch a chord with the masses. He wanted to create music that would be part of the common man's everyday life, his joy and sorrow. Though it made him happy to hear other singers and connoisseurs talking about his songs and singing them, his real satisfaction lay in commoners like workers, cobblers, paan shop owners and the like singing his songs. All through his life this remained his yardstick for successful music. Only if the most ordinary people lent their voice to his songs would he be able to think of himself as a successful composer. In this context he has said:

> While I was composing the music for my first film *Shikari*, everybody in the studio kept praising my music. But I could not feel happy, I do not know why. Outside the studio, there was no response from the public. There was no popular reaction from the general mass of people. Sometime after the release of *Shikari*, Jamini Dewan's film *Ratan* was released. The entire city of Bombay started reverberating with the songs from *Ratan*. The masses had

taken the songs to their hearts. One day I was busy in my room composing something on the harmonium. Suddenly, I heard my manservant singing a song while making tea, *'Jab tumhi chale pardes, lagakar thes, O pritam pyare duniya mein kaun hamara'*. It was a song from *Ratan*. Those days, the song was heard often on the streets of the city. I stopped working for the day. I thought—here is this man who has been working for me for so long. Day in and day out, he listens to my compositions. But I had never heard him humming my tunes. After a few days, everything became clear to me. Eureka! A few days later I was busy composing the music of a song for my next film *Do Bhai*, whose first line was *'Mera sundar sapna beet gaya'*. Suddenly, I heard my servant singing the same song in the next room entirely lost in his work. The greatest realization of my film life dawned on me then and there: a hit film song needs the simplest of tunes, the less ornate the better, because only then will the ordinary folk be able to give their voice to the song. My first guru in film music direction was that servant of mine. (*Sargamer Nikhad*)

Sachin's second film, Filmistan's *Eight Days*, released the same year. It included the song *'Ummeed bhara panchhi tha khoj raha sajni'* sung by Sachin. The song was not shot on any actor or actress but was presented as a background number. It became immensely popular and marked the entry of East Bengal's folk music into Hindi films. Sachin sang another song in the film, a duet with S. L. Puri, *'Babu, babu, oh babu re dilko bachana'*. Ameer Bai brilliantly sang *'Pehle na samjha'*. The film's success and the popularity of its music established the presence of the man who wanted to introduce the sweetness of East Bengal's folk music into the world of Hindi cinema. Sachin proved that Western orchestra was not essential, that it was possible to reach the audience using the flute, stringed instruments and the tabla.

The year was 1947 and no one had heard of this girl from Faridpur. But Sachin had gauged the immense possibilities in her voice from just one line she had sung in chorus in the film *Bhakt Prahlad* (1946). That she belonged to his beloved East Bengal only made Sachin even more determined to bring her talent to the fore. He used her to great effect in *Do Bhai* to create one of Hindi film's most memorable numbers, *'Mera sundar sapna beet gaya'* which became a super hit and made a star of Geeta Roy (later Dutt). She became the first in a series of fellow Bengalis—Kishore Kumar, Manna Dey and Hemant Kumar—whom Sachin introduced to Hindi cinema with great success, and often much against the wishes of producers who insisted on using established names; and he was able to establish each one as a star. *'Mera sundar sapna'* also marked the culmination of his earlier experimentation with music. The song was written on the lines of a ghazal but the music was that of a modern song. The song's incredible success infused him with confidence and from then on his experimentation continued unabated. He made every song a different experience, by introducing changes in the beat, tempo, rhythm and of course the melody which formed the core of the song. And he brought in the influence of his Bengali roots again and again. In *'Mera sundar sapna'*, for example, the influence of Rabindra sangeet is noticeable. S. D. Burman's touching melody for *'Mera sundar sapna beet gaya'* can scarcely hide the haunting echoes of Rabindranath's song *'Rodon bhora e bashonto'* not in the words but in the melody that murmurs like a longing reaching us from a time long forgotten. Geeta put her heart and soul into this song. She never had to look back again. She became a part of S. D. Burman's unit and remained so till the end.

Besides *Do Bhai*, Sachin also composed the music for *Chittor Vijay* and *Dil Ki Rani* in 1947. Both films were directed by Mohan Sinha. These films did not do as well as *Do Bhai*. The year 1947 witnessed a prolific Sachin bring out a number of Hindi records. The songs in these included a duet by him and S. L. Puri ,*'Babu babu re'* and a solo *'Ummeed bhara panchhi'* (*Eight days*). The other popular numbers are *'Prem kiye bin raha na jaye'*, *'Kaun aaya sapno mein'*, *'Sooni sooni laage'*, *'O mere raja'* and *'Janewale sunta ja'*.

Interestingly enough, most of these records, as indeed the records of *Shikari*, *Eight Days* and *Do Bhai* were brought out by HMV. For quite some time now, HMV's management had been requesting Sachin to record his songs through their company. It took him a while to forget the insult of being rejected all those years ago. But finally he decided to forgive and forget, thus revealing the greatness of his royal character, and responded politely to HMV's request.

With his arrival in Bombay, Sachin brought in significant changes in his style of music composition. Forging a new sound of music that blended classical-based, classical, folk music and bhatiyali songs, he abandoned intricate twists and turns in his songs, preferring a simplicity that touched the heart and belied the mastery behind the fusion of disparate streams. He broke the established stereotype that popular North Indian beats were essential for the success of a film's music. He fused Bengal's bhatiyali, murshidi, baul and jari songs with Western folk songs, and created a lively musical world devoid of ornamentation, or with limited ornamentation. He simplified intricate classical tunes in songs like *'Dakhina paban'* and *'Alochhaya dola'* united modern and traditional music and created a new pattern of songs in which melody, which made the song accessible to one and all, was of primary importance.

Film music operates within certain limitations. The music has to be in sync with the drama unfolding on screen otherwise it will fail to strike a chord. This imposes certain restrictions on the musician's creativity, while at the same time challenging him to synchronize his/her creativity to patterns dictated by the screenplay. For example, the screenplay may include a cabaret, the music for which needs to be of a certain type, calling for heavy orchestration, which should be able to intoxicate the audience. This often requires the musician to learn to let go of classical indoctrination. The list of great music directors in Hindi films will show that only those who were able to adapt their classical training to a film's requirements were able to succeed. Sachin was one such music director who accomplished this difficult feat and that too with remarkable finesse. If he was instrumental in introducing Bengali folk music to Hindi films, he also mastered Western beats and jazz which would have his audiences in raptures. Even as he enriched Hindi film music with his creativity, his foray into the same brought his sheer versatility to the fore. But for Hindi film songs, we might not have had the multifaceted artist in Sachin Dev Burman.

It was Sachin who introduced the concept of 'music first, words next' in Hindi cinema. He would first work out a tune in sync with the sequence and then ask the lyricist to write the words to match the tune. This has become the custom now. Towards that end, he could be regarded as a pioneer, someone who was far ahead of his time.

In 1948, only one film with his music was released, *Vidya*, directed by Girish Trivedi. It boasts ten songs. The film wasn't very successful but the songs '*Bhagwan tere sansar mein hai khel nirale*' (sung by Ameer Bai) and '*Jhoom rahi jhoom rahi khushiyon ki*' (sung by Suraiya) became quite popular. The tune of the song '*Pyaar banke mujhpe koi chha gaya re*' was lifted from his own Bengali song—'*Prem Jamunai hoito keu'*. This song too drew the attention of the connoisseurs of music. But if it wasn't a prolific year for film music, he more than made up for it with seven non-film records, including two which had songs written by the doyen of modern Bengali songs, Gouri Prasanna Majumdar.

Gouri Prasanna had long nurtured a desire to have Sachin's music set to his songs. But so far Sachin had not liked any of his songs till the young lyricist came up with the perennial classic *'Bondhu go ei madhumas'* through which Sachin ushered in a new era in Bengali modern songs outside the purview of classical-based compositions. From then onwards, Gouri Prasanna became Sachin's favourite lyricist.

SD always tried to challenge the limits of classical music introducing new method and improvisation to make it simple and likeable for general people. In *'Bujhi ba bifal holo'* he stretched the tune in such a way in *'lo'* that it did not blend with any raga, but the raga was there in its subtle form. It came through wrenching the heart; in the form of wailing.

Mohini Chowdhury's lyric *'Ei chaite sandhya jai britha'* had been inspired by Rabindra Sangeet. The mukhda of the song is similar to a Tagore song. The passage from the mukhda to the antara and vice versa was through different words, interjections and tunes. He composed a very simple tune in *'Aankhi jal diy-e-e-e'* and made the song bloom like a flower.

'Prem Jamunai hoito keu' is an example of East Bengal's vivacious folk song. The song starts on a long measure, o-o-o, which is Sachin's style. The 'bol' of khemta and jhumar give a new dimension to this song. The song fades away with a soft punch on *'dhew dilo'* which, creating ripples, allows Sachin to effortlessly go to the mukhda.

Sachin sang *'Hai ki jey kori e mono niya'* in a soft baritone because of its light-hearted nature. Although it was a modern song, the tune of 'Jari gaan' was embedded in it. The orchestra was also played in the style of dhap yatra. *'Nirobey aankhi jaley bharey keno'* is also a modern song on a fast measure, based on theka taal. *'Keno alayarey bondhu bhabi'* is a pure and simple village song.

These seven records also included three in Hindi comprising five songs, in one of which he sang a duet with Meera Dev Burman *'Kali badariya chha gayi'* (the reverse side of this album contained Meera's solo *'Dali dali phool'*). Yet another popular album included the songs *'Ud gaya bhawra'* and *'Prem ka pinjra ho gaya'*, both written by esteemed lyricist Raja Mehdi Ali Khan. Another album opens with *'Gun dhaam hamare Gandhiji'* and *'Sab desh ki janata tumhein ro ro ke pukare'*, both dedicated to Mahatma Gandhi, with the latter being a lament on the demise of the Mahatma.

In 1949 were released the films *Kamal* directed by Suraj Kumar and *Shabnam* by B. Mitra. *Kamal* flopped but the songs of *Shabnam* became hits. Speaking of the latter, Sachin has said: 'While composing the music for *Shabnam*, I surreptitiously tried to find out my attendant's response to the tunes. Needless to say, the songs which my attendant used to hum became hits.' (*Sargamer Nikhad*). These included *'Mera dil tadap ke kahan chala'* (sung by Gita Roy), Shamshad Begum's *'Yeh duniya roop ki chor'* and *'Ik bar tu ban ja meri o pardesi'*. Duets by Gita—Mukesh (*'Kismat me bichhadna tha'*) and Mukesh—Shamshad Begum (*'Tumhare liye huye badnam'*) also became quite popular.

The success of *Shabnam* added to S. D. Burman's increasing respect in the world of Hindi films, but the music director himself was not happy. He felt that Hindi film enthusiasts had not yet taken to his style wholeheartedly. Despondent and unhappy in Bombay, Sachin seriously thought about returning to Calcutta. Cine star Ashok Kumar has written about this difficult phase in Sachin's life in his autobiography *Jeevan Naiya*:

> Just as I had brought Bimal Roy from Calcutta, so had I a hand in making Sachin-karta stay back in Bombay... I had asked him to compose the music for *Shikari*. He composed the music for *Eight Days* too. But he did not get off to a flying start in Bombay. In three to four years, none of his songs, barring '*Mera sundar sapna*', became very big hits. He decided to go back to Calcutta. At Bombay Talkies, we were shooting *Mashal* at that time. I told Sachin-karta, 'Why not do the music for this film and then go?' He replied, 'No, nothing is happening here. I'd rather go back to Calcutta'. I said, 'Well, go if you must, but at least do the music for this film.' I decided I would somehow get Sachin-karta to score the music for *Mashal*. At long last he agreed, saying, 'Well, I shall return to Calcutta after doing this film.'

Three records were released this year. Sachin sang two duets with Meera Dev Burman—'*Banshi tomar hatey dilam*' and '*Ke dilo ghum bhangaye*'. The lyricist was Mohini Chowdhury. These two duets and '*Dali dali phool*' (solo, 1948) sung by Meera amply proved her talent as a singer. She should not have forsaken singing at such an early stage. She had the potential to become a great singer.

Sachin sang four songs penned by Gouri Prasanna Majumdar, out of which '*Aami patho cheye robo*' and '*Bajey na banshi go*' deserve special mention. The songs '*Maramiyarey ei udhas madhumasey*' and '*Basarer phool gelo jey shukaye*' are trademark S. D. Burman songs, but in '*Aami patho cheye*' and '*Bajey na banshi go*', Sachin excelled himself and heralded a new era in modern Bengali music. He achieved what one can call 'absolutely going outside the purview of norm' and created magic. Whenever he sang a stanza, he never repeated the same procedure again. For example, in '*(Aami) patho cheye robo*', 'Aami' is a magical word used for the sake of emphasis before and after the sentence. In this song, Sachin sang antaras '*Jeyo na jharey*' as '*Jeyo na-na jharey*'. The extra '*na*' works as a magical note in this composition.

After going to Bombay, Sachin seemed to have opened his box full of enchanting melodies. He started the *dhun* of the song '*Bajey na banshi* go' with a wave like '*o-o-o-aa*'. He sang '*bajey na*' on various measures without repetition and '*banshi go*', '*hasi go*' and '*parabashi go*' in different metres to avoid monotony. The jawari of his voice was very prominent in this song. It strikes the ear with a soothing effect like the waves of the sea. His broken voice is abundantly clear in the lines '*Durai rahilo she mrignayana*' and '*Malakhani holo jey go phul jharano*'. The wailing voice in '*rahilo*' and '*holo*' has given a new dimension to the song.

As it turned out, fortune smiled on Sachin-karta in the year 1950. He had to abandon the idea of returning to Calcutta. Producers started flocking to him. If the hit songs of *Shabnam* led to a renewed interest in the musician from Bengal, the demand for Sachin soared with the super success of *Mashal*.

It is rare for all the songs of a film to become hits. Normally, it is one or two songs which become chartbusters and it is on the popularity of these songs that the film and its other songs ride. *Mashal* was an exception. Almost all songs of *Mashal* became big hits, including '*Aaj nahin toh kal bichhad jayenge*' and '*Aankhon se door door hai*', both sung by Lata Mangeshkar, and Geeta Roy's '*Kitni sach hai ye baat*'. But it was Manna Dey's rendition of '*Upar gagan vishal*' that set new standards for the success of a song in

Hindi films. *Mashal* became a turning point not only for Sachin but also for Manna Dey who had come to Bombay around 1943 with his uncle and Sachin's erstwhile guru, K. C. Dey. In the course of finding his feet as a singer, he had become an assistant to Sachin, who fondly called him 'Mana' and affectionately nurtured the extraordinary talent of the budding singer. Manna Dey was, in fact, the assistant music director of *Mashal*. His own words reveal the extent of Sachin's single-minded devotion to the creation of music:

> I was then working with Sachin-da as assistant music director. No, not just that, I was an assistant to him in everything. As directed by him, I took down notations, arranged for the rehearsals, I got the singers and musicians to practise and adapt to his tunes. Besides, I was an errand boy for him. Sachin-da was fond of bananas. I often used to buy bananas for him.
>
> It was he who taught me to attain perfection by singing the same song over and over again. Just after he composed the music for a song, he would sing it from morning till night. He would try it out before select audiences. He would extract from the singers exactly what was required. Lata, Asha, Geeta, Rafi, there were no exceptions. He had a youthful mind and a very East Bengali sense of humour.
>
> Sachin-da asked me to sing the song '*Upar gagan vishal*' which he had composed for *Mashal*. I sang and with it I announced to the world of Hindi film music: 'I have arrived. I have arrived at the durbar of the audience with the message of a new dawn. It is I who will sing from now on. I shall fill the world of music with my songs and tunes. I have arrived."

> My successful march began with that song. I can never repay my debt to Sachin-da for my career in music. I have seen him from close quarters for many years. As a singer too he was unrivalled, extraordinary. But even as a man Sachin-da was incomparable. What struck me most was his simple lifestyle. I have seen the agony he went through while composing music. He would try each and every line of a song in different styles and tunes just to see which worked best. He would ask for my opinion on each and every line of a song. When I said, 'Oh, splendid!' he would ask again, 'Do you like it? Do you really like it a lot?' It was almost as if before giving birth to a song, before exposing it to the light of this world, he wanted to bestow the best possible combination of beauty and melody on it, so that this child of his could win everybody's heart, so that it would be remembered over generations, it would transform itself to time-tested music. And that was exactly what used to happen. With repeated honing, every tune he composed reached a state of perfection enabling it to carve a niche in the minds of millions. (*Jiboner Jalsagharey*)

While *Mashal* strengthened Sachin's place in the world of Hindi film music, forcing him to reconsider his decision to leave Bombay, the film established Manna Dey as a singer. Sachin chose the little-known Manna Dey in spite of the fact that Mohammad Rafi was, by this time, the preferred choice of all music directors. Over the next couple of decades, Sachin would fall back on Manna Dey to render some of his most accomplished compositions, often going against the wishes of the producer. In the words of Sachin:

> Manna Dey was my assistant as music director. He was open-hearted, modest and soft-spoken. Bombay's Hindi

film songs have become somewhat mechanical these days. The singers are often busy recording. They don't have time to practise or rehearse. But Manna is the sole exception. Even at the zenith of popularity and fame, he is an artist who practises daily in the morning with his tanpura, rarely ever missing on this routine. Such devotion and reverence for music on his part have fascinated me. That is why I like him so much. Manna has worked in many of my films and is still working. He can infuse life and energy into any song. (*Sargamer Nikhad*)

Apart from Bombay Talkies' *Mashal*, directed by Nitin Bose, there were three other films that year for which S. D. Burman scored the music. The three films—*Afsar* (directed by Chetan Anand), *Pyar* (directed by V. M. Vyas) and *Samar*, the Bengali version of *Mashal* (directed by Nitin Bose)—did not run long, but the songs (Suraiya's '*Man mera hua matwala*' in *Afsar* and Geeta Roy's '*Woh sapnowali raat*' in *Pyar*) left their mark on audiences. In fact, *Pyar* happens to be probably the only film where Kishore Kumar sang as the playback for Raj Kapoor. But it was *Afsar* which had greater significance in terms of the future of Hindi film music. Its importance lay in the fact that it was the maiden venture of the production company Navketan established by Dev Anand and his brother Chetan Anand. The Navketan—Sachin partnership would result in some of the most enduring melodies in Hindi cinema over the next couple of decades. Sachin talks about the beginning of this association in these words:

> I first met Dev Anand in 1948. He had just become a hero in films. Dev was crazy about my songs. He used to live in Bombay's Pali Hill with elder brother Chetan, younger brother Vijay (Goldie) and his sisters. We used to have our evening rendezvous at his house; our common

friend Guru Dutt was also a frequent visitor there. He was another of my fans. There were hardly any other admirers of mine in Bombay as devoted as Dev and Guru. They used to frequent my flat in Sion to listen to my songs. Over many such evenings, we discussed the possibility of establishing a film production company of our own. We even conjectured that our organization would set a new path and not adopt the traditional approach. Dev, Chetan, Vijay and Guru used to encourage me to create music in my own style without any compromise. This association made me confident that someday I would be able to popularize my music all over India through the medium of Hindi films. The opportunity I was waiting for came soon enough. Dev created his organization and called it Navketan. *Afsar*, directed by Chetan, with Dev and Suraiya as hero and heroine was the first film of the banner. I was the music director. The year was 1949. The film did not do well. But the song *'Man mera hua matwala'* in Suraiya's voice became very popular. (*Sargamer Nikhad*)

Sachin-karta's star was on the ascendant. Two of his records of Bengali songs released around this time gained popularity like never before. If Gouri Prasanna surpassed himself with the lyrics of evergreen numbers like *'Aankhi duti jhare hai'*, *'Malakhani chhilo haatey'* and *'Aajo akasher path bahi'*, Sachin excelled with a virtuosic amalgamation of the various styles of thumri, khayal, kirtan and folk, often within the same song.

Sachin Dev brought an impish teenage twinkle to his creations. One only has to hear snappy lilts of this year to discern how spryly he was in tune with the times. Such crisp numbers as *'Aankhi duti jharey hay'*, *'Aajo akasher patho bahi'* and *'Khulia kusum saaz srimati jey kandey*' prove that Sachin had discovered the secret of eternal youth in his art. He has plucked the choicest flowers from the bower of music, whose fragrance is still fresh.

Sachin Dev Burman is the bearer of India's cultural tradition. The song of the minstrel which finds expression in his nasal baritone is, in fact, indicative of Bengal's cultural heritage. Those who have heard puthi gaan, pala gaan, kabi gaan and the songs of dhap yatra, etc., would realize the depth of Sachin-karta's musical world. The glory of the 'bol' is delightfully present in this year's songs. The songs *'Aajo akashero patho bahi'* and *'Aankhi duti jharey hay'* are sung in the same fashion. How beautifully he draws the pictogram of *'teer bendha pakhi'* (bird shot with arrow) when he sings *'rudherey rangano aami'* (bleeding profusely) stressing on the syllables of the word *'Ru-dhi-re'*!

'Malakhani chhilo hatey' and *'Khulia kusum saaj'* are classical modern romantic songs. Sachin starts *'Malakhani chhilo hatey'* on a long measure in the khayal style *'O-o-o'*. He sings the 'nai' of the line *'jharey tabo jharey nai'* first in his normal nasal voice, but in the next moment *'nai'* transforms to *'n-a-a-i'*. In *'kshma she to kandey nai'* he stops for a while in *'kshma'* and then repeats the sentence in a wailing baritone for not being excused. After that too he does not return to the mukhda but instead sings the antara's *'jaley aankhi bharey nai'* which is simply exceptional. This is absolutely necessary for bringing out the emotions of the song.

'Khulia kusum saaj' is beautiful song. The experimentation is unique. In the form of the alaap of khayal, the song begins with *'a-a-a'*; but soon after that, the song seems to be coming down in torrents. Sachin gives a sudden emphasis to the word 'kanu' in such a way that one can't help but be amazed. The raga-raginis are utilized to exhaustion. If you notice closely, you would observe that in this song there is the bandish of khayal, the bol of thumri,

the swing of folk songs, the cymbals of kirtan and, above all, the symptoms and mood of a modern song.

In 1951, Sachin scored the music for six films: Shahid Latif's *Buzdil*, O. P. Dutta's *Ek Nazar*, Mahesh Kaul's *Naujawan*, M. V. Raman's *Bahaar*, Fali Mistry's *Sazaa* and Navketan's *Baazi* (the directorial debut of Guru Dutt with Dev Anand and Geeta Bali in the lead.) *Baazi* marked the beginning of one of Hindi cinema's most celebrated lyricist—music director combinations. Sahir Ludhianvi was an unknown entity at that time as far as film songs were concerned. With his instinct for backing the talented but unknown, Sachin brought in Sahir as the lyricist for *Baazi*. The authorities at Navketan who had profound confidence in Sachin welcomed the rookie lyricist. Thus was born a partnership that, over the next five years (till *Pyaasa*), gave Hindi cinema some of its most celebrated songs in *Jaal*, *Taxi Driver*, *Funtoosh* and *House No. 44*, among others. In *Baazi*, Sachin showed his extraordinary creativity by turning Sahir's ghazal '*Tadbeer se bigdi hui taqdeer bana le*' into a fast-paced seductive number. Hardly had the film been released than the song became a raging hit. Thanks to Sachin's experimentation, Sahir arrived in a big way. Geeta Roy poured her soul into the song as well as into the other popular number '*Suno gajar kya gaaye, samay guzarta jaaye*'.

The singer listed this song *(Tadbeer se bigdi)* as one of her ten favourite songs from amongst those she had sung till 1957. It is also a song that changed her from a singer (largely) of bhajans and classical tunes, to one who could handle western tunes—a genre she was soon dominating. Not that '*Tadbeer se bigdi hui*' is strictly western: the tabla and the general tone of the music is very much Indian but the guitar strummed between the stanzas makes the song simply superb. The combination of S. D. Burman's music, Majrooh

Sultanpuri's lyrics, Dev Anand and the luminous Geeta Bali on screen and her 'voice', Geeta Dutt (then Roy) in the movie is alluring. The success of *Baazi* went a long way in establishing Geeta Roy as a solo singer. Besides, Kishore Kumar delivered his first hit with '*Mere labon pe dekho aaj bhi tarane hain*'. The film marked out Sachin as a non-conformist musician who wasn't afraid of experimenting either with new singers or with musical styles. It also established Navketan's reputation for great music, something that would be seen in a number of films over the couple of decades.

If *Baazi* set the tone for the year, Sachin consolidated his position with the songs of *Bahaar*, where Shamshad Begum's song '*Saiyyan dil mein aana re, aa ke phir na jana re*' and Kishore's '*Qusoor aap ka huzoor aap ka*' become huge hits. These songs, like '*Tadbeer se bigdi hui taqdeer bana le*', are examples of Sachin's sense of rhythm and beat. Listening to '*Saiyyan dil mein aana re*' one cannot help tapping one's feet even today. It remains one of Shamshad Begum's most popular numbers in Hindi films. It is a tribute to Sachin's genius that the song continues to be one of the biggest chartbusters among remixes even in the new millennium. Other hit songs of the year which helped Sachin reach the summit of success as a music director included Lata Mangeshkar's '*Jhan jhan payal baaje*' and '*Rote rote guzar gayi raat re*' (*Buzdil*), the Rafi—Lata duet '*Mujhe preet nagariya jana hai*' (*Ek Nazar*), and the evergreen Lata number '*Thandi hawayein lehra ke aayein*' (*Naujawan*), which gave a glimpse of Sachin's equally strong hold on melody.

The background to the birth of '*Thandi hawayien lehra ke aayein*' is quite interesting. Director Mahesh Kaul did not like the first tune that Sachin had composed. Even as Sachin came up with one tune after another, the director remained unhappy with each. Irritated with himself at not getting the desired tune, Sachin went for a walk which took him to Juhu beach. He kept humming one tune after another even as he strolled down the beach. A little later, he entered a restaurant for a cup of tea. Suddenly he heard a tune on a piano, *'sa-re-sa-sa-pa'*. He liked what he heard, ran to the piano and saw a waiter playing the same keys repeatedly, *'sa-re-sa-sa-pa'*. And this is how *'Thandi hawayein'* was born. This time the director loved the tune. If there's one song that can be highlighted in Sachin's repertoire as reaching across generations, it is this. Around fifteen years after Sachin composed *'Thandi hawayein'*, music director Roshan used the same tune for Lata's immortal *'Rahein na rahein hum'* in *Mamta*. Nearly twenty years later, R. D. Burman created *'Saagar kinare dil yeh pukare'* in Ramesh Sippy's *Saagar* based on his father's composition. A tune that created waves in 1951 continued to mesmerize listeners even in the 1980s.

The music of *Sazaa* deserves special mention because it was with this film that Sachin brought Hemanta Mukhopadhyay into the limelight in Hindi cinema. Hemanta Mukhopadhyay (known to Hindi film lovers as Hemant Kumar) sang a popular duet, *'Aa gupchup gupchup pyar karein'* with another great Bengali singer Sandhya Mukhopadhyay. Sandhya had earlier sung a duet with Lata Mangeshkar in *Tarana* under Anil Biswas's music. Let us hear about Sandhya's experience in her own words:

> We had great fun during the making of *Sazaa*. I had a duet in it with Hemanta Mukhopadhyay. Of course, with Sachin-da composing the music, we had to do something special. He had a remarkable sense of humour. For example, while recording *'Aa gupchup gupchup pyar karein'*, he added two or three funny lines like *'hathe mukhe chunkali /Naake mukhe chunkali'* in chorus preceding the song. Later, when the film's record was released, we realized that the lines had been retained. I also had a solo in *Sazaa*. (*'Ogo More Gitimoy'*)

The lines Sachin had put in, quite meaningless in the context of the song, came from a folk song of Tripura. It is difficult to resist quoting it here:

> *Tongwali go tongwali*
> *Hathe mukhe chunkali*
> *Tumi ma jagater Kali mara patha khao*
> *Shiber buke pao*
> *Shiber buke pao diya vengchi dhaira rao*
> *Jagadamba go!*

Roughly translated, it addresses Goddess Kali as someone whose face is smeared with lime and soot, who partakes of the sacrificial goat, and tramples on Lord Shiva and grimaces with embarrassment. Sachin had used the folk tune earlier for the song *'Sundari lo sundari'* in the Bengali film *Samar*. Interestingly, much later, in the Bengali film *Anusandhan*, R. D. Burman used the same tune in the song *'Phulkali go phulkali'* (its Hindi version in *Barsaat Ki Ek Raat* was *'Manchali o manchali'*).

'Tum na jaane kis jahan mein kho gaye' and *'Hum pyaar ki baazi hare'*, rendered impeccably by Lata Mangeshkar, emits a musically urban romantic expression. The first song bears witness to the influence of Himangshu Dutta, who was probably the first in the subcontinent to consciously use European musical elements in songs produced in the Indian music industry. The melody of *'Tum kahan'* echoes the movement of *'Tumi kothai'* in Himangshu Dutta's *'Rater mayur chhoralo je pakha'* in its touching crescendo. Sachin's *'Tum na jane'* also shares the gentle movement of waltz that Himangshu Dutta used for his *'Rater mayur'*.

Only one non-film record by SD was released this year. Mohini Chowdhury penned two marvellous songs for it. The first song *'Sei jey dinguli'* is a nostalgic ode to bygone days which has the imprint of Sachin's childhood days. Though the words are Mohini Chowdhury's, the idea is quintessential Sachin, a lament for the unforgettable memories of roaming the countryside, playing the flute. The song ends with one of the most extraordinary laments put in verse and set to music 'Pichhu daake, pichhu daake'. How Sachin's sweet tremor fills the air beckoning the days gone by is a real treat. The prelude starts with some rhythmic words giving company to the reed of a harmonium playing incessantly. The tune is based on padabali kirtan. The last part of the song is heart-rending. Village instruments never used before are used as orchestra. The moment 'Takdum takdum bajey' begins its fray, dhak (big drums) and cymbals play the rhythm in full swing and create a unique ambience. This song is timeless and is popular even today.

The song 'Jhilmil jhilmil jhiler jaley' is lifted from the folk song of East Bengal, 'Gayer badhu dul duliya jai'. Sachin's improvisation has changed the song and given it a new rhythmic feel. When Sachin sings, the words and tune of the song become images. He sang this song in a broken voice, keeping its elemental nature intact.

Sachin's purple patch continued with super-hit songs. But the icing on the cake came in the year 1952 with a film that broke all records of the time, *Jaal*. Directed by one of his ardent admirers, Guru Dutt, and starring another close associate, Dev Anand, *Jaal* was a milestone in the careers of all three as also its lyricist Sahir. However, the one person who benefited most from the success of the film's music wasn't even in the picture when the film was being planned and shot.

One of the things that set Sachin apart from his colleagues was that he demanded absolute freedom as music director and followed his instinct in deciding on the voice which would suit a particular song. Unlike other music directors of the era who largely depended on the known voices of Rafi or Lata for all songs, Sachin set little store by reputation. This is probably why he was able to usher in so many new talents in Hindi film music. Never one to compromise on excellence, he paid scant heed to any recommendations on which singer to take for a song. He knew that not all voices were suited to all songs. Something that is impossible to imagine today, he would try out a song with several singers before choosing the one he felt was most appropriate. In a remarkable show of respect for his stature as a composer, the singers of the era not only did not feel offended by this but were proud to be able to sing for him. In this context it is worthwhile to quote eminent Bengali lyricist Pulak Bandyopadhyay:

> Everyone accepted him as an elder brother. Hemant-da used to tell us with his disarming smile, 'I'm off to rehearse for Sachin-da's song. But nobody knows who will ultimately get to sing it. Manna-babu, Talat, Mukesh, Rafi, everyone will try. But the song will be recorded only in the voice Sachin-da finds most appropriate for it.' The artists of the era willingly accepted this state of affairs. No one had any complaint against dada either. (*Kathay Kathay Raat Hoye Jay*)

Thus it came about that despite the presence of established singers like Rafi and Mukesh, Sachin chose Hemant Kumar for what turned out to be the most popular song of *Jaal*. Though Hemant had sung a solo in the 1941 film *Irada* and had rendered a duet with Sandhya in *Sazaa*, he was still not very well-known. But the connoisseur in Sachin sensed that the resonant voice of Hemant was best suited for the song; that it was in his voice the song would reverberate in the heart of the audience. Hemant became famous overnight in the world of Hindi film music with this one song in *Jaal*: 'Sun ja dil ki daastaan'. Sachin himself recorded later:

In this film [*Jaal*] I composed a song for the hero which I absolutely loved. I had been thinking about whom to choose for the hero's voice. Rafi, Talat, Mukesh were famous names then. But just around that time Hemanta had come to Bombay and had joined Filmistan. He hadn't yet got a chance as a playback singer in films. I decided to get him to sing the song. Whenever I set a song to music I also decided whose voice would suit it best. Hemanta established himself in Hindi films with this song. Apart from Geeta and Manna, Hemanta was another singer I helped establish in Hindi cinema. The song's popularity also boosted my confidence. (*Sargamer Nikhad*)

It needs to be mentioned here that few people at the time remembered Hemant's song in *Irada*. Sachin himself was not aware that '*Sun ja dil ki daastaan*' was not Hemant Kumar's first solo in Hindi films. *Jaal* had other hit numbers by Geeta Roy and Lata, while the Kishore Kumar—Geeta Roy duet '*De bhi chuke hum dil nazrana*' was also fairly well received. But Hemant's solo overshadowed everything else in the film and proved once again that when it came to sheer melody, there was no one who could hold a candle to Sachin.

The other movie *Lal Kunwar*, although not a hit, had a few songs which became quite popular. The song '*Raja jani lage mohe nayanwa ka baan re*' based on a folk song and sung by Shamshad Begum and Suraiya's '*Tum jo mile arzoo ko dil ki rah mil gayi*' won the hearts of the people.

During 1952—55 Sachin did not record any Bengali songs. Neither did he compose any non-film songs in Hindi. In the wake of the success of *Baazi*, Sachin became extremely busy composing music for many films. Finding it difficult to cope with the stress, he decided to reduce his quota to three films per year. He would not agree to do more even for a higher payment. Pulak Bandopadhyay narrates an incident where the composer turned down what was a most generous offer:

> An interesting incident took place one morning at 'Jet', the residence of S. D. Burman. Lyricist Pulak Bandopadhyay was an eye-witness. There were a number of people in the room. One gentleman opened his suitcase and showed S. D. Burman bundles of currency notes. SD said in his own style, 'You may show me as many bundles of notes as you want. But I'm not going to do your film.' The gentleman pleaded a lot but SD did not budge. After a while, the disheartened gentleman left the place.
> One of the people sitting in that room said, 'Dada, you shouldn't have thrown away so much money at such an hour. SD replied, 'Have you seen a draw-well? If you draw out all the water from a well, it dries up. You have to give time for water to collect again. Music direction follows the same principle. If I become greedy and take a heap of films, I'll be finished in no time. I've got a fixed yearly quota. I don't do more than that. My quota for this year is complete. Whoever gives whatever money, I'm not going to do any more films this year'. (*Kathay Kathay Raat Hoye Jay*)

S. D. Burman did what he said. There were many music directors who created a stir for a short while and disappeared from the scene, unnoticed. But it was S. D. Burman who was in demand as a music director till the last days of his life.

Most people are unaware of the fact that if a film-wise average is taken, S. D. Burman holds the record for the highest number of hit songs scored by a music director. He used to nourish his compositions and refused to do films for which producers insisted on hit songs. He used to say, 'I score good songs and not hit songs.'

It would not be a digression from the topic if we talk about his son R. D. Burman in this context. Here lies the difference in attitude between the father and his son. It takes nine months for the development of a child; the mother has to suffer the throes of labour before she gives birth to the baby. There is no way you can cut down on this time or there will be a miscarriage. This was responsible for the downfall of R. D. Burman in the 1980s and 1990s. He did not allow water to gather in the well. He was in a hurry, and therefore, the conception did not take shape properly. Quantity should not be considered as a measure for talent, it is the quality which matters. S. D. Burman never accepted any offer indiscriminately. He used to study and understand the story meticulously and score music accordingly. That is why he never lost his popularity in his lifetime.

The year 1953 was a moderate one for SD. Music lovers appreciated his songs but none of the songs was a big hit. Four films were released this year. They were Fali Mistry's *Arman*, Agradoot's *Babla*, Mahesh Kaul's *Jivan Jyoti* and Amiya Chakrabarty's *Shahenshah*. It would be difficult for anyone to offer such successful for films one after another. Sachin was not an exception. His songs in the aforesaid films, such as Talat's '*Jag mein aaye koi*' and Lata's '*Raat khushi ki aayi*' in *Babla*; Asha Bhonsle's '*Balma ne man har le na*' in *Jeevan Jyoti* and '*Main pankh lagake ud jaaun*' in *Armaan*; and Lata's '*Khaak hua dil jalte jalte*' in *Shahenshah*, were received well by the audience but none of these were as big a hit as the songs of *Baazi* or *Sazaa*.

If this upset Sachin, it surely did not deprive him of his sense of humour. Probably looking for divine intervention to leave behind what was by his standards a lean phase, he decided to visit the Ramakrishna Mission at Khar and seek God's blessings. Just before entering the temple, he did something strange. Instead of keeping his shoes together at one place, he kept one shoe in one place and the pushed the other under a heap of shoes in another corner. His companion asked in surprise, 'What are you doing, Karta? Why are you keeping your shoes like that?'

Karta replied, 'Cases of theft of shoes are increasing by the day.'

'What if the thief traces both pieces?' the friend asked him, still incredulous.

With his disarming smile, Sachin said, 'Brother! If the thief goes to such elaborate lengths, he deserves to have the pair.'

This is just one example of Sachin's jovial, fun-loving nature which all his near and dear ones attested to. So much so that he even infused many of his songs with his trademark wit and sense of humour. Though he took his work very seriously, he never lost sight of the lighter side of life and was always game for a session of adda. Many close associates, including singers like Manna Dey, Asha Bhonsle and Lata Mangeshkar, have often referred to his joviality and childlike nature. Salil Ghosh says:

> One afternoon I found Sachin-da sitting alone at the dinner table, legs folded on the chair, wearing a lungi and a pair of socks, a light shawl wrapped around the body. He was enjoying a cup of tea and toast with honey. Meera boudi was in Calcutta. An exercise book wrapped in brown paper, with the words 'Bibagi Bhanwara' written on it in Hindi, was lying on the table. The usual exchange of pleasantries over, I lifted the exercise book and asked him if it was the story of some new film he was composing for. Sachin-da

said in his special East Bengal dialect, 'What can I say? There's a story here that I liked. I read it to a producer. He also liked it but wanted some changes. While I want to fill the story with the aroma of sandalwood, the producer would have nothing but the odour of garlic and onion. I told him bluntly, 'I won't do it. I will not allow him to use the story.' I couldn't help laughing out at the way he said it. Introduction to (*Sargamer Nikhad*)

Sagarmay Ghosh, elder brother of Salil Ghosh and editor of *Desh*, narrates another incident which demonstrates Sachin's unique take on the way the Hindi film world operated. Ghosh had arrived in Bombay on a holiday. Sachin was looking for some story for a new film. The topic came up during conversation. Sachin told Ghosh:

Give me some good stories. Dev Anand respects me. If I get some good stories I can ask him to make films on them. But one has to be careful with the kind of story one chooses. You know what the heroes and heroines here are like? We cannot emphasize one at the cost of the other. Both must have equal footage. If the hero has eighty scenes and the heroine twenty, or vice versa, it will lead to a clash. The proportion may at best be sixty to forty, not more than that. (Introduction to *Sargamer Nikhad*)

Subal Mukhopadhyay, father of honourable Biman Mukhopadhyay, was a friend of Sachin. He mentions another incident that shows this side of Sachin's character. When in Calcutta, Sachin insisted on buying biscuits from a young boy who had a stall on the pavement at Gariahat. One day he asked the boy to pack one ser of biscuits, telling him, 'Look here my boy, I am from a Vaishnava family. I don't have beef. Don't give me cows.' It took a nonplussed Subal-babu a few moments to realize what Sachin meant. In those days some local biscuits were made in the shape of animals and birds. Sachin wouldn't accept cow-shaped biscuits.

This aspect of his nature gives a charming spin to this royalty turned composer. On the one hand, he could be temperamental, obstinate and stubborn but on the other he was as simple as a child, publicity-shy and sagacious.

In 1954, S. D. Burman received his first national-level recognition, the *Filmfare* award for best music director. In a year where he had rather nondescript scores for films like *Angaar*, *Chalis Baba Ek Chor* and *Radhakrishna*, it was again a Navketan film, *Taxi Driver*, which brought Sachin glory. In his own words:

> In this film I made Talat Mahmood sing a favourite song of mine. Rafi, Mukesh and Hemanta were then eager to sing for me. But I had a feeling that this particular song would sound best in Talat's voice because the tune had a series of small and light tremors. Talat's voice had a special tremulous quality to it and a refined Lucknowi style. Talat sang what turned out to be the most popular song of the film. (*Sargamer Nikhad*)

This particular song, '*Jaayein toh jaayein kahan*', deserves a special mention. Sahir's exquisite words became very popular with the romantic fraternity of the era. The agony of unrequited love found doleful expression in the one-of-a-kind voice of Talat Mahmood. Dev Anand's passionate lip-syncing raised the song to a symbol of grief-stricken loneliness. The first line has some similarity with Sachin's Bengali hit '*Prem jamunar pare*' rendered in raga Bhairavi but it better approximates Rabindranath Tagore's '*Hey kshaniker atithi*'. Like many others of the era, Sachin was deeply influenced by Rabindra Sangeet and would often dip into the vast ocean of Tagore songs for inspiration.

SD's views on plagiarism are very clear. In one of the music sessions, someone close to him remarked that Salil Chowdhury had copied two western songs and adapted them in Bengali. The song *'Clanti name go'* is a Bengali version of *'Happy birthday to you'*. The other Bengali song *'Duranta ghurni tai legechhe pak'* is a lift from Pat Boon's style. Lastly, he added that the adaptation was done with artistic workmanship.

S. D. Burman was reserved by nature and never spoke much. He interrupted the discussion with a serious note. He said:

> What did you say, artistic workmanship? That's what matters and nothing else. Everyone from Rabindranath Tagore to D. L. Roy to Kazi Nazrul Islam borrowed from others in their own artistic workmanship. I have also copied. Remember the song, *'Jaane wo kaise, log the jinke, pyaar ko pyaar mila/ Humne toh jab kaliyan maangi, kaanton ka haar mila'* sung by Hemant Kumar in *Pyaasa*? Before I talked about it, could anybody guess that the tune of the second line of this song was copied from our national anthem *'Punjab, Sindhu, Gujarat, Maratha, Dravid, Utkal, Banga?'* Let it be. The less we talk about it the better for us. (*Kathay Kathay Raat Hoye Jay*)

I do consider that in the creative world we owe each other consciously or unconsciously and thus the chariot of creation progresses in its mission to explore the unknown.

Other songs of the film became immensely popular too, making *Taxi Driver* the musical hit of the year. For *'Chahe koi khush ho'*, sung by Kishore Kumar at his zaniest best with Johnny Walker and others, Sachin was inspired by the Italian folk tune of Tarantella. While

Lata sang '*Dil se milake dil pyar kijiye*', '*Dil jale to jale*' and '*Aye meri zindagi, aaj raat jhoom le*' with her trademark expertise, Asha also did not lag behind, rendering '*Jeene do aur jiyo*'with great compassion. Though the most soulful and well-known of the film's songs was '*Jaayein toh jaayein kahan*', I personally prefer the excellent club song '*Dil se milaake dil pyar kijiye*'. This one is in a class of its own; a simple, uncluttered tune that stays true to its picturization. The tiny orchestra in this bar room consists of a piano, a guitar, a clarinet and maracas. *Taxi Driver*'s great music once again proved that Sachin reserved his best for a banner and director that understood him and his music and gave him a free hand. It had taken Sachin almost a decade since his arrival in Bombay to reach the position he had. Sachin wrote about his experiences after the Filmfare Award ceremony:

> You enter a garden house with a beautiful garden and congratulate the gardener. What about the master of the house?' said Sri Ramakrishna. In our film world the same question is often asked, though in different words.
>
> However, let me assure you that as a director of film music, I do not envy the film stars or playback singers, except when I am called a 'bundle' [a word of unknown origin heard in Bombay which means a good-for-nothing fellow].
>
> One day I had some business at Kardar studio. A fairly big crowd was waiting at the gates for a glimpse of the star and I drove in. 'Who is it?' they anxiously asked and peeped in. 'Oh!' came the loud voice of a disappointed fan, and then, 'Arre, he is a bundle.'
>
> But I have my admirers too. Once I was waiting at Bandra station to catch a train for Malad. Suddenly, I

discovered that the train had come, halted and left. I didn't even realize. What was I doing? Well, I was lost in the enjoyment of my own tune of a song from *Shabnam* which a gang of labourers were singing to the rhythm of the movements of their hammers and shovels.

Talking of rhythm, I am tempted to repeat an old story. I had just joined Filmistan and I was giving a recital of my songs before S Mukherji, the Filmistan chief, Ashok Kumar (Dadamoni to all of us), Pradeep the lyric poet and others at an informal gathering at Malad. In the midst of it I heard a jarring sound which was supposed to be a message of appreciation from an admiring listener. Who could it be? I looked in the direction of the sound and turned pale. The culprit was none other than my boss, Mr Mukherji, whom I knew to be a true lover of music and whose style of singing was like my own. How could I satisfy his ears?

As days went by, I made further discoveries regarding his sense of rhythm and harmony. Every day after lunch I had to carry my harmonium to his room. Lying comfortably on a sofa, he listened to my compositions, then closed his eyes, and snored! The snore was a signal that my composition had been disapproved of.

This ordeal continued for nearly two months and I couldn't bear it any more. I also came to the conclusion that if I could not please my boss, there was no point in my staying on at Filmistan, just to sing lullabies to him. The next day I went prepared for a showdown.

As usual I started playing the harmonium and went on humming my new tune till my boss's eyed closed. There was nothing more to do. I had only to wait for the inevitable snore. But suddenly the boss woke up and said, 'Mr Burman, why not record it?'

'Record what?' I asked.

'I mean this tune. You may call the musicians and start rehearsing right now,' he said.

I was puzzled and wondered why he had liked this one of all the tunes I had composed for him all this time. I found out the same evening. As I was coming out of the rehearsal room, the 'room-boy' (doorkeeper) was humming the tune and quite correctly too! This gave me an idea. From that day I made it a point to get my tunes 'approved' by the 'room-boy'. It worked. In almost all cases the room-boy's approval carried.

The secret of Mr Mukherji's judgement was, as he told me one day, the formula of universal appeal. He said, 'You see, Mr Burman, you have your own style of music, which I like. By all means, keep it up, but present it in such a way that film lovers may like it and feel at home with it, not only in Bombay or Bengal but all over the country.'

With this and many other pieces of sound advice the man who had apparently no rhythm or harmony, guided me over the difficult road to success for which I shall always remain grateful to him.

My present work is nothing but trying to weave patterns of universal appeal in my own style, and in doing this, I think, I am doing my duty to the film industry and no disservice to the country. For me no reward is bigger than the pleasure of hearing my tune from the lips of a stranger.

Fishing is one of my hobbies. Once, I was fishing at a village about twenty miles from Calcutta. It was an unlucky pond, and at the end of a fruitless day I had only my patience to flatter. Thoroughly disappointed, I was about to call it a day, when a boy of about ten jumped into the pond and started singing my *Baazi* song (*Tadbeer se bigdi hui*) not knowing that the man who composed its music was on the opposite bank with his fishing rod. It was the biggest catch of my life. It is not the composition of music alone that makes a 'hit' song. One is on the tenterhooks for fear that a thousand and one calamities may spoil the song. For instance, imagine everything set ready for the final 'take' but the singer nonchalantly enjoys ice cubes before singing an important song. And who could be it but Dadamoni? The idol of the Indian screen was to sing a song in *Shikari* and he had been ordered that he should have ice before singing my song to improve his voice! But, believe it or not, to my great amazement and unbounded relief, Dadamoni's voice did improve and become quite steady as lumps of ice went down his throat.

I cannot explain the medical theory, but I would like to tell my friends, the playback singers who sing my songs: 'For heaven's sake, don't ever try Dadamoni's trick on me. I am already a 'bundle' ... of nerves. ('The Road to Success', *Filmfare*, 1955)

After the relatively low-key years of 1953 and 1954 (although he won the Filmfare Award for *Taxi Driver*) Sachin bounced back strongly again in 1955 with five films, three of which—Bimal Roy's *Devdas*, Navketan's *House No. 44*, and Subodh Mukherjee's *Munimji*—saw the composer in great form with compositions ranging from Vaishnava kirtans to those based on Western Latin American beats. Nabendu Ghosh, the screenplay writer for *Devdas*, talks of the film's music:

Devdas was an instant hit. Sachin-da's music also was a big success. The song of the Vaishnava pair *'Aan milo Sham sanware'* (Manna Dey—Geeta Dutt), Chandramukhi's *'Ab aage teri marzi'* and *'O aanewale rukh ja koi dam'* (Lata Mangeshkar) and Devdas's own *'Mitwa, mitwa'* (Talat Mahmood) were on everyone's lips. On meeting him, I said, 'Karta, it's simply wonderful.' Raising his folded hands upwards, Karta simply said 'Allah meherbaan.'

Nabendu Ghosh has written about his experiences with Sachin-karta in an article 'Dakhina Paban' published in the Calcutta-based literary magazine *Prantik* edited by the author of this book. Let us hear him:

> It was Bimal-da who introduced me to Sachin Dev Burman. I hadn't met him before. So when Bimal-da said, 'Nabendu-babu, let's go and meet Sachin-karta and see if he consents to do the music for my film,' I agreed immediately. He was already a well-known name in the world of Hindi film music. I had been listening to his songs for quite some time. I accompanied Bimal-da to Sachin Dev Burman's Bandra house [...] He was dressed in a spotless white dhoti and panjabi, tall, fair-complexioned and with no trace of fat anywhere on his body. I thought he could not be above fifty. Without uttering a word, I simply bowed before him. He said, 'Namaskar!' and asked Bimal-da who I was. Bimal-da said, 'He has written the screenplay for my films *Maa, Parineeta, Biraj Bou,* and *Naukar.* He has also written for other directors. He is one of the forceful young writers in Bengali.'
>
> Sachin Dev replied, 'Well, well, these are all famous films; I shall now remember his name. But to tell you

the truth I have not read any of his literary works.' By now he was talking in the Bangal dialect... Bimal-da took his seat and said, 'Please do not disappoint me. I want to film Saratchandra's *Devdas* anew, and you will have to take charge of its music.'

'Saratchandra,' Sachin-babu said, folding his hands in salute and in the same posture told Bimal-da, 'Saratchandra, and Bimal Roy directing it. I am doubly blessed. Yes, thank you, I'll do it with pleasure.'

His face glowed with the simple joy of a child.

That Sachin Dev's mind was as simple as a child's was revealed before Nabendu Ghosh on another occasion when the latter had gone to meet the maestro. When he asked for a glass of water, Sachin, in keeping with his plain-speaking nature, which was part of his earthy simplicity, said, 'Sure, water you shall have, but no tea.' Perhaps Sachin could sense Nabendu's discomfort, so he said, 'People keep coming all the while. Making tea is tiring—boil water, pour tea, mix milk and sugar, and you know we have no cook, my wife does the cooking herself.'

But, when Nabendu met Sachin next, he was offered not only tea, even snacks were served. By then, Sachin and Meera had managed to procure and read Nabendu's books from the Bengali club of Shivaji Park. Nabendu writes:

> I remember Sachin-karta saying, 'Have tea, Nabendu, you write well.' It was a memorable day. So many readers have praised me and I have derived some pleasure from this, even pride. I have silently saluted Goddess Saraswati. But I just cannot express the feeling of joy and inspiration when I heard such words of praise from the learned and famous of the land.

When I told Bimal-da, [about this experience] he responded, 'He is a great human being and a wonderful artist. He is like royalty in his personality and behaviour, yet has a simple, childlike mind.' I then told him how Karta and Boudi had taken the trouble of sourcing my works and reading them. Bimal-da said, 'This is another example of his humanity. There are many talented people, but not many show due respect to others.' (*Prantik* Jan-Feb 2006)

Apart from *Devdas*, 1955 became a memorable year for Sachin's music with great songs like Hemant Kumar's '*Chup hai dharti chup hai chand sitare*', '*Tere duniya mein jeene se*' and Lata and Asha's '*Faili hui hai sapnon ki baahein*' and '*O bhole piya tumhein meri kasam*' respectively in Navketan's *House No. 44* and Kishore Kumar's evergreen hit '*Jeevan ke safar me rahi*' in *Munimji*. This song, inspired by the music of 'Mexican Hat Dance', changed the course of Kishore Kumar's life in Hindi films. The original composition of 'Mexican Hat Dance' by Jose Ortega and his Mariachi Band is a fast-paced rhythm-based piece. Sachin changed it completely to a slow measure. The difference in beat is so great that at first it is difficult to recognize that the two songs have the same origin. Never one to copy anything blindly, Sachin used his mastery over various genres of music to adapt the Mexican beat, measure and tune to the Indian context. This is where his greatness and his individuality lie, in his remarkable ability to assimilate diverse streams of music.

Apart from Kishore's '*Jeevan ke safar mein rahi*', two other *Munimji* songs—'*Nayana khoye khoye tere dil mein*' and '*De diya toh ley le dil*' sung by Lata Mangeshkar, S. D. Burman and Geeta Roy respectively are masterpieces. Geeta Roy is simply incomparable. Kishore also sang '*Pehli na dusree tisree pasand hai*' (*Mad Bhare Nayan*) very well with the characteristic modulation of his voice. Lata's song 'O leke jiya piya kahan' (*Mad Bhare Nayan*) is a unique example of SD's improvisation.

Sachin has written about how he introduced Kishore Kumar to the Hindi film music scene:

> I was then with Filmistan, working on Dadamoni Ashok Kumar's own production, *Eight Days*. The year was 1946. Kishore used to visit his elder brother's film studio occasionally after his matriculation examination. Once, Dadamoni asked me to listen to Kishore singing. Kishore was never a regular practitioner of music, never rehearsed regularly. I was charmed with his natural God-given voice. Then and there, I made him sing a song for the film. I had to okay him at the first take. I told Dadamoni, 'Better not send him to college for further studies. Let him take up music.' (*Sargamer Nikhad*)

Sachin liked the youthfulness in Kishore's voice. Unlike other established singers of the era, Kishore had not practised under a guru ever in his life. He did not even know anything about ragas and raginis. But Sachin made no mistake in evaluating the magic in the young man's voice. In Kishore's own words:

> I came to Bombay to act in and produce films. I never dreamt of singing. But the old man just wouldn't give up, kept chasing me. I felt quite annoyed. I used to keep away from him.
>
> It so happened one day that I was travelling by car. It halted at a traffic signal. All of a sudden, I heard, in chaste Bangal, 'Ah! Is it not Kishoira?' Before I could say anything the old man simply opened the door of my car

and entered. He asked the driver to drive out of town.
We drove for quite some time till we reached some green
meadows on the outskirts of the city. The fellow alighted
and proceeded on foot towards the fields. He lifted his
dhoti and started walking along the earthen boundary of
the fields. He went on singing one song after another. I
felt as if it was all a dream. I don't remember being in my
senses. Only then did I realize that this was the man I had
been looking for all along. I decided that from that day on
I would always do his bidding. (*Sa Re Ga*, Dec—Jan 2001)

This episode suggests that before bringing Kishore to the limelight, Sachin wanted him to experience the earthiness of his music in his heart. One has to have a feel of the soil, an understanding of the common folk's life and livelihood, before one can render a song with any feeling. It is essential to be one with nature to be able to sing in a way that it moves the listener. Then and only then will people embrace a song. Is there anyone who has not held Kishore's songs set to tune by Sachin-karta close to their heart?

Immediately after '*Jeevan ke safar mein*' Sachin gave Kishore another hit with '*Dukhi man mere sun mera kehna*' in Navketan's *Fantoosh* directed by Chetan Anand, Sachin's only film in 1956. This song is a standing testimony to Kishore's unrivalled felicity even in melody-dominated songs. He had so far been slotted as a singer of comic and fun songs, much like his image as an actor. But now, those who dismissed him as a singer had to grudgingly accept that if given the opportunity, Kishore could outshine the well-known names of the era.

The other Kishore song in the film, '*Aye meri topi palat ke aa*', has an interesting story associated with it. Sachin's son Rahul was only sixteen then. He would often insist on composing music only to be rebuffed by his father. So imagine his surprise on seeing *Fantoosh* and listening to '*Aye meri topi palat ke aa*'. It was he who had composed the music and had played the tune before his father! An excited Rahul almost asked his father for an explanation. Sachin's nonchalant reply was, 'Sachin Dev Burman himself has chosen your music. Remember, this is a stroke of good luck for you.' Rahul realized that his father was not only a father, but a competitor too. He decided that from now on he would never let his father listen to his tunes.

That year Sachin came out with a Bengali record during the pujas, after a gap of four years. The record included two of his most loved songs—'*Mano dilo na bondhu*' and '*Tumi ar nei she tumi*'. The first, a thumri, a delightful fusion of folk with ragas, will be familiar to Hindi film lovers for its similarity to the song '*Jaane kya tuney kahi*' in *Pyaasa* which released in 1957, the year when almost everything Sachin touched turned into gold. '*Tumi ar nei she tumi*' is not only a song of verbal tricks but also a song where Sachin takes it to such a vocal climax that one has to be on one's toes to keep up with the song. He created a fine balance between the lyrics and the tunes composed. He sang '*Tumi ar*' in different styles giving particularly stress to '*ar*'. In the stanza '*Tomar saaper beni doley na hawar banshi shune*' he drew a phonic image of a floating pig tail. It is an experimental song sung in a unique style.

Four movies were released in 1957. Except *Miss India*, all were hits. It was not that the songs of *Miss India* were not popular. Popular they were but not so when compared to the songs of the other three. The songs '*O mere sajna aya re aya*' (Lata), '*Jaaon main kahan*' (Lata, Manna Dey) and '*Albela main ek dilwala*' (Asha) deserve mention.

This was the year of Vijay Anand's *Nau Do Gyarah*, Subodh Mukherjee's *Paying Guest* and Guru Dutt's *Pyaasa*. The music of all three films, dramatically different from each other, became instant hits and remains popular to this day, fifty-six years after they were released. The success of the music of *Nau Do Gyarah* and *Paying Guest* established the team comprising Sachin Dev Burman, Kishore Kumar, Asha Bhonsle and Majrooh Sultanpuri. These films revealed a new facet of Sachin's music as he came up with several light numbers befitting the situations in the film. These included the Kishore—Asha duet *'Aankhon mein kya ji'*, Kishore's *'Hum hain rahi pyar ke'*, and the Rafi—Asha duet *'Kali ke roop mein chali ho dhoop mein'* in *Nau Do Gyarah*, Kishore's *'Mana janab ne pukara nahi'* and the super-hit Kishore—Asha duet *'Chhor do aanchal zamana kya kahega'* in *Paying Guest*; the last mentioned song becoming an anthem for young lovers of the era. In this song, Sachin introduced an 'Ah!' sound at the very beginning. Given his total involvement with and understanding of the mood of the sequence that the director had envisaged, he asked Asha to articulate it as if someone was pulling at her sari. The effect was electric and drove listeners crazy. This was something he did regularly in his Bengali songs. Now he started introducing interjectory sounds in Hindi songs too. Many of us may not know that in *'Chunri sambhal gori'* (music by R. D. Burman, *Baharon Ke Sapne*, 1969,) it was Sachin who advised the use of 'Huh-A!' with each line of the mukhda. How it gives the song its seductive appeal! At the same time, it needs to be mentioned that even in the midst of these light-hearted numbers, Sachin could come up with the glorious melody of *'Chand phir nikla'* (Lata, *Paying Guest*) and the lilting folksy number *'Aaja panchhi akela hai'* (Rafi—Asha, *Nau Do Gyarah*).

I have forgotten to mention one superb score of *Paying Guest*. The song is *'O nigah-e-mastana'*. It has been filmed fabulously with a handsome Dev Anand serenading a gorgeous Nutan with a wonderful song—romantic and playful at the same time. The tune in the background is subdued, rippling and tilting, until it swells in a way that is almost mischievous in its transition from gentle to swift. The words are all sung by Kishore with Asha's humming used at strategic points. The song fades away gently with a glorious combination of whistling and humming.

In *Pyaasa*, Sachin composed what many consider the last word in melody. The film showcased Sachin at his versatile best, its songs ranging from the playfully romantic *'Hum aapki aankhon mein'* to the heart-stopping lament of *'Jinhein naaz hai Hind par'*, from a kirtan-inspired *'Aaj sajan mohe ang lagalo'* to some of the finest nazms ever in Hindi cinema. If Geeta Dutt had two super-hit solos in *'Jaane kya tuney kahi'* (the Hindi version of *'Mano dilo na bondhu'*) and *'Aaj sajan mohe ang lagalo'*, and a duet with Rafi, *'Hum aapki aankhon mein'*, Hemant rendered the heart-rending *'Jaane woh kaise log thay'*. But the undoubted star among the playback singers was Rafi who sang some of the best songs of his entire career for this film. These ranged from the irresistible *'Sar jo tera chakraye'* (the tune for the line *'sun sun sun arey baba sun'* was taken from Ghazi's song of East Bengal *'Gun-gun-gun, tabal paak, kanchakala bote, dukha tum-tum nagrani baper sagarali bap'*) to *'Yeh duniya agar mil bhi jaaye to kya hai'*.

There are some songs that give us gooseflesh everytime we listen to them. *'Yeh duniya agar mil bhi jaaye toh kya hai'* is one of them. The cynicism of Sahir's words is palpable, and S. D. Burman's music complements it perfectly. The song starts off very slow and soft (Rafi's voice literally trails over the first few lines), then gradually gathers momentum, building up till the finale, when the dead-alive poet Vijay's fury boils over in a thunderous denouncement of the world, with the voice and music both reaching a sudden crest.

The film marked the coming together of the finest work of Sachin, lyricist Sahir, and director—actor Guru Dutt who immortalized the songs, particularly '*Yeh duniya agar mil bhi jaaye to kya hai*', with his innovative picturization.

The songs of *Nau Do Gyarah*, *Paying Guest* and *Pyaasa* catapulted Kishore Kumar, Hemant Kumar, Asha Bhonsle and Geeta Dutt to dizzying heights of popularity. Geeta in particular reaped immense benefits from the success of *Pyaasa*. Till now she had the image of a singer of sad songs and bhajans. Sachin stunned one and all by radically altering her style, giving a delectable sex appeal to her voice which seemed as comfortable in a kirtan-style song as in a Western refrain. Likewise, Kishore was largely seen as someone suitable only for fun songs. The songs of *Nau Do Gyarah* and *Paying Guest* changed that perception and even established him as the voice of the 'hero' Dev Anand.

Sachin's choice of Asha during this period owed itself to a rift with Lata. As a music director, Sachin could be quite demanding about how he wanted a singer to render his compositions. He believed that as a composer it was his primary responsibility to bring out the best in a singer, to bring to the fore what the singer was capable of. It was his job to extract the essence of a tune in the voice of a singer. If he could not do that, it would amount to his failure as a music composer. This belief and his insistence on ensuring what he thought was the best possible rendering of a song resulted in a falling out with his favourite Lata Mangeshkar. Between 1957 and 1962, he did not ask Lata to sing any song for him.

It so happened that after Lata had recorded a song for *Sitaron Se Aage*, Sachin thought it would be better to record it again. But Lata was a busy singer. Besides, she was scheduled to leave for a foreign tour soon. Busy as she was completing jobs she had on hand, she could not assign any date to Sachin despite his repeated calls. Probably piqued at this behaviour by someone he had given his finest compositions to sing to, Sachin dropped Lata altogether and called upon Asha. Around this period, Asha, despite her considerable talent, was entirely eclipsed by her formidable elder sister who used to be the preferred choice of all music directors. She was struggling to make a name for herself, largely unsuccessfully, getting to render only cabarets or leftovers that Lata would not sing. Sachin's call gave Asha the big break she was looking for and she grabbed the opportunity wholeheartedly. Over the next four to five years, Asha, thanks to Sachin, emerged out of Lata's shadow and made a place of her own, rendering popular numbers in films like *Chalti Ka Naam Gaadi*, *Kala Pani*, *Insaan Jaag Utha*, *Sujata*, *Bambai Ka Babu*, *Kala Bazaar*, *Manzil* and others.

This tiff with Lata went on till 1962. Sachin Dev Burman's 'Lawta' (this is how he used to pronounce her name in his East Bengal accent) returned with her dream voice in *Bandini*, which incidentally had two fine Asha numbers too. In a radio interview, Lata spoke about the episode:

> After we had recorded the song, Burman-dada praised it profusely and okayed it. Once a music director okays a song, a second recording is generally not done. But Burman-dada was fastidious—a perfectionist to the hilt. Though willing, I could not spare the time. Such tiffs are nothing new among artists. But since there is mutual respect for each other, there are no problems in reunion. I admired Burman-dada.

It is, however, telling that when Lata listed the top ten favourite songs she had sung in 1967, none of Sachin's composition found a place, even though she included songs composed by newcomers Laxmikant-Pyarelal.

The song for which Lata was dropped and Asha inducted was

'*Pag thumak chalat balkhaye haye saiyyan kaise dharun dhir*'. Interestingly enough, Asha too could not render the song the way Sachin wanted. So, finally, the original Lata version was retained for the film. Almost a decade later, Sachin would use the same tune for one of Hindi films' classic songs, to be sung by Lata. If Sachin was unsatisfied with Lata's rendering of '*Pag thumak chalat balkhaye*', she more than compensated for it with the latter.

One record was released during puja in 1957. The songs included in that were '*Ghum bhulechhi nijhum ei nishithey*' and '*O jaani bhanwara keno katha koy na*'. Ardent fans of S. D. Burman might have noticed that in each of his songs an admixture new tune is involved. The embedded emotion is expressed in different modes; modulation of voice changes the style of singing and floating words and emotion embroil each other. He had, by now, mastered the art of presenting his songs in a new form not akin to others. Dakshina Mohan Thakur's dilruba and Karta's voice have become synonymous in this song.

The song '*Ghum bhulechhi nijhum*' starts with the grave, sonorous recital of the sarod. It seems as if the song does not have taal. The return from the antaras to the mukhda and vice versa is through different tunes, not similar to each other which have enhanced the beauty of the song manifold. At the end of the song '*Ghum bhulechhi*', he sang 'bhulechhi' once; and after that with a soft meend 'ghum', the song fades away.

'*O jaani bhanwara keno katha koy no*' is a light-hearted song. Sachin sang '*Jhilmil jhilmil*', '*jhar jhar jhar jhar*' and '*jhiri jhiri jhir jhiri*' in such a style that they render a pictorial view before our eyes. After giving stress on '*mahua keno*' his singing '*Mataal hay na-a-a*' with a pause is a unique improvisation. The pleasant drowsiness of the folk song demands our attention when Sachin sings '*chokh gelo, chokh gelo boley re*'. The use of vowel sounds and interjections have made this youthful song lively.

If having as wide a variety of songs as those in *Pyaasa*, *Nau Do Gyarah* and *Paying Guest* in one year wasn't enough to prove his versatility, the very next year (1958) he revolutionized the world of Hindi songs with compositions as varied as those in *Chalti Ka Naam Gaadi* and *Kala Pani*. Friends, fellow-composers and the lay listener all were rendered equally dumbstruck with his compositions for *Chalti Ka Naam Gaadi*, delectably sung by Kishore and Asha.

Nobody could have imagined such an intimate blend of Western music with Bengal's folk music. The film's songs were a perfect fit between the playful lyrics and beat-based, rhythmic music, with the beautiful voices to match. No wonder the songs of *Chalti Ka Naam Gaadi* created a sensation. Till now, the general feeling was that Sachin was more at home with serious, classical-based and folk songs. Despite some of his compositions for *Baazi* (most notably 'Tadbeer se bigdi hui'), *Paying Guest* and *Nau Do Gyarah*, no one had thought him capable of frothy, light-hearted numbers with a sustained Western beat. But those who accuse Sachin of old-fashioned melody-dominated music must listen to his songs from *Chalti Ka Naam Gaadi*. His music was capable of bursting the banks of the river of music to flow along ever new courses. If he were devoted to a single style of music, it would not have been possible for him to reign for thirty long years over the world of Hindi film music. Just think of the Kishore Kumar—Manna Dey duet '*Babu samjho ishare, horan purkare*', Kishore's '*Ek ladki bheegi bhaagi si*' and '*In haathon se sabki gaadi chal rahi hai*'. Can any of these be compared with anything he had composed so far? That is why Sachin is a genius and a genius can never be measured with the routine measures in vogue. Listen to the musical accompaniment in the last mentioned song. Given that the protagonists of the film are owners of a garage, the song is accompanied by music from a xylophone which reproduces the sound of a car mechanic's wrench on the body of a car. Was this possible without an amazing power of the imagination? Kishore Kumar is always at home in frothy songs, but listen to Manna Dey, the singer of *'Upar gagan vishal'* and other weighty classical numbers, in *'Babu samjho ishare'*. This is clear proof of Manna Dey's versatility and his expertise with various genres of songs.

It is said that *'Ek ladki bheegi bhaagi si'* is inspired by the classic country song 'Sixteen tons'. But I feel that Sachin has made the song livelier by composing something diametrically different from 'Sixteen tons'. Kishore and Asha had two duets in *'Haal kaisa hai janab ka'* and *'Paanch rupaiya barah aana'*, both playful numbers benefitting immensely from the singers' lively rendering and which continue to be as popular to this day. If it comes to using musical idioms of popular Western music, S. D. Burman shows us how to do that in *'Haal kaisa hai janab ka'* (Asha and Kishore), complete with yodelling and big-band-style inflections that a trumpet performs. In this song he uses musical phrases that are highly entertaining but also highly sophisticated. The antara is a delicious departure from the tonal mood of the sthayi and there Sachin uses, as though with a knowing smile, a melody that is entirely Indian in flavour. *Chalti Ka Naam Gaadi* opened up a new horizon for the modern song in Hindi films.

Diametrically opposite in texture was Navketan's *Kala Pani*, directed by Raj Khosla. The film's story was developed by Anand Lal based on the Bengali film *Sabar Upare* scripted by Nitai Bhattacharya. Sachin experimented with a different style in almost every composition. Asha Bhonsle's *'Nazar laagi raja tore bangley par'* and the Rafi—Asha duet *'Achchha ji main haari chalo maan jao na'* became extremely popular, the former in the pattern of a mujra, the latter in a quintessentially mischievous Sachin tune. In true Sachin style, when Asha articulates *'maan jao na'*, breaking it into syllables in a mock-offended indulgent voice, it is not at all difficult to guess who the composer is. Rafi sang what is arguably the best song of the film, '*Hum bekhudi mein tumko pukare chale gaye*', based on Sachin's hit Bengali composition '*Ghum bhulechhi nijhum nishithey ki jege thaki*'. Though the song is generally regarded as one of the finest ghazals of Hindi cinema, it is interesting to see what Sachin has to say about it:

> In *Kala Pani*, in one particular song, I preserved the ghazal style in the mukhda and composed the music for the antara in perfect geet style... Rafi sang the song exactly as I had envisaged it. (*Sargamer Nikhad*)

Among the other popular songs of the year, special mention needs to be made of Hemant's '*Hai apna dil toh awara*' in Raj Khosla's *Solva Saal* and a string of popular Asha numbers in *Lajwanti*. Hemant's song, with its memorable mouth organ refrain by R. D. Burman in the background, gave life to *Solva Saal*. The singer's deep baritone conveys the romance and sweetness of the composition, making it an evergreen hit which people hum to this day. Another noteworthy song in *Solva Saal* was Asha's '*Yeh bhi koi roothne ka mausam hai*', possibly inspired by the Rahbani Brothers' song '*Ya ghozayel*'. Adding to Asha's growing list of popular numbers were two songs from *Lajwanti*, '*Koi aaya dhadkan kehti hai*' and '*Ga mere mann ga*'. In the span of two years, 1957-58, thanks to Sachin's rift with Lata and his belief in the capabilities of Asha, the latter emerged from the shadows of her sister and established her very own style with her songs in *Nau Do Gyarah*, *Paying Guest*, *Chalti Ka Naam Gaadi*, *Kala Pani* and *Lajwanti*.

Sachin himself emerged as the frontrunner among the composers of the era, not a mean feat considering that this was the era of stalwarts like Naushad, Shankar-Jaikishan, Madan Mohan,

O. P. Nayyar and C. Ramachandra, among others. Sachin's music resonated in every nook and corner of India and catapulted the films to box office glory. His fame was no longer restricted to Tripura or Bengal. He was fast becoming one of India's internationally famed personalities. The honours flowed in thick and fast, beginning with the Sangeet Natak Academy Award in 1958.

He sang two songs during the Pujas that year. By this time, a change in his Bengali songs was discernible. Gone were the rigorous classical effects and the virtuoso play of notes to lend extra sweetness to the composition. What was left was a subtle experimentation with tunes resembling a topsy-turvy sea, the waves breaking and gathering once again. So subtle was his approach to Bengali music now that his expertise was almost invisible but it was there, audible to the true connoisseur of music. He had learnt the art of simplifying his music so as to make it accessible to the common man. What remained was a resonance of folk music, the reverberations of Bengal's folk songs, his cherished jewel since childhood, his inheritance and ultimate bequest to posterity. If he lost that there would be nothing left for Kumar Sachin Dev Burman.

There is rarely a folk song without the syllable 're', for example, '*Sujan bandhu re...koi gela re*'. Sachin often broke the rhythm of his song and inserted the syllable '*re*' which gave the song the resonance of a folk tune. In one of the songs, '*Na, na, phutona re phul*', he combined '*re*' with '*chand*' and at the very beginning, in the mukhda, sang '*na-na-na*' in different tunes. It is noticeable that while returning to the 'sthayi' (the final stave), Sachin changed the tune. This was also no exception. In '*Ekhono banshite ishara shuni ni*' he emphasized '*ekhono*', almost stopped and then sang the rest in a playful manner emphasizing neither '*i*' nor '*ra*' of the word '*ishara*' but '*sha*'. Singers will know how difficult it is to put the emphasis on the middle syllable of a word. In '*Se pradip nibhe jai*' he pronounced '*pradip*' as '*pradip-o*'. The song reached a different level altogether.

One may justifiably point out that it is essential to emphasize certain words to bring out the nuances of the composition and that every singer does this, so what's new? Yes. But if one listens closely, one will realize that other singers never alter the words. They stick to the core. But Sachin makes his own additions and alterations to the lyrics. He plays with them in such a way that the words become inseparable from the tune in the magical web he weaves. When he returns to dwell on the words, the theme becomes clear; one gets a kaleidoscopic presentation. This breaking and making of lyrics was part of Sachin's style. Instead of emphasizing on the usual word or syllable, Sachin used his creativity to provide the listener with ever-new experiences while listening to him.

The second song of the year '*Katha diye ele na*' falls in the category of songs he preferred Asha Bhonsle to sing in Hindi films. In it he so forcefully articulates the word '*na*' that it reverberates in the listener's consciousness long after the song is over. The subtle change from '*tumi kothay, tomi kothay*' to '*tumi-tumi kothay*' conveys the distress of someone helplessly looking for his beloved. The way he articulates the word '*abasad*' in the line '*shesher prahare elo abasad*', brings out the extreme physical fatigue through his voice. While the first song has a touch of folk to it, the second is a modern song.

1959 was another successful year, memorable for two films in particular, Guru Dutt's *Kaagaz Ke Phool* and Bimal Roy's *Sujata*. Equally accomplished, though lesser known, are his songs for Shakti Samanta's *Insaan Jaag Utha*. Let us hear from Shakti Samanta how sincere and diligent Sachin Dev Burman was in composing the songs and ensuring they matched the situations in the film:

> The man was a workaholic. He would listen to the situation in the film again and again. If I had any reservations about the tune he played for me, he would work on it immediately. In *Insaan Jaag Utha* there was a song 'Janu janu re'. The Nagarjun Sarovar dam was under construction then and we were shooting there. I explained the situation to Sachin-da. There would be two tractors at a distance of eight to nine feet from each other. The heroine would sing there, and so on. I noticed Sachin-da measure the distance a few times during our conversation. He rang me up a few days later. 'Make a detour to my house on the way to office,' he said. Accordingly, I reached his house 'Jet' in Bandra. I could hear the sound of music from outside. Once inside, I found a marking over a length of eight to nine feet. And to judge whether the interlude was in sync with the distance, Sachin-da himself was singing with eyes closed and measuring the gap. He did not even notice me enter the room. Opening his eyes a little later, he looked at me and asked 'When did you come?' I said, 'About ten minutes ago.' 'You should have called me,' he said and then sang a part of the song asking for my opinion. He was such a warm-hearted gentleman and had such control over music that everybody respected him [...] He was fun-loving but when it came to work, he was extremely serious. He liked his work and was devoted to it. His voice, his style was different. Music lovers all over India could feel the touch of his magic. He was unparalleled.
> (*'Ananya'*, *Aajkal*, 25 Sept. 2005)

Asha Bhonsle, who sang *'Janu janu re'* with Geeta Dutt, says:

It was Dada who first taught me to laugh in a song. In '*Janu janu re*', there is a portion where I was required to laugh. He himself demonstrated how to. I followed his instructions. He did not like it and told me, 'If you draw in your breath after laughing it will sound much better, more natural.' I did likewise. It was splendid. And from then on my laughter became quite famous.' (*Bhati Gang Baiya*)

No doubt, this duet in *Insaan Jaag Utha* remains its most popular number but let us not forget Rafi's dulcet voice in '*Chand sa mukhda kyun sharmaya*' (with Asha) and '*Yeh chanda Rus ka na ye Japan ka*', two forgotten gems which could be classified as belonging to Sachin Dev's gharana. Rafi uncannily echoes Sachin's style. The second song reminds us of 'Barefoot girls' in Rahbani Brothers' *Music for an Arabian Night*.

Sachin invariably put his heart in every Guru Dutt film. For as long as Guru Dutt made films, he remained a devoted admirer of Sachin who always brought out that little extra while composing for Guru Dutt. *Kaagaz Ke Phool* was no exception. Be it the justifiably celebrated '*Waqt ne kiya kya haseen sitam*', possibly Geeta Dutt's greatest song ever, or the philosophical underpinnings of '*Dekhi zamane ki yaari, bichhde sabhi baari baari*' in Rafi's nuanced baritone, *Kaagaz Ke Phool* was a more than worthy follow-up to the earlier films of the Guru Dutt—Sachin partnership—*Baazi*, *Jaal* and *Pyaasa*. And lest one thinks that the film was all about serious songs, there were the delectable frothy numbers '*Haar kabhi jeet kabhi kaheko rona re*', '*San san san chali hawa*' and '*Hum tum jise kehte thay shaadi*'. *Kaagaz Ke Phool* had one breathtaking song after another and choosing just one is a problem. I like '*San san san woh chali hawa*' (Md. Rafi, Asha, chorus) the most. I adore the sheer joie de vivre of this song. Waheeda Rehman's hair streaming in the wind, the papers flying, the happy crowd in the truck in front and the song of course. It is marvellous to notice how everything comes together in this song, the whistling, the chorus singing in parts, even the musical 'screeching' of tyres in the beginning. Guru Dutt's death was an irreparable loss to the music director who recounted:

> Starting with *Baazi* and up to *Kaagaz Ke Phool*, we shared a special relationship. The void that his death has left can never be filled. The moment he came to know that I had composed a new tune; he would stop shooting and come over to listen to it. Listening to the song he would immediately sit with his script to create a situation for the song. I feel so lonely whenever I remember this evergreen, stoical personality, he had an understated sense of humour.
>
> (*Sargamer Nikhad*)

This was also the year when Sachin lent his voice once more to a song in a Hindi film, the second time in thirteen years. The last time he had sung a Hindi film song was in *Eight Days*. Aptly enough, the song Sachin lent his voice to was a bhatiyali '*Sun mere bandhu re*' in Bimal Roy's classic, *Sujata*. This was probably the first true bhatiyali composition in Hindi cinema, complete with a '*re*' at the end which is a must in folk numbers, especially the boatman's song. These are songs in which boatmen just hold on to the helm of the boat and sing their heart out. It does not follow a particular rhythm. The song flows like a river in ebb. Nobody had ever composed such music in the Hindi film world before this. The sound of the boatman's oars splashing against the water accentuates the heart-rending quality of the song. The tune reflects the Indian philosophy of maya or illusion. Spiritualism has always been an essential part of life in India. In the daily battle for existence, one has to go through the entire gamut of emotions—happiness, sorrow, pain, ecstasy, hope, despair, expectation, disappointment—look upon all of them as maya and dedicate oneself fully to God. Happiness and sorrow alternate like tides in a river. Hence the heartfelt call to the friend: *'Sun mere bandhu re...'*

Before proceeding to discuss the music of *Sujata*, let us hear what Sachin has to say about bhatiyali:

> I have my own definition of bhatiyali, though in no way does it intend to change the general concept of the same. Bhatiyali is the tune of the earth. Its roots are in the earth, it flowers in the earth. Bhatiyali is the song of the river. Its notation, its words, its pathos and its delight remind us of the rivers of Bengal as do Rabindranath's poems. Again, bhatiyali is the song of love be it of the common peasants or of Radha-Krishna. Bhatiyali's mood, its passion is bathed in philosophic melancholy but it has no similarity with the philosophy of baul. (S. D. Music: Classic Aesthetics of Folk)

According to Sachin, the difference between baul and bhatiyali is on account of their theme. The change in subject matter is manifest in a change of mood and expression. Baul has its own philosophy. Bhatiyali speaks of the mind, the mood. Usually, bhatiyali describes human feelings and moods of the mind discernible through the senses in a captivating tune. For example, in the baul song *'Ami bandhur premagune pora, ami morle poras ne re tora'*, the sad tale of love can also be explained philosophically. Another, *'Chintaram darogababu karle jalatan'* in its figurative overtones is philosophic in all senses. Compared to this, the desire of an adolescent bride to return to her parental home in *'Tora ke jaas re'* makes for a mystic bhatiyali song.

When Sachin sang Hindi songs, for some of which he has

achieved immortality ('*O re manjhi mere sajan hain us paar*' is one of these) one could distinctly hear the unique voice, style and pronunciation of the non- Hindi speaking Sachin Dev Burman who never tried to hide his linguistic origin and identity. His singing style and pronunciation had something unabashedly and refreshingly rural about them.

The fifth note is prominent in folk songs. But it is not so in the case of bhatiyali. In '*Sun mere bandhu re*', it is the use of the seventh note that lends elegance to the tune, making it soar and reflect the restlessness of the human mind. Through the lyrics and the music of the song, the listener becomes one with the aspirations and sufferings of the hero and heroine of the film. For the tune, Sachin was inspired by a little-known song of separation from East Bengal—'*Tomar laagiya re/ Pran amar kande re/ Pranbandhu kaliya re*'. But for Sachin's efforts to popularize it through his music and his voice, the elegance and effervescence of Bengal's folk songs would have remained unknown outside the state. Sitting on the shore of the distant Arabian Sea, Sachin's heart still beat to the rhythm of his native land, his land of birth, his golden Bengal.

Nabendu Ghosh, the scriptwriter of *Sujata*, remembers:

> Sachin-karta poured his heart into the songs of *Sujata*. Also, Bimal-da's splendid direction and diversity of shots, wonderful acting by the entire cast from Sunil Dutt, Tarun Bose to Sulochana and Shashikala and, above all, the memorable performance by Nutan as the eponymous title character made the film a super-hit immediately on release in 1959. Sachin-karta's contribution to the film's success was no mean one. The songs were all extremely popular at the time and continue to be remembered—'*Tum*

jiyo hazaaron saal', '*Kali ghata chhaye mora jiya tarsaye*', and the boatman's song at Gandhighat, '*Sun mere bandhu re*' which personified the restrained but deep love between Sujata (Nutan) and Adhir (Sunil Dutt). Finally, there is Talat Mahmood's immortal '*Jalte hain jiske liye*', perhaps the most popular example of a telephonic love song in the history of film-making. When I talk of songs, I include background music also. Sachin-karta used to compose his music strictly keeping in mind the nature of the characters, their mutual affection and attraction, their joys and sorrows, their separation and reunion.' (*Prantik* Jan-Feb 2006)

Many people may not be aware that the idea of the telephonic song sequence came not from Bimal Roy but from Sachin himself. It was picturized on his suggestion and he was drawing on his personal experience for the idea. Singing over the telephone was nothing new for Sachin. In 1937, he had made a trunk call from Darjeeling to Calcutta to his friend Sukumar Dasgupta, the director of *Rajgi*, and proceeded to sing a new song he had composed. Eyewitness Haraprasad Mukhopadhyay records:

> I think it was his friend from Calcutta who requested that Rajkumar Sachin Dev Burman sing over the telephone. The song was '*Saje nawal kishore*'. I had heard Kamala Jharia, Angurbala and Indubala's songs. I had been charmed by Pankaj Mullick's voice. But this was something else. I hadn't heard such a song, such a special voice, before. I kept hoping the trunk call would never end; the song would go on and on. (*Prantik* Jan-Feb 2006)

Sachin himself has spoken about the telephone song in *Sujata*:

> I made the suggestion to Bimal-da even though it seemed

odd. After the Gandhighat scene, Sujata returns home. After some time Adhir rings Sujata and sings a love song on the phone. This song created quite a stir. It was not a song for a song's sake. The audience loved it and many people congratulated me. Talat sang the song *'Jalte hain jiske liye'* with all his heart. ('Tumi jey Giyachho bakul bichhano pathy', *Anandlok*)

Like so many of Sachin's compositions, this too has retained its popularity even fifty years after it was composed. It is a time-tested song that reminds one of long-lost youth, makes one close one's eyes and ruminate on the passion that engenders such creativity. This is undoubtedly one of the finest romantic songs ever in Hindi cinema.

If Talat was pure gold in *'Jalte hain jiske liye'*, Asha rendered what was one of her best so far—*'Kali ghata chhaye mora'*. The song is structured as a mix between a kirtan and a folk tune. Then there was Geeta Dutt's *'Nanhi kali sone chali'*, an unparalleled lullaby. Asha—Geeta's sweet duet *'Bachpan ke din bhi kya din thay'* is no less endearing. Asha's *'Tum jiyo hazaaron saal'*, which is to this day the staple birthday song at many gatherings, has an unsavoury controversy associated with it. Though it was Asha who sang the song, many believed for a long time that it was rendered by Geeta Dutt. So much so, that after Geeta Dutt's death the record issued by HMV in homage listed Geeta as the singer of this song. While Asha kept a dignified silence over the matter, it was Rahul Dev Burman, Sachin's assistant in *Sujata*, who finally revealed that though Geeta had originally recorded the song, her version was scrapped and it was recorded by Asha all over again. After twenty-seven years, Asha also admitted that indeed it was she who was the singer. HMV later made amends for the unfortunate error by listing Asha as its singer in future compilations.

It was a time for awards and recognition. If in 1958, SD was honoured with the Sangeet Natak Academy Award, 1959 saw him receive the Asian Film Society Award for his music in *Pyaasa*. His untiring labour over the decade was at last bearing fruit.

During the puja this year, one record was released with *'Sun mere bandhu re'* (*Sujata*) sung by S. D. Burman and *'Nanhi kali sone chali'* (*Sujata*) sung by Geeta Dutt.

In 1960, Sachin scored the music for seven films. Mohan Sehgal's *Apna Haath Jagannath*, Raj Khosla's *Bombai ka Babu*, I. S. Johar's *Bewaqoof*, and Vijay Anand's *Kala Bazaar*, Shanti Burman's *Manzil*, Jyoti Swarup's *Miya Bibi Raji* and Raj Rishi's *Ek Ke Baad Ek*. One reason for this prodigious output in one year was that some of these films had got stuck midway in the past resulting in a delayed release. Again, demonstrating the magic of the Dev Anand—Sachin combination was the fact that four of these seven films starred Dev Anand.

Sachin introduced the Bengal dhol in Hindi films in one of the songs this year and the audience appreciated it. Manna Dey sang the lilting *'Takdum takdum baje'* in *Bombai ka Babu*. Interestingly, after the independence of Bangladesh in 1971, the same number, written by Meera Dev Burman and sung by Sachin, with minor changes in tune, took an altogether different form, *'Takdum takdum bajai Bangladesher dhol'*.

The other songs of *Bombai Ka Babu* also deserve mention. Whereas the ticklish tunes of *'Deewana mastana hua dil'* (Md. Rafi, Asha) and *'Aise mein kachhu kaha nahi jaaye'* (Asha, chorus) appealed to the lighter side of the audience, the pathos of *'Saathi na koyi manzil'* sung by Mohammad Rafi made their eyes moist.

One of the biggest musical hits of the year was, of course, *Kala*

Bazaar. Rafi's popularity skyrocketed with his intoxicating rendering of '*Khoya khoya chand*'. He also left a deep impression with '*Apni toh har aah ik toofan hai*'. Asha Bhonsle's '*Sach huye sapne tere*' and the Rafi—Geeta duet '*Rimjhim ke tarane leke*' became very popular. Waheeda Rehman's wonderful dance on the beach to the infectious beat and the sweet voice of Asha Bhonsle in '*Sach huye sapne tere*' remain embedded in the memory of audiences even after half a century. The tune, the beat and the tempo merged intricately with each word in the song to create a mesmerizing effect. Rafi's '*Teri dhoom har kahin, tujh sa yaar koi nahin*' emphasizes the beauty of a mukhda one feels like diving into again and again. The melody of '*Na main dhan chahoon na rattan chahoon*' sung by Geeta Dutt and Sudha Malhotra is simply captivating. '*Sanjh dhali dil ki lagi*' is a lovely duet by Manna Dey and Asha Bhonsle.

Among the other songs this year, mention may be made of Asha Bhonsle's popular numbers '*Ghanshyam Ghanshyam Shyam Shyam re*' (two parts) and '*Tujhe mili roshni mujhko andhera*' in *Apna Haath Jagannath*. The first is a bhajan and the second is a song full of pathos. Asha's articulation in both the songs is unparalleled. *Bewaqoof*, although a light movie, had memorable songs like *Tumi piya chikara hu*' (Kishore, Asha), '*Dhadka dil dhak se*' (Manna Dey and Asha) and '*Mubarak ho mubarak ho*' (Asha, chorus). The first song has a mesmerizing melody and an effective rhythmic pulse. The second is a club song and the third a qawwali. The romantic vibe of the song '*Batao kya karoongi main jo gham ki raat aayegi*' Mohammad Rafi, Geeta Dutt) and Rafi's '*Thumak thumak thumak hai chali tu kidhar*' (*Ek Ke Baad Ek*) are beautiful songs that lead you to a land of romance where the lover assures the beloved promising to come as 'sleep' to her eyes. Hemant Kumar's lively baritone in '*Yaad aa gayee woh nasheeli nigaahein*' and Manna Dey's articulation in the qawwali '*Banao batiyan hato kahe ko jhoothi*' (*Manzil*) are simply mind-blowing. *'Chupke se mile pyaase-pyaase' (Manzil)* sung by Rafi and Geeta Dutt has a romantic tune that combines humming, music and vocals with sections half-recited, half-sung by Geeta. It is lovely to notice the two voices come together, then drift away, one humming while the other sings the words, and then blending back in again. Suman Kalyanpur's steeped-in-sorrow *'Chhodo chhodo mori baiyaan sanvare'* from *Miya Bibi Razi* is a heartrending rendition.

Never before had so many films under Sachin Dev's music direction released in one year. This took its toll on his health. He suffered his first heart attack in 1960.

Sachin had only one record of Bengali songs in the year. For lovers of Hindi films songs, it is worth mentioning that Sachin used this tune later in *'Wahan kaun hai tera'* in *Guide*. *'Dur kon parabase'* is a perfect example of how to use a folk tune in a modern song. Rural Bengal comes alive in our mind's eye even as one soaks in its words and tune. The pain of separation pierces the heart with the plaintive wail of the music. In the early stages, Sachin introduced folk tunes in classical music to give the latter a wider appeal. Now, he gave a new spin to the modern song by assimilating folk music into it. One can even discern an imaginative strain of tappa in the song.

The other song in the record was the incomparable *'Banshi shune aar kaaj nai'*, which Hindi film song aficionados will recall as the Lata song *'Neend churaye'* in the 1972 film *Anurag*. In the Bengali version, Sachin brings out the unshackled intensity of love with his voice even as the flute pierces the silence of the night and beckons an anxious Radha to a rendezvous with her beloved.

Because of the heart attack in 1960, he had no Hindi film releases in 1961. But his love for Calcutta knew no let-up despite his illness. He gave an exquisite performance in the city in April 1961, rendering two of his most popular Bengali numbers '*Saite pari "na" bala*' and '*Bane phagun mane agun*'. Here, I'd simply like to mention Sachin's mastery in rendering a song in free verse, which '*Saite pari "na" bala*' essentially is. It is very difficult to return from the antara to the mukhda without a rhyming end. Sachin performs this impossible task with facile ease by introducing his trademark indeclinables, 'O ho' and 'Ah', to return to the mukhda. The second song '*Ki kari ami, ki kari/ bane phugun mane agun*' begins with a classical-based tune, before acquiring a light touch of a thumri. The song also incorporates folk elements in the antara in a large measure.

The year 1961 was almost a blank year as far as S. D. Burman's work was concerned. Let me fill up the blank by talking about what I have forgotten so far—the arrival of great musician R. D. Burman, son of equally great S. D. Burman and its impact on the father-son relationship. It was 1955. R. D. Burman joined his father as an apprentice and later on as an assistant or associate music director. Pancham aka R. D. Burman worked as an assistant to his father from 1955 till his father's death. On paper, the movies were—*Pyaasa* (1957), *Chalti Ka Naam Gaadi* (1958), *Kaagaz Ke Phool* (1959), *Bewaqoof* (1960), *Naughty Boy* (1962), *Tere Ghar Ke Samney* (1963), *Bandini* (1963), *Ziddi* (1964), *Teen Deviyan* (1965), *Guide* (1965), *Jewel Thief* (1967), *Talash* (1969), *Aradhana* (1969) and *Prem Pujari* (1970). After Rahul's joining his father, there was a radical change in S. D. Burman's music. A new sound emanated that was full of vigour and youthfulness. There was the ghost hand of R. D. Burman in the making of several songs of S. D. Burman. Rahul talked about the period when he learnt the subtle nuances of music from his father thus:

> From then on my father started grooming me. He taught me how to mould a song to the satisfaction of a producer

or a director. For instance, if someone narrates a 'situation', you are to immediately compose a tune to suit it, and today, after having done it for 25 years, it's become a habit. If the situation is bad, you have to come up with the best you can. Of course, you can try suggesting a change in the situation but you don't always succeed.

Another thing my father inculcated in me was never to be overexcited about what I composed. He had a habit of composing the mukhda and passing on the antara to his two assistants (Jaidev Verma, Surit Kaur) and me. A sort of healthy competition prevailed while we tried to outdo each other.

My father would choose the best and sometimes I scored too. If I felt happy about it, he'd snub me and call the servant and ask his opinion. The moral of this was: simple is beautiful. While composing, he used to say, we can get carried away and add a bit of everything which finally makes it less appealing.

He also advocated introducing new sounds. The producer or director may not immediately take to it but a novel idea can click in a big way. When a situation was narrated to him, my father would visualize it and even dance it out. In the song 'Chhod do aanchal' (Paying Guest) by just adding that 'Aah' at the beginning he changed the whole complexion of the song. He explained that's how a girl will react when the hero teased her.

An important tip I leant from my father was picking up cues. When you heard a bird chirp and started humming, you thought of a particular aspect of life. You had the situation and the tune that went with it. When I told him that I sometimes dreamt tunes, he asked me to immediately get up and hum it into a tape recorder or jot down the notations. The next morning, he said, you can improvise on it. The tunes of *'Kanchi re kanchi re' (Hare Rama Hare Krishna)*, *'Tum bin jaoon kahan' (Pyaar Ka Mausam)* and *'Duniya mein logon ko' (Apna Desh)* have all come to me in my dreams. (*Filmfare,* June 16-30, 1984)

The teachings of S. D. Burman had immensely benefited Rahul. RD's entry into Bollywood saw a revolution in the way music was composed here. RD is credited with injecting a fresh style and technique into Hindi songs. Rahul completely revolutionized Bollywood's music and later on brought Bollywood onto the world map.

Now let me come back to 1961. During his illness, all the producers and directors left SD. Let me quote Rahul in this context:

> That the film industry is full of fairweather friends I came to know in 1961 when my father had a heart attack. At that time he'd already composed about five songs for Guru Dutt's *Baharen Phir Bhi Aayengi*. My parents told Guru Dutt that I was capable of getting the songs recorded but he declined and said sorry but he couldn't wait. After that one by one all the producers left my father. The only one to stick with him was Dev Anand. He told my father not to worry, that he'd delay the film. That's something nobody will ever do for a music director today.
>
> Five months later, when my father had recovered, we finished all the *Guide* songs in five days and will you believe it, at the first session, Dev Anand okayed four tunes! Shailendra even penned three songs right there—*'Aaj phir jeene ki tamanna hai'*, *'Din dhal jaye'* and *'Tere mere spane'*. (*Filmfare*)

It is a shame for the film industry to treat its eminent music director like this. After 1961, S. D. Burman had become a prudent man.

In 1962, three films with Sachin's music were released. The songs 'Na tum humein jaano' and 'Sheeshe ka ho ya patthar ka dil' from *Baat Ek Raat Ki* directed by Shankar Mukherjee were greatly admired. The first song remains one of Hemant Kumar's most popular songs. In this song, we get a different SD mood and approach. The song has a four or eight beat rhythm. The tempo is slowed down a wee bit. The composer uses the musical idioms and phrases that were developed during the growth of the modern Indian song. These compositions have nothing to do with any folk music tradition, nor do they have anything in common with the classical music of the subcontinent. S. D. Burman focussed on the urban romantic expression that modern Indian songs developed after the impact of European classical, light classical and popular music genres. He seems to apply the tonal principles of serenades that are gentle, soft and deep and reproduced them on Indian musical terms.

Rafi's 'Akela hoon main' in the same film also created waves. In *Dr Vidya*, Lata rendered the super-hit 'Pawan diwani' which was set to the same tune as Sachin's Bengali hit 'Alochhaya dola'. Shakti Samanta's *Naughty Boy* had Sachin and Kishore Kumar repeat the fun act one had seen earlier in *Apna Haath Jagannath*, with songs like 'Hai hai yeh matwali ada' and 'Sa-sa-sa-sa-re, ga-ga-re' (with Asha), among others, all of which attained a fair measure of success. Sachin did not record any Bengali song in 1962.

This was the year Sachin was selected as a member of the jury for an international music competition held in Helsinki, Finland. In that connection, essayist Robin Sengupta, who chanced upon the maestro in faraway Helsinki, has narrated an interesting anecdote which shows what Tripura meant to Sachin even after all these years spent away from 'home'. Sengupta says:

> I happened to accompany a team of youth representatives from India to the International Youth Festival held in Helsinki in July 1962. One morning, Salil Choudhuri and V. Balsara told us about a proposed visit by S. D. Burman to the Indian representatives. Along with Sudha Malhotra from Bombay, Amar Shaikh, Salil Choudhuri, Purna Das Baul and many others, I was eager to meet the master. At last he arrived. There followed sundry introductions and exchange of courtesies. When he approached me, I bowed before him, bending my knees and offering my pranam, touching his knees with my hand as is typical of the culture and etiquette of the inner courts of the Tripura raj family. He was almost dumbstruck and looked at me for a few moments before asking in Bengali, with a distinct East Bengal intonation, 'Where are you from?' I said, 'Agartala'. Surprised, he asked further, 'Whose child are you?' I said, 'Prafulla Sen.' His eyes widened even further as he asked, 'Prafulla Sen? Magician Prafulla Sen?' I replied, 'Yes, karta.' The next moment he embraced me in front of the whole gathering and told his wife, Meera Debi, standing nearby, 'Look! Someone from home!' Then he started enquiring about Agartala. He asked about Rabi Nag, about Pulin Thakur, Lalu-karta, whether those tall trees in front of his old house in Agartala were still there, and so on. Others present took me as a VIP. I realized that a large-hearted man like him who had spent his infancy and childhood so close to the earth, drawing upon the smell of earth and the aroma of wild flowers for sustenance, can never be indifferent to the common man. (*Prantik*, Jan-Feb 2006)

Sachin returned to top form in 1963 with three hit films which are still considered among the ones having the finest music ever in the history of Hindi films, *Bandini* directed by Bimal Roy, R. K. Ralhan's *Meri Surat Teri Aankhein* and Vijay Anand's *Tere Ghar Ke Saamne*. But apart from the overwhelming success, what was indeed music to the ears of lovers of Hindi films songs was the news of the patch-up between Sachin Dev Burman and Lata Mangeshkar.

The tiff between S. D. Burman and Lata Mangeshkar continued for five years up to 1962. Rahul was instrumental in patching up and bringing them together again. Rahul told his father, 'I am going to ring up Lata didi to sing my first song as a music director'. R. D. Burman wanted no one but her to sing his first composition for the movie *Chhote Nawab*. Lata's singing of *'Ghar aaja'* had initiated the process of their reunion.

Letting bygones be bygones, Lata returned to her favourite music director Sachin-da in *Bandini*. And what a return it was! Sachin reserved the finest for her in *'Jogi jabse tu aaya'* and *'Mora gora ang lai le'* and Lata obliged with her tender rendering of the two classics which did justice to Sachin's efforts. The second song has become a classic, thanks to Gulzar's lyrics, the divine elegance of Nutan, Lata's voice and the mesmerizing beat of the tabla. The glow of fireflies at night, the chirping of crickets, a tempest, the swinging symbolic beat, all these come alive in Lata's perfect rendition of Sachin's classic tune! Both songs are based on Bengal's kirtan and represent Sachin's efforts to bring the sounds of his native place to the world at large. But, even while giving Lata the finest, Sachin did not forget to provide two uncut gems to the singer who had given him some of his biggest successes in the last few years when Lata did not sing for him. How can one forget Asha's passionate voice in 'O panchhi pyare' and 'Abke baras bhej bhaiya'? It is incredible how Sachin composed a tune that expresses the pathos of the situation of a female prisoner in the voice of a fellow inmate of the film's protagonist Kalyani (Nutan). It is interesting to note that Asha was made to sing songs which were laden with sorrow while Lata sang what were essentially playful modern songs structured on the kirtan. Normally, most music directors do the opposite, giving the serious songs to Lata while Asha got the frothy numbers. But Sachin always believed in going against the grain. 'O jaane wale ho sake toh' was a splendid rendition in the plain and simple voice of Mukesh. And the icing on the cake was 'O re manjhi, mere sajan hain us paar', rendered by Sachin-karta himself. The song was used in the background which only adds to its poignancy and heightens the dramatic potential, particularly where Sachin renders the high-pitched words *'mera kheenchti hai aanchal'* and stops for a fraction of a second as the heroine goes for a rendezvous with her beloved. This song is very appealing, with Sachin's wonderfully nasal and somewhat raw voice blending superbly with the sweet notes of a flute and the seemingly incongruous sounds of a train's piercing whistle and the sonorous boom of a boat's foghorn. Gulzar's lyrics are very poignant, and the combined effect—music, voice, words, the chance meeting between two separated lovers now destined for different paths—never fails to give one a lump in the throat.

The beat is the life of a song. Most musicians use this beat as a measure to meet the demands of the orchestra or to scale down from a higher to a lower beat. Often this controls the singer, as in O. P. Nayyar's music in which the singer's free movement is halted by the unalterable trap of the tune (music). Between these two extremes, the third option is to allow the singer the freedom to stretch his voice in favour of the beat of the music; also to harmonize the beat with the tune, identifying with the singer, as often happens in duets. None other than Sachin Dev Burman could apply this third option successfully. *Bandini* is its perfect example. The music immerses you in its uninterrupted flow and yet it remains elusive, beyond reach. The lilt of the elusive tune overwhelms you and your heart dances to the tune, the song captivates you and then plays truant, as if immersing in the sea of delight.

Gulzar, who debuted as a lyricist in *Bandini* with '*Mora gora ang lai le*', remembers:

> Sachin-da was upset with Shailendra at the time. It worked to my advantage. Bimal-da [Roy] advised me to go to Sachin-da to work on the songs for *Bandini*. That was how I also got to meet my lifelong friend Pancham. After meeting Sachin-da I wrote the songs all right. But who would sing them? Sachin-da was not on speaking terms with Lata. But things changed in the interest of the film. Lata sang the songs. What was amusing about Sachin-da getting annoyed with someone was that the reason was never substantial. He would get upset on some insignificant issue. He was unusually childlike in this, as well as in many other respects. Perhaps highly talented people have this kind of childishness. Nachiketa Ghosh once narrated an incident. It was during the Second World War. The two of them were returning to Howrah by train. Some time before they reached Howrah, a few British soldiers boarded the train. At the sight of the soldiers Sachin-da pulled his chadar over himself and stayed absolutely still. Shortly before the train was to reach its destination,

Nachiketa Ghosh asked Sachin-da to pack his belongings. Sachin-da whispered from under the sheet, 'Have they gone?' Nachiketa replied in the negative. In a trembling voice Sachin-da said, 'Please tell them I am not Japanese.' That is why I used to address Pancham as gorkha.

Sachin-da had a royal temperament. Every evening after his bath, he would dress in dhuti-panjabi and sit with his harmonium. He would have a glass of drink. All evening he would remain intoxicated with his music. Drinks would be limited to that single glass. All my life I have regretted not being a singer, and Sachin-da was the first one who made me feel sorry about my lack of talent in this respect. After the lyrics for *Bandini* were composed, he wanted to know, 'Do you know how to sing?' I said, 'No.' He said, 'Then you need not go to Bimal-babu to talk about the songs. I will do the explaining.' Of course, ultimately I joined Sachin-da during his meeting with Bimal-da. I could not resist the temptation of listening to my songs being composed by him. (*Satabarsher Alokey Sachin Karta*)

Sachin's second film of the year, *Meri Surat Teri Aankhen*, had six songs in all. Two of these were a class apart when it came to classical-based songs in Hindi cinema. Sachin himself has spoken thus about them:

> Whenever I compose a song based on classical music, I prefer Manna's voice. I have always depended on his talent when it comes to carrying off a classical tune as dictated by the situation [...] *Meri Surat Teri Aankhen* was produced in 1961 [released in 1963] and was based on the Bengali film *Rikta* [Sachin was mistaken here. The film was *Ulka*]. Ashok Kumar himself requested me to take charge

of the music. The story was about an ustad of classical music who taught his son a song when the latter was but a child. This boy grows up (Ashok Kumar) and later in life sings the song he had learnt as a child. I composed a song written by Shailendra. It was based on raag Ahiri Bhairav—'*Poochho na kaise maine rain bitayi.*' In the film, it was sung by Manna Dey. And what a song it turned out to be in Manna's voice! It was a serious song, in a slow measure, and very difficult to render. Manna sang it with such finesse that it remains popular even today. I have a strong feeling that connoisseurs and laypersons alike will adore this song for ages to come. (*Sargamer Nikhad*)

'*Poochho na kaise maine rain bitayi*' reminds one of Kazi Nazrul Islam's '*Arunakanti ke go jogi bhikhari*'. I don't find it surprising that Sachin Dev Burman coolly used the entire melody of this to create the unforgettable Hindi film song '*Poochho na kaise*'. He hardly changed any notes of the composition. The changes that did take place were owing to the differences in the sound of the two languages.

Sachin knew it was very difficult to popularize a classical-based song. And because he was aware of this, he never fought shy of experimenting with music. He had already experimented with classical music in the mukhda and by using the kirtan style in the antara of the same song. Let us see what he has to say about his experimentation in *Meri Surat Teri Aankhen*:

I conducted another such experiment in the film *Meri Surat Teri Aankhen*. Shailendra had written a song whose first line was '*Nache mann mora magan tigdha dhigi dhigi*'. You might wonder about the origin of these words. Kathak maestro Shri Bindadin Maharaj, while training his nephews, used to utter the words '*tigdha dhigi dhigi*', to give them a sense of rhythm with the words. These words touched a chord in my mind. I created a tune based on them and got Shailendra to write the song. I told him that the first line had to bring alive the idea of a peacock dancing, the mind as a dancing peacock. He wrote the words 'Nache mann mora magan' and I added 'tigdha dhigi dhigi' to it. It was necessary to have a good tabla beat to bring about the tempo signified by the words 'tigdha dhigi dhigi'. Pandit Shanta Prasad from Varanasi accompanied on the tabla for the song. This song was specially commended by connoisseurs because of its kathak-style tabla accompaniment. (*Sargamer Nikhad*)

'Nache mann mora' was sung by Mohammad Rafi. In the memorial service on TV after Sachin-karta's death, Maruti Kir played '*Nache mann mora*' with all his heart and immediately thereafter broke down, overwhelmed. Mohammad Rafi sang the single line '*jhule jhule sakhiyon*' with such feeling that the audience was overcome with emotion at the simple greatness of Sachin's music. Though the other songs of this film are more difficult and classical-based, '*Nache mann mora*' has something about it that touches the heart.

All the songs of Sachin's third film in 1963, *Tere Ghar Ke Saamne*, were huge hits and each song continues to be as popular even today. The fact that Sachin was equally at ease with Western music is brought out by the very first song '*Dil ki manzil kuchh aisi hai manzil*'. Strongly reminiscent of '*cha-cha-cha*' in its rhythm pattern, the song is a splendid amalgamation of Western beats and quintessential folk tunes. The instruments that Sachin used in the song's background music are noteworthy—flute, Nepali drum, violin, guitar and clarinet—a delectable combination of the East and the West. Asha rendered the song splendidly in a voice that oozes oomph. Then, there is '*Dil ka bhanwar kare pukaar*'. There is probably no one of the whole generation at the time who has not lent his voice to the song, hummed it at some time or the other. It is difficult to decide what enchants us more, the lilting tune or the enchanting voice of Mohammad Rafi. And the moment Lata's voice breaks free in *'Ye tanhai hai re hai'*, the feet seem to develop a mind of their own, tapping away despite one's best efforts to control oneself. Such is the intoxicating charm of the tune. The delectable mix of kirtan and a modern tune and the feeling of utter surrender one feels as Lata utters the refrain *'thaam lo baanhein'* has never been heard before.

One record of Hindi film songs was released in 1963. Two songs of the film *Bandini*—*'O re manjhi more sajan'* and *'O jaanewale ho sake'* sung by S. D. Burman and Mukesh respectively were released.

The next year, 1964, was memorable for the film *Kaise Kahun*, for which Sachin Dev Burman was decorated with the Sant Haridas Award by Sur Singar Samsad. He scored the music for two other films in the year—*Benazir*, directed by S. Khalil and *Ziddi*, directed by Pramod Chakravarti. While fairly successful, the music of these films did not create the waves that his films had in the previous years. Ziddi's *'Teri surat se nahin milti'* (Rafi), *'Raat ka sama jhoome chandrama'* (Lata), and *'Pyar ki aag mein tan badan jal gaya'* (Manna Dey) became quite popular. Though Atma Ram's *Kaise Kahun* boasts of some superlative songs like Lata Mangeshkar's *'Kaise kahun, kaise kahun'*, *'Haule haule jiya dole'*, *'Tum humein pyar karo'*, and Mohammad Rafi's *'Zindagi tu jhoom le zara'* which are unforgettable, the film did not do well and so the songs haven't found a place in the memory of music lovers. If a film is not strong enough, only the songs cannot sustain it. Though important to a film, songs are essentially a secondary attachment. It says something about

Sachin's exalted position as music director that he received the prestigious Sant Haridas Award for the film despite its moderate box-office success.

As a composer, Sachin anchored the most evanescent human feeling and the wildest passion in his world of sensitive music. The heart seeks to expand and envelop the whole world when music becomes one with the world of feelings. This is the mantra with which Sachin conquered the heart of humanity fatigued by daily routine.

Sachin did not record any Bengali song in 1964.

In 1965, he composed the music for two films: *Guide* directed by Vijay Anand and *Teen Deviyan* directed by Amarjit. A new horizon opened up for Hindi film music with the songs of these films. He was adjudged the best music director for 1965 by BFJA (Bengal Film Journalists' Association) for his work in these.

In *Guide*, Sachin sang two background songs '*Wahan kaun hai tera, musafir*' and '*Megh de, pani de, chhaya de re tu*'. The first one resembles his timeless Bengali hit '*Dur kon parabase, tumi chole jaiba re*'. Rooted in the folk tradition, this song effortlessly conveys the feeling of someone wandering in search of one's own self. Sachin renders the word 'musafir' in myriad styles, weaving a musical web each time he says it. The song remains an all-time hit. His style and technique in this song evoke a question that is essentially existential, therefore all-encompassing. The second one, a prayer for rain, is based on popular Bengali folk singer Abbasuddin's timeless classic.

Listening to Lata's rendition of '*Piya tose naina lage re*' and '*Aaj phir jiney ki tamanna hai*' one realizes that nobody else comes even close to Lata when one thinks of doing justice to Sachin's music. Sachin too had immense faith in her. As he says:

> Lata Mangeshkar is especially remarkable among playback singers. Perhaps no one else possesses a voice so suited to a microphone; no one ever had in the past, and perhaps no one will have in future. Lata's voice fits all genres of songs, irrespective of the tune and the mood. She can render all kinds of songs and tunes effortlessly. Even today, in these days of parochialism and provincialism, she remains equally popular in every region. Her songs in different languages have made a place in the hearts of people everywhere. In fact, behind the success of many of my songs is Lata's voice. (*Sargamer Nikhad*)

This is a significant appreciation of Lata's voice. Even when she sings today, the enchanted listener cannot but bow in respect. *Guide* happens to be the pinnacle of Sachin's partnership with Lata. She brings '*Piya tose naina lage re*' to life in an extraordinary manner when she suddenly stops after '*piya tose*', in accordance with the style of folk music, to the rhythm of dance and the mesmerizing 'bol' of the tabla. It is a very different song; it is lavish, a celebration of life and love that chronicles the rise to fame of the dancer Rosie/Nalini, and her simultaneously growing intimacy with Raju in the film. Waheeda Rehman's dancing is reason enough to admire the song. SD manages to introduce a slightly different touch in each stanza. The stanza about Holi, for instance, has a cute squirt sound in the beginning very like pichkaris (water guns). And the combination of the tabla and payals at various points is lovely. Shiv Kumar Sharma, the famous santoor player, was on the tabla. The song is eight minutes long. But still one wishes it had gone on for a few more minutes. '*Aaj phir jeene ki tamanna hai*' is of course a classic where melody cascades like flowers falling from a tree at the onset of spring. The extraordinary feeling of freedom, the lust for life, discernible in the first words of the song, '*kaanton se kheench ke yeh anchal*', has never been replicated in another Hindi film song. The other Lata song in the film, '*Mose chhal kiye jaaye, hai re hai, dekho saiyan beimaan*', has an interesting story to it. Almost a decade ago, Sachin fell out with Lata over the song '*Pag thumak chalata balkhaye hai saiyan kaise dharu dhir*' in *Sitaron Se Aage*. Now, in *Guide*, Sachin reworked the tune of '*Pag thumak chalata balkhaye*' for '*saiyyan beimaan*', written by Shailendra, Sachin's favourite, whom he considered the greatest of all lyricists. In his own words:

> Whatever Shailendra wrote for me was plain and simple. Even with my limited knowledge of Hindi, I could fully visualize his songs. I had this tune that was perfect for Lata's passionate voice. I sent Shailendra to the roof of my bungalow. Shailendra sat there for some time and came down with a song that would match the passion in Lata's voice. This was '*Mose chhal kiye jaaye*'. (*Sargamer Nikhad*)

The artistry in Rafi's voice need not be articulated. Yet, even by his exalted standards, he excelled himself with three songs which rank among the finest of his oeuvre. Even today, people hum the exquisite ghazal '*Din dhal jaaye*' while '*Tere mere sapne ab ek rang hai*', with its touch of the classical but a modern song by all accounts, remains one of the finest romantic songs in Hindi films. Then there is the climactic '*Kya se kya ho gaya*' which takes off from Lata's '*Saiyyan beimaan*'. As if such gems by Lata and Rafi were not enough, Sachin surpassed himself with the sole Kishore number in the film, a duet with Lata. Connoisseurs of music will never forget '*Gata rahe mera dil*' where the dew-fresh voices of the two singers produce a beautiful song. It is to Kishore's credit that in a film that has such an embarrassment of riches from Lata and Rafi, it is his song which is probably the most well-known. The youthfulness of Kishore's voice brings a rare effervescence to the song.

Now let me narrate two incidents that followed *Guide*. On the eve of the release of *Guide*, a popular Bombay weekly published a review of the film without a word about Burman's music. SD was upset. 'I don't mind a critic tearing my work to pieces if he does not like it. But I want to know, is the music in *Guide* so bad as to be completely ignored?' he asked.

Most reviewers acclaimed Burman's work in *Guide* the following weekend as one of the most outstanding musical scores of his career. What more, it appealed to both the masses and the classes.

Guide had led to another interesting episode. A local film publicist-cum-agent approached SD with a proposal that both shocked and enraged him. 'Give me a certain amount of money,' the man said, 'and you'll get the award'. He had come hoping that the old man would fall for the offer readily. He was in for a surprise.

> 'Now look, young man,' S. D. Burman told him, 'I will be honest and tell you that I'm interested in getting this award, though I never knew it could be manipulated or bought. I can afford the money that you are asking for. And I also know that compared to the gains the award might yield, the money you ask for is nothing. But I would rather give it away to those who had acclaimed my music than buy the award.' ('Maestro who was a misfit')

In reply to a question, 'Even amidst his [S. D. Burman] best scores, *Guide* remains a milestone,' Dev Anand said:

> Yes, S. D. Burman would get deeply into the core of every subject. I remember how we had recorded a song sung by Rafi. After this, both Goldie and I were completely dissatisfied. We called up Dada and told him about it. 'I find

the song very good,' he countered. We said that perhaps it could be better. Dada insisted that it was absolutely okay and hung up. Half an hour later, Dada called up and said that maybe we had a point. He said that he was coming over the next morning and that I was to arrange for a harmonium. And he played the melody of *'Din dhal jaaye'*. We instantly told him that was it. He smiled, flattered by the praise and said, 'That's why I'm here.' This showed that he had been restless because of the thought that we were unhappy. Incidentally, we immediately summoned Shailendra, who wrote the mukhda in five minutes flat.

I also remember how he implored us to trust him when we had to leave for Jaipur for the shoot of the film, and a song was not ready. 'Please depend on me. I'll send a tune that the world will remember,' he said. A few days later, with Goldie and I far away from Bombay, he sent us *'Aaj phir jeene ki tamanna hai'*. He did this again in *Jewel Thief* and the song was *'Honthon pe aisi baat'*. (Dev Anand on S. D. Burman, *Screen,* Nov 2002)

As a film, *Teen Deviyan* is strictly average fare. But it is a glaring example of a most ordinary film becoming a box office hit only by virtue of its music. If in *Guide,* Sachin largely took the classical and folk route, here he goes modern, though again the best songs here are the two Rafi ghazals, *'Kahin bekhayal hokar'* and *'Aise to na dekho ki humko nasha ho jaye'*. The passion in Rafi's voice articulates longing in a manner that intoxicates the listener. These numbers again demonstrate that though it is generally believed that Rafi's finest songs came with other composers, Naushad and Madan Mohan in particular, it is Sachin who gave him some of his most beautiful numbers. *'Aise to na dekho'* is based on raga Khamaj and is structured as a medium-paced, modern song influenced by the two Hindustani music genres, thumri and ghazal. Kishore does not lag far behind. In fact, if in *Guide* he stole the thunder with '*Gaata rahe mera dil*' despite the other classics in the film, here he overshadows every other song with '*Khwab ho tum ya koi haqeeqat*', in which his god-gifted voice conveys the feeling of a landscape drenched in moonlit joy. This is a wonderful song especially in the way it starts. Kishore's voice is beautiful by itself, without any musical instruments to support it. After that, in sharp contrast to the beginning, the song is a rollicking, fast-paced one but is still romantic. The piano notes between the stanzas are lovely. With Lata, he sang the duets '*Likha hai teri aankhon mein*' and '*Uff, kitni thandi hai ye raat*'. And then there is the seductive Asha-Kishore duet '*Arre yaar meri*'.

Sachin recorded two private albums in 1965. One of these had the songs '*Je na jane biraher mane, balo se ki jane*' and '*Keno je hai bolo na katha ami ki jani*'. The first begins as a classical number in the Kalawati tradition in which Sachin incorporates various classical styles before bringing in a touch of thumri with the words '*balo se ki jane*'. The play of ragas in the mukhda gives way to the kirtan in the antara. While one can discern the use of stringed instruments as long as the style is classical, the moment he incorporates kirtan into it, it is the mesmerizing beat of the tabla which takes over. The other song, '*Keno je hai balo na katha ami ki jani*', begins with a swift flow. In the antara, folk tunes and kirtan are intermingled intricately. There is also a hint of bhatiyali in the words '*O bondhu re*', which generates a trembling sensation in the heart. The other record had his song from *Guide*, '*Wahan kaun hai tera*'.

Sachin was not keeping very well at the time. His body was no longer being able to keep up with the constant pressure of work.

S. D. Burman Composing Music

S. D. Burman with Lata Mangeshkar and Mohammad Rafi

S. D. Burman with Lata Mangeshkar and R. D. Burman

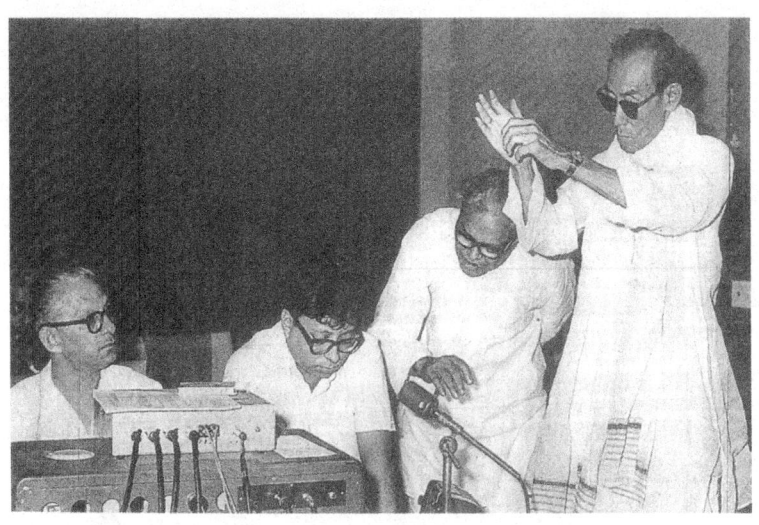

From L to R: Robin Chhatterjee, R. D. Burman, Majrooh Sultanpuri and S. D. Burman

From L to R: Mukesh, Majrooh Sultanpuri, Talat Mahmood, S. D. Burman, Lata Mangeshkar, Nargis, Madan Mohan and Mohammad Rafi

S. D. Burman with Madan Mohan, Majrooh Sultanpuri and Hridaynath Mangeshkar

From L to R: Geeta Dutt, R. D. Burman, S. D. Burman, Badal Bhattacharya and Guru Dutt

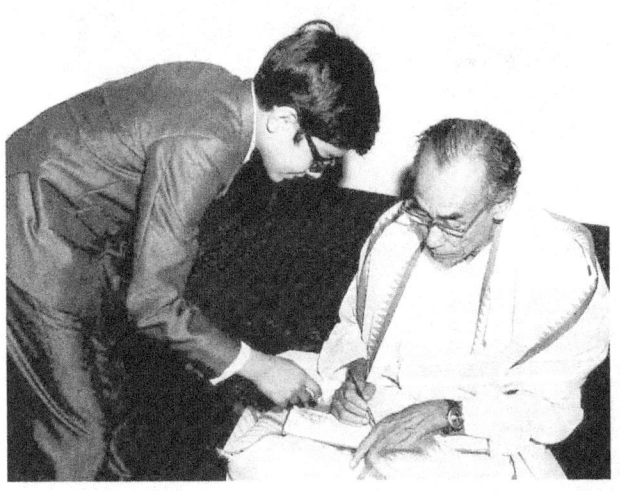

S. D. Burman Giving an Autograph

He had to forego many films because of his health after his heart attack. Not many producers were willing to give him time to recuperate. They could not be blamed. In films, more than in any other field, time is money. Dev Anand, however, was an exception. He waited for over six months for Sachin to get better to compose for *Guide*. He was insistent that if at all *Guide* was to be made, it would have music by Sachin; otherwise he would scrap the film altogether. No wonder Sachin repaid such faith and love with what is among the greatest musical scores in Hindi films.

As things stood, Sachin's illness prevented him from taking up any films. Neither did he record any Bengali songs in 1966. For the first time in the past decade-and-a-half, he had no contribution to make to the world of music. Not well enough to lift his baton, he picked up his pen. On 8 September 1966, film journal *Cine Advance* published his article 'The Role and Indispensability of Music in Indian Films'. Reading it, one can see how well he understood the importance of music in our films:

> The main factor in the film is its story. Everything else, including songs and background music, serves only as fine embroidery to improve and enhance the impact and beauty of the content. Hence, it is a logical argument that if the film has a powerful and gripping script that holds the audience interest from beginning to end, the other paraphernalia like songs, dances and even other allied embellishments are not a must.
>
> While songless films are a rarity in Hindi, they are common on the Bengali screen. For the reasons I have enumerated above and because being regional films with limited markets which stands in the way of their affording costly production values, they have powerful story content

instead, which balances the absence of songs in these films. There is also the case of Satyajit Ray who makes internationally acclaimed films, and most of his films don't have songs. As I said, he compensates for this with his camerawork and engrossing direction.

But songs are very necessary in musical films. Even here, care has to be taken in their use. If songs are not properly utilized and merged with the film as a whole, they hinder the continuity of the story. It's not that people don't like and enjoy songs as such; it's how they are presented in the film which matters to them while watching a film.

Many a time the best of songs are wasted either by placing them in odd situations or by picturizing them badly. People get disgusted with the results and adopt the surgical course of saving themselves from the evil being inflicted on them. They walk out of the auditorium and have a quick cup of tea or a smoke. The fault in this lies not with the music director. The matter is out of his hand the moment a song has been recorded. But even before that, it is the director who decides the necessity of a song in a particular sequence. And what type or kind of song it should be. It is also left to him to ensure that he gets the required results as far as the picturization is concerned.

I personally believe that instead of placing a song where it is not required, it should be removed entirely. An out-of-place song is the most horrible thing imaginable in a movie. Finally, the question of having songless films as a regular feature in India is a very risky proposition. In fact, it's the songs which are the main prop of an ordinary film with a weak story and inefficient direction. Even in the case of films having powerful themes, should direction lack deftness, the characters do not register properly, the sequences lack the easy flow of continuous motion; under such circumstances, suppose by a stroke of luck or calculation, if the songs prove popular, they become the sole saving grace of the movie. They may save the film from becoming a fantastic flop. This is the silver lining which will make songs a must in Indian films for years to come.'

In 1967, Sachin had only one film to his credit—Vijay Anand's *Jewel Thief*. Starring his favourite star Dev Anand, the film was a super hit, particularly for its songs. Kishore Kumar, Lata, and Asha Bhonsle kept the audience enchanted. Two songs by Kishore, a solo, '*Yeh dil na hota bechara*' and a duet with Lata Mangeshkar, '*Aasman ke neeche,*' are unforgettable. In the competition between Kishore and Rafi, the former was moving, inching ahead slowly but steadily, with Sachin now utilizing him not only for simple songs but also for those which required a measure of expertise. Asha Bhonsle learnt about the origins of '*Yeh dil na hota bechara*' from Rahul Dev Burman and spoke about it on Vividh Bharati. One night, Sachin and Rahul were returning from a show of David Lean's *Bridge on the River Kwai*. Sachin kept beating the film's memorable whistling tune 'Colonel Bogey March' on the car's dashboard and humming the same in a different style. The same tune found a resonance in '*Ye dil*'. The song's antara matched astonishingly well with the mukhda of Alberto's Spanish classic 'Perfida', though 'Perfida' moves to a much faster measure. This is a lively melody, fast-paced and colourful. However, the application of *komal ni* in the second line adds a sudden touch of sadness which is more romantic than sad. The quick run involving *dha, komal ni,* the upper octave *re,* and *sa* takes care of an unexpected lift that enlivens the melody. S. D. Burman always took care to give his listeners refreshing surprises in his melody lines, though he preferred to be brief in keeping with the economy required of modern songs.

There is much to be said about Asha's rendering of 'Raat akeli hai'. This was the first time Asha was singing a song like this, one that oozed oomph, for Sachin. Let us hear what Sachin had to say about the song:

> In Navketan's *Jewel Thief,* a certain sequence made it necessary to experiment with a new style of tune. There were two heroines, Tanuja being one of them, indomitable in character, unrestrained, vivacious. Director Vijay Anand asked for a special song for her. Usually, Hindi film songs start with what is called a mukhda and then we have the stanzas or antara to return to the mukhda. Not treading that path for this song, I created music for a prose-poem. I wanted the tune to match the character. The scene—the restless heroine sings a song for the hero; the first lines—'*Raat akeli hai, bujh gaye diye, aake mere paas, kano mein mere/ jo bhi chahe kahiye*'. I set it to music. The heroine would croon the first four lines. And then suddenly she would sing the last line '*jo bhi chahe kahiye*' in a theatrical and loud voice in the top scale. After the first line comes music, the antara is in the verse in prose. Asha Bhonsle sang the song. My attempt met with enormous success.
> (*Sargamer Nikhad*)

Let's hear what Asha has to say about this song:

> There's an interesting anecdote about '*Raat akeli hai bujh gaye diye*'. I began singing it in the normal manner. Dada said, 'Asha, do something. In our childhood while whispering in someone's ear we would suddenly shout a

loud *ku-u-u-u*. You also do likewise. Accordingly, I sang the first four lines in a low voice and from the fifth line onward raised the voice to a high pitch. It turned out to be a memorable song. ('Bhati Gang Baiya' — Shyamal Chakraborty

Sachin has commented:

> Lata's sister is a top-class artist. She has a youthful vigour in her voice. With these two sisters, whatever experimentation you do with a tune, once you explain it to them they pick up the nuances with effortless ease.

This song is a favourite with so many of us. We love Tanuja's sparkling eyes and her irrepressible vivacity. We love Asha's voice and the way it flows seductively through low notes and then powerfully through very high notes, seemingly without any effort. It has loveable music: soft, slow and enticing, then rising into a joyful crescendo before dropping into a whisper again. Which other composer could compose such a song, create a cabaret music effect with appropriate notes, languid and erotic, in the first verse (sthayi) and then take us further into a mysterious languidness by unexpectedly applying the *teevra madhyam* (the raised fourth), associate it with the *pancham* (the fifth), *shuddha gandhar* (the third) and the *shuddha re* (the second), creating a touch of raga Yaman! Sachin Dev Burman uses his compositional chemistry in this song to exploit the hidden erotic nature of raga Yaman and mix it with notes that have nothing to do with this raga and produce an effect that is both physical and cerebral.

One of the most widely talked-about songs of the film was '*Hothon pe aisi baat*' sung by Lata, Bhupinder and chorus which, through its thrilling accompaniment of the Nepalese drum, conveyed the sense of mystery and suspense that forms the crux of the film. The use of drums in this song is a benchmark in Hindi film songs. Then there was the typical folk-inspired Lata—Rafi duet '*Dil pukaare aa re aa re*' and Lata's classic number '*Rulake gaya sapna mera*', the musical accompaniment in the latter was muted and fragile to bring about the helplessness and agony of the protagonist.

This year Sachin sang two Bengali songs during the pujas: '*Asamaye bajao banshi*' and '*Jadi dako akarane*'. With lyrics by Rabi Guha Majumdar both the songs became very popular. The first one starts '*O, O, kala*' to the accompaniment of a fine tune from a flute. This is Sachin's personal style. Starting with '*O, O, kala*', he stretches the tune and in perfect technique brings about a beautiful harmony between the lyrics and the music. How well has he captured Radha's restlessness on hearing Krishna's flute in this folk tune! While articulating the words '*rakam dekhe hasahasi*', the jolt he introduced after '*rakam dekhe*' can be heard only in the Kabigaan style, a genre of Bengal's many folk forms. He sang the last line '*pran to mane na re kala*' breaking the words into single syllables '*ma*', '*ne*', '*na*', '*re*', '*ka*', '*la*', conveying a delectable picture of Radha's restlessness to the listener. The other song, '*Jadi dako akarane*', starts with the baul's ektara. The tune is somewhat reminiscent of the manastattva genre of songs (philosophical) of Bangladesh, but the baul tune is predominant. Yet it cannot be categorized as a baul song as the style is modern. It is astounding to see how many different genres Sachin mingled for the same song! The tune that pierces the heart is caught in one line, '*Kare dosh debo balo balo na, O bandhure*'. Haltingly alternating between a high and low pitch, his rendition is bound to overwhelm the listener.

With Sachin not keeping well and having to follow a strict regime of rest and diet, he had no Hindi films to his name in 1968. But Sachin the singer did not forget Bengal. This time he presented four songs to his Bengali-speaking fans. These songs make it evident that his voice was becoming increasingly youthful with age. The first song, '*Tumi esechhile porshu*', is a modern song in all respects, which transports the listener to a world of romance. Sachin eschews his normal practice of weaving in classical and folk elements to give us an unadulterated love song. Though such modern songs were quite common in Bengali music of the era, what sets this apart is Sachin's special style, which puts his Bengali songs on a separate footing as compared to those by his contemporaries. No other singer has so far dared to copy his style of breaking a word and playing with the tune.

The second song, Rabi Majumdar's '*(Ore O bondhugo) koi koi re ghungur*', starts in the Khatki style. Sachin loved incorporating the symbolic sounds of dance in his songs. And here he sings '*ta-ta-thai-thai*' in a way that is reminiscent of the bol of the Nataraj dance. He renders '*Koi, koi re ghungur*' in delayed and medium measure with long and short vowels as if he is lovingly looking for the ghungroo which is so dear to him. He splits '*Jadu korechhili re amare*' into '*Jadu korechhili/ re amare amare*', adding an extra '*amare*' in order to control the measure, thus adding to the pleasing grace of the song.

Sachin opted for a simple, uncomplicated tune in Meera Dev Burman's '*Bhangite taba nesha, jhim hoy dasha disha*'. He had learnt the value of simplicity from experience. A plain and simple tune often made a lasting impression in the minds of common people. The song starts with the jingle of a sitar and the tune of a flute. The emphasis on '*nesha*', '*disha*', etc., at the end of each line is absolutely Sachin's own. In the middle antara, the tune is entirely different, touched as if by a poetic grace. There is an artistic playfulness about the song which is irresistible. The fourth song he sang in the year was '*Chander aloy kalo kankol*'. Unfortunately, I haven't been able to procure this song and hence I am not able to comment on it.

The year 1969 turned out to be a memorable one in the life of Sachin Dev Burman. Three films with his music were released. While the Government of India awarded him with the Padma Shri, this year saw the unprecedented success of his music in Shakti Samanta's *Aradhana*. The film has already gone down in the history of Hindi films for the manner in which it turned star ratings topsy-turvy. Its unknown hero Rajesh Khanna became a superstar, and gained unprecedented popularity. The film also gave a new singing star to Hindi cinema. Trailing behind Mohammad Rafi for long, Kishore Kumar leaped ahead with his chartbusters in *Aradhana*, leaving all competition languishing. For the next two decades, till the end of his life, Kishore remained the undisputed leading singer in Hindi films. Going against the wishes of his producers, Sachin had consistently opted for Kishore for a number of his songs, helping the singer grow under his tutelage. With *Aradhana*, Kishore opened a new horizon in the world of Hindi film songs. The most heartening aspect of the success of *Aradhana* was the victory of earthy tunes. S. D. Burman, who had arrived in Bombay with his stock of plain and simple Indian music, surpassed the Big Band represented by the likes of Shankar-Jaikishan, O. P. Nayyar and Madan Mohan who charged three times the fee charged by Sachin Dev Burman. Their films, particularly Shankar-Jaikishan's and O. P. Nayyar's, used to reverberate with Western music and orchestra. Sachin had only his stock of melody and creative talent. At last, Bengal's folk tunes had overcome Western music. The melody of flute, sitar, sarod, dhol, kansa, and tabla defeated Western beats. He also demonstrated with super hits like '*Mere sapnon ki rani*' and '*Roop tera mastana*' that when it came to Western beats, he was in the same league as the best!

Aradhana was initially titled *Subah Pyar Ki*. Taking the cue from the words of Sachin Dev Burman's song in the film, writer Sachin Bhowmik changed the name to *Aradhana* much after work on the film had started in full swing. There is an interesting incident behind the appointment of S. D. Burman as music director for the film. Shakti Samanta reached his Bandra residence one morning accompanied by his companions. The songs of his previous film, *An Evening in Paris*, had become raging hits. Shankar-Jaikishan had scored the music for it. As such it made sense for Shakti Samanta to go with the same composers. At first, Sachin could not guess why the film-maker had come to him. It was Shakti Samanta who broached the subject, 'I am planning a low-budget film, can't afford Shankar-Jaikishan. If you could kindly…'

Sachin responded in his typical East Bengal intonation, 'I understand. You want me to do the music for a pittance, isn't it?'

Shakti Samanta knew Sachin's temperament. Wringing his hands he said, 'No, no, not exactly. Please don't misunderstand me, Karta. We have a very limited budget. So, finding no other way…'

'Finding no other way, you have come to me. That does not make me feel very good about myself, does it? Say that you want to have me as the music director. Why digress?'

'That's right, Karta. I have come with high hopes. If you kindly…'

Usually, Sachin never talked about money. Haggling about such matters was inimical to his royal character. But something happened that day. He said, 'All right, in the last film you paid me seventy-five thousand. This time you have to pay eighty thousand.'

Shakti Samanta submitted in all humility, 'Sir, we have a provision for a lakh.'

Sachin was ecstatic. He responded, 'One lakh? Just wait and see; my music will talk, break all records.' (*Start Sound Camera* Action)

Sachin himself sang a passionate background song in the nature of 'vivek' in a Jatra play—'*Safal hogi teri aradhana*'. After the untimely demise of the hero, the unwed pregnant heroine and her father are shown the door by the hero's uncle. The song unfolds against this background. All the songs he had sung so far in Hindi films were bhatiyali, but not this one. The tune follows the style of old Bengali folk songs in the genre of songs of separation. The original song goes '*Ami bandhur premagune pora sai go/Ami maile poras na tora*'. Keeping the basic appeal intact, he created an unparalleled song with a new structure, in his own style.

Sachin was sensitive about the instrumental accompaniments to his songs. He considered orchestra as secondary to the song. It had to remain in the background and not overshadow the song. He used to advise Pancham, whose fascination for orchestra is well known, 'Don't forget the song for the sake of the orchestra.' He was fond of the softer accompaniments like flute, santoor, sitar, sarod, and folk instruments such as ektara, madal, etc., which gave his songs a dew-fresh appeal. His understanding of and ear for musical instruments matched his grasp of the tune itself. He was more at ease with Indian instruments in general. His sharp ear ensured that instruments and orchestra never overshadowed the tune itself. Shakti Samanta speaks of SD's dislike for excessive instrumental accompaniments:

> Only once have I seen Sachin-da really angry. It was during the recording of '*Safal hogi teri aradhana*' in *Aradhana*. Sachin-da told Pancham not to have more than eleven musicians. Poor Pancham could not decide whom to drop

and had to keep twelve on the floor. Sachin-da was livid with anger. He said, 'Pay the extra hand and release him.' Pancham reported the incident to me. I asked him to do as Sachin-da desired. The musician was paid off and asked to leave. (*Ananya* Shakti Samanta

One of the biggest hits of the film, and the song that made the biggest impact, was Kishore Kumar's '*Roop tera mastana*'. Let us now hear what Brajen Biswas, the tabla maestro, has to say about the story behind the song:

> Many of Karta's songs originated from the songs we heard in our countryside. Those songs were the foundation of his musical output. [...] I remember, Karta had come from Bombay to Calcutta. People had assembled at his South End Park residence, a gathering of luminaries from the world of music. In between the conversations, Karta kept playing the harmonium. Suddenly he stopped and said [in his East Bengal accent], 'Do you know Shakti is making a film? He has asked me to direct the music. He also wants me do a sexy number. I was reminded of an old story. I had gone to a fellow's house. I kept calling him, but he would not come out. When he did not answer my call for a long time, I scolded him. He said, 'Forgive me, Karta. I am getting my son married today and was helping him with his dhuti.' I noticed a small girl playing with an earthen oven. When she saw the boy she started laughing. I asked, 'Are you marrying off this small boy?' The fellow replied, 'It is better now, or else he might go astray.' Hearing this, the small girl's laughter knew no bounds. She started singing, '*Kalke jabo shoshur bari, aajke khai garagari*' ['Tomorrow I go to my in-law's place and so

am rolling in joy today']. Listening to Shakti, I suddenly remembered this song. I decided immediately that I would slow down the tempo a bit and ask Kishoira [meaning Kishore, in East Bengal dialect and tone] to sing. I would ask him to sigh and punctuate the lines with deep breath and it would then be a sexy song.' That is how the famous '*Roop tera mastana*' was born. So many songs came to life in this manner. ('Sachin Kartar Shangey', *Anand lok*)

But this was not the end of the matter. The song was to be picturized on Rajesh Khanna and Sharmila Tagore scorching the scene with their passion, and Sachin's tune did not quite reflect that. Pancham, who was assisting his father, and Kishore, who was to sing the song, both felt the same way about the tune and were wondering how to raise the issue with Sachin. Pancham set '*Kalke jabo shoshur badi*' to a new tune, making liberal use of Afrotal and cha-cha-cha styles. At last, Pancham himself gathered enough courage to sing the song before his father. Sachin saw that the boy had grasped the essence of the scene. This was when he realized that there was no holding back Pancham. He was already famous and would be more famous one day soon and that it was time he took up music direction independently rather than attach himself to his father as an assistant. It is indeed Pancham's unseen hand that transformed '*Kalke jabo shoshur badi*' lock, stock and barrel to something as evocative as '*Roop tera mastana*'. And what about Kishore's performance? With what effortless ease does his voice convey the feverish longing of the body, the fire of passion! There is probably no other singer in Hindi cinema who would have managed to bring a song like this to life in the manner he did. The rhythm, the melody and the rendition style along with the nature of orchestration evoke physical movements of erotic nature.

According to playback singer Bhupinder, *'Roop tera mastana'* from *Aradhana* was not composed by Pancham as is commonly believed, but by Dada Burman himself. But dada would very frequently 'steal' his son's tunes and tell him that he was testing them on the public.

There is no denying that the story behind the creation of a song is always fascinating. *Aradhana*'s other hit song *'Mere sapnon ki rani kab aayegi tu'* has an equally interesting tale. Those jealous of Sachin's success accused him of copying the tune of 'Tequila'. In this context Pulak Bandyopadhyay mentions what Sachin told him:

> After *Aradhana* became a super hit, I once heard Sachin-da say, 'Tell those who say that I have copied *'Mere sapnon ki rani kab aayegi tu'* from 'Tequila' that I have indeed based it on another tune, but not copied it. And it is not 'Tequila'. The tune is inspired by a song sung during the boat race of Comilla. I am a Bengali. There's a lot of musical wealth scattered all over my Bengal. I will first take all of those before turning to the West.' (*Kathay Kathay Raat Hoye Jay*)

The song commences with the sound of a train passing by, the train's whistle, as the strains of a mouth organ, flute, and sundry instruments produce the effect of a train in motion. Interestingly enough, in an effort to convey the effect of a train setting off, Sachin begins the song with a jolting motion. Before creating a tune, Sachin took into account the minute details of the situation like the character singing the song. He had an uncanny ability of creating tunes which matched the situation. He would visualize the scene in his mind's eye and then choose a tune which would make the audience correlate the song to the scene. Kishore Kumar rendered the song with an extraordinary sense of joie de vivre. The sequence with Sharmila reading a book on the train winding its way through the hill landscape and Rajesh Khanna serenading her in an open jeep remains one of Hindi film's iconic sequences, and the credit for this largely goes to Sachin's tune and Kishore's voice which captured the imagination of the young. People were all praise for Kishore. The success of *'Roop tera mastana'* and *'Mere sapnon ki rani'* catapulted Kishore to the top and like a marathon runner he left all his competitors behind. It is interesting that in his mid-sixties, Sachin created two songs which spoke so eloquently to the young generation of the era.

The other songs in *Aradhana* also became immensely popular. Kishore had another exceptional number, the memorable duet with Lata, *'Kora kaagaz tha yeh mann mera'*, in which the unforgettable echo of the hills weaves a mesmerizing web of romantic dreams. Though Kishore walked away with all the honours, Rafi had two delectable duets in *'Gunguna rahen hain bhanwre'* and the playful *'Baagon mein bahaar hai'*. In any other film, these would have stood out on their own. But such was the effect of the Kishore songs that even such melodious numbers were overshadowed. Rounding off the score is Lata's touching lullaby *'Chanda hai tu'*, which has for years remained the epitome of a mother's love in Hindi films songs.

The year 1969 saw the release of two more films—*Talash* and *Jyoti*. Among the several popular numbers of *Talash*, the most remarkable is probably Manna Dey's *'Tere naina talaash kare jise'* in raga Mishra Khambaj. It is one of those ironies of fate that despite a string of immensely popular songs, success eluded Manna Dey. Unlike his contemporaries like Rafi and Mukesh, he always remained a niche singer and never quite managed to become a mainstream one. In spite of the sensation he created with his very first song *'Upar gagan vishal'* and following it up with such all-time great numbers like *'Puchho na kaise maine rain bitayi'*, he was never the first choice of either producers or composers. According to Bengali lyricist Pulak Bandyopadhyay:

> Manna Dey once told me about the effort he had to put in just to get a foothold in the industry. Even when he got it, his struggle continued. With tears in his eyes he said, 'Do you know, I had gone to Sachin-da's music room to rehearse "*Tere naina talaash kare*". The director of the film also came to listen to the song. Sachin-da asked Manna Dey to sing the song for the director. In the presence of Manna Dey himself, the director told Sachin-da, 'Will Manna Dey sing this song? What about Mukesh?' Sachin-da replied, 'Mukesh cannot sing this song.' The director asked Sachin, 'Why have you composed a song that Mukesh cannot sing?' But Sachin-da remained firm. 'If you want S. D. Burman's music for *Talash*, this song will have this tune and it is Manna who will sing it. If you don't like this, you better look for another music director.' In a way, Sachin-da forced the director to accept Manna Dey for the song and the outcome is known to all. On the occasion of the silver jubilee of the film, the director said, 'S. D. Burman sahab, you are our dada—our eternal dada.
>
> (*Kathay Kathay Raat Hoye Jay*)

Any more discussion on the song is futile and it is needless to say that the song was well-accepted. Despite the fact that this is primarily a raga-based song and thus more likely to appeal to the connoisseur, it became immensely popular even with the common folk. This is in no small measure due to the inherent simplicity of the tune despite its foundation in the ragas, a blend that only Sachin could manage so effortlessly.

We have already mentioned the genesis of '*Khayi hai re humne kasam*' in Sachin's Bengali number '*Shuno go dakhin hawa, prem korechhi ami*'. The Hindi version, sung by Lata in her divine voice, became as popular as Sachin's Bengali one. In fact, Lata rendered the tune so beautifully that Sachin quite forgot having ever sung it himself. It was as if his tune had been born again.

Sachin himself had a song in *Talash* which, like almost all his Hindi film songs, played in the background. The song was '*Meri duniya hai maa*'. Whenever he sang for a Hindi film, Sachin invariably took recourse to the folk tune of East Bengal. And this song is no exception. No other musician of Bengal has done so much to disseminate the music of his motherland in the rest of the country. Interestingly, the nasal, hoarse voice which caused HMV to reject him all those years ago became his signature in later years. '*Meri duniya hai maa*' continued the tradition.

Dulal Guha's film *Jyoti* did not do well at the box office. It boasts five songs, of which Lata's lullaby '*Munne mere aa main tujhe pariyon ki*' and the Lata Mangeshkar-Manna Dey duet '*Soch ke yegagan jhume*' deserve special mention.

Sachin sang three Hindi songs in 1969: '*Meri duniya hai ma tere aanchal mein*' (*Talash*), '*Safal hogi teri aradhana*' (*Aradhana*), and '*Prem ke pujari hum hain*' (*Prem Pujari*). He also had two Bengali records which included the following songs: '*Ganer kali surer duri te*', '*Subal re bolo bolo*', '*Shono go dakhin hawa*' and '*Barne gandhe chandhe gitite*'. Meera Dev Burman wrote all the four songs. The first song has a brisk measure where the indeclinable '*hun-hun-hun*' plays a major role as Sachin uses it to move from the antara to the mukhda. Hindi film lovers will recognize the tune in Mohammad Rafi's solo '*Mehbooba teri tasveer*' in *Ishq Par Zor Nahin*. '*Subal re bolo bolo*' is a folk song, with Sachin returning to a song of separation from East Bengal after a long time. It was nothing new for Sachin to add extra words to a song. He did it in almost all her songs. But never before had he added a full line just in order to express the feeling. He further added '*re*' and '*dada*' with '*Subal*', raised the pitch of the tune, and infused the feeling of tearfulness in the listener. He ends the song with '*ainya de, ainya de*', words that are nowhere in the original lyric. Only the listener can feel how successful such words have been in expressing the feeling of separation in the song.

'*Shono go dakhin hawa*' is one of his most famous songs where Sachin mixes a folk tune in a modern song in a way that is difficult to make out unless one is absolutely attentive. Sachin used the tune for the popular Lata solo '*Khayi hai re humne kasam*', in *Talash*.

In '*Barne gandhe chhande gitite*', Sachin delectably utters each word individually. The entire song is composed in one tune with the mukhda having practically the same tune as the antara, much like one hears in a nazm. But simply by altering his style of singing from the mukhda to the antara, Sachin makes it sound different. Two particular lines in the song have given a measure of immortality to it: '*Mukta jemon shuktir buke temni amate tumi/ Aamar parane premer bindu tumi shudu tumi*' (Like a pearl inside an oyster you reside in me/ the touch of love in my heart, that's you, only you.) He comes back to these lines again and again. Sachin used this tune to compose one of Kishore Kumar's most beautiful romantic numbers, '*Phoolon ke rang se, dil ki kalam se*' in *Prem Pujari*.

The year 1970 saw the release of two films for which Sachin scored the music: Ramesh Saigal's *Ishq Par Zor Nahin* and Dev Anand's *Prem Pujari*. As was the case for all his films with Dev Anand, Sachin delivered yet another brilliant score for *Prem Pujari*. Apart from such hit evergreen numbers like '*Phoolon ke rang se*' and the irresistible blend of the modern and the folk in Lata's '*Rangila re tere rang mein*' and the youthful duet of Lata and Kishore '*Shokhiyon mein ghola jaye phoolon ka shabab*'. Sachin too sang a background song, '*Prem ke pujari hum hain*' for this film. This time he invoked his folk collection to come up with a patriotic song. Though the film failed at the box office, *Prem Pujari* continued the tradition of superlative music that had become the hallmark of the Navketan banner. Paying his respect to Sachin, Dev Anand has said:

> Sachin-da was a genius. I cannot remember anyone else who had such a repertoire of tunes. Sachin-da was one of the chief architects of our banner. I have no hesitation in declaring that during the zenith of my career, it was his music that made Navketan stand out as a banner. (Dev Anand on S. D. Burman — *Screen*, Nov 2002)

Ishq Par Zor Nahin had a moderate run at the box office. It boasts eight songs of which four are worthy of mention. *'Mehbooba teri tasweer kis tarah main banwaun'* is a Hindi version of Sachin's Bengali song *'Ganer kali surer duri tey'*. Like its counterpart, the Hindi version was also very popular. The dhun *'hun-hun-hun'* is the lifeline of this song. Lata's *'Mere bairagi bhanware mujhe tadpao na'* is an extremely melodious composition and *'Tum mujhse door chale jana na, main tumse door chali jaaungi'* is an exudation of pathos and Lata almost broke into tears while singing it. Lata's other song *'Main to tere rangrati mere mitwa mere saathi'* is a product of experiments and improvisation by S. D. Burman. It is an admixture of bhajan, kirtan and a modern song.

Sachin recorded four Bengali songs in 1970, the lyrics for which were written by Meera Dev Burman. *'Biraha baro bhalo lage'* begins on a melodious note in Kafi style after 'bhalo lage' only to segue to folk after the mukhda. What a splendid coexistence of the classical and the folk! He returns to the raga with *'habe eto madhur'* with such a honey-laced play on the word 'madhur' that the pain of separation became personified for the listener. One should listen to his rendition of 'lage' in 'bhalo lage' in different styles while keeping to the purity of the raga to realize Sachin's command over his muse. When prosody comes in the way of the tune, he adds indeclinable or extra words. The whole effect the song creates reminds one of Tennyson's words, 'It is better to have loved and lost than never to have loved at all.' What synergy between the theme and the tune of the song! Only Sachin could have achieved this.

The second song was *'Ghate lagaiya dinga paan khaiya jao…Allar dohai'*, one of the many Sachin songs that have a universal appeal. This song demonstrates his deep love for the flute. Though the word 'banshi' (flute) does not find a place anywhere in the lyrics, Sachin introduces it right at the start, beginning with *'O-o-o-o banshi'*, thus laying the ground for the flute motif that dominates the song. This bhatiyali song is a prime example of the play of his trademark hoarse voice. In *'paan khaiya jao'* he pronounced 'paan' and 'jao' in a manner that had never been heard in folk songs and perhaps never will be in future. The way he utters the words *'Allar dohai'* gives the feeling that he has just let the words afloat in the breeze of Bengal's countryside. There is no doubt that Bengal's folk music was in his blood.

Listening to *'Raater aatare bhijaiya aadare'*, one would at first have a feeling of a classical-based modern song. But it is only in the first line that one finds a whiff of khayal. Then Sachin Dev comes to his true self. With special emphasis on *'du'* in *'durer'* and *'le'* in *'bhulechhilam'* in a swift folk tune, he renders such a Khatki twist in the style of a Jhumar that the listener can only gasp. Using the third word of the mukhda as a prop, he shifts from antara to sthayi.

Listening to this song *'Kalsaape dangshe amay'*, I was reminded of an oft-heard song of my childhood. Ratanmani revolted against the king of Tripura in the 1940s and was arrested and killed. The people of Tripura still remember him as a revolutionary who bought for the cause of common people. In those days, bards used to go around singing the exploits of Ratanmani to the accompaniment of drums. The song was *'Ora juddho kare/ Mare dhare/ Bhaish murag katiya khay/ Ghare ghare agun diya/ Juddho karte chay'* (They fight/ kill and capture/ slaughter buffaloes and chicken/ burn down houses and want to fight). This song belongs to the tradition of Dhaker gaan (a song of the drum) and its tune is similar to *'Kalsaape dangshe amay'*. In Dhaker gaan, the tune is usually fixed; there is not much of a change. It needs to be noted that Sachin employed a hoarse voice in special casesa and the use of hoarseness is intentional. In his rendering of the words *'harailam'* in *'gourbarna harailam'*, one can hear him scream in a hoarse voice. For the lyrics of these four songs, special credit must go to Meera Dev Burman. It is but natural for one's songs to be spontaneous if one's wife is a poet and lyricist!

Director Sudhir Mukhopadhyay's Bengali film *Chaitali* was released this year under the music direction of S. D. Burman. It comprises eight songs of which Lata's songs, *'Phoolon mein se phool chuna, Shyam bhoi bine shyam hai'* and *'Hay payal baj gayi aaj meri'* deserve mention.

In 1971, four films were released under Sachin's music direction, *Gambler* directed by Amarjeet, Pramod Chakrabarti's *Naya Zamana*, Samir Ganguli's *Sharmilee*, and *Tere Mere Sapne* by Vijay Anand. This discussion will be limited only to the hit songs from these movies. Kishore Kumar did wonders in gambler. For many years, Sachin did not give Kishore flowing melody-dominated songs to sing. Rather, he always wanted Rafi for these. Under Sachin's tutelage, Kishore, however, mastered various genres of songs and their pitch of delivery, and thus flowered into a complete singer. With time it became clear that nobody other then Kishore could bring to life the artistry behind Sachin's music. Those who thought that Kishore was good for only plain and simple songs were astonished to listen to the expertise with which he rendered the songs of *Gambler*, particularly the nazm-like *'Dil aaj shayar hai'*. Even a few years ago, Sachin would have probably given this song to Rafi, but now he had enough faith in Kishore's ability to pull off the difficult number. Kishore sang another solo, *'Kaise hai mera dil tu khiladi'*. The song had two parts. In one part, Kishore played his usual comedian's role; the other part contained a variety of the ghazal. Kishore had other popular numbers like the duet with Lata *'Apni hothon ki bansi bana le mujhe'* where the flute played a vital role and the frothy solo *'Churi nahi yeh mera dil hai'* which was a chartbuster. Though by now Sachin had more or less decided on Kishore as his primary singer, he gave Rafi one of the most memorable songs of his career in *Gambler*, *'Mera mann tera pyaasa'*. And with what passion did Rafi render the song!

One song from *Naya Zamana* deserves special mention. We have repeatedly mentioned Sachin's love for Bengal's folk songs. Whenever he got an opportunity, he never fought shy of spreading the magic of rural Bengal's earthy tunes. In a dance sequence in *Naya Zamana,* he unfurled the flag of Bengali culture in all its glory. The song was *'Rama Rama gazab hui gaya re'*. Exceptionally sung by Lata, this song steeped in youthful exuberance is redolent of Bengal's folk tradition. Just before the second antara one hears the sound of Bengal's dhol and kansa (the drum and bell-metal dish). And those acquainted with his oeuvre of Bengali songs will remember hearing these instruments in his immortal *'Sei je dinguli, banshi bajanor dinguli'*. Other songs from this movie were important too. *'Kitne din ankhin tarsenge ek din to badal barsenge'* (Lata) is a song of positive realism, *'Naya zamana aayega'*. Lata's articulation in *antara* is impeccable. The futility of life is depicted in the song '*Duniya o duniya tera jawab nahin*' sung by Kishore with pathos that filled the air.

All the songs of *Sharmilee* became huge hits, another example of Sachin being a music director who delivered hit scores rather than only hit songs. Kishore Kumar's versatile genius was amply demonstrated in two diverse songs, the ghazalish '*Khilte hai gul yahan*' (Kishore renders this in an unusually melodious voice) and the fun number '*O meri, o meri sharmilee*'. These also gave another glimpse of Sachin's mastery over all kinds of music. Though in essence Sachin Dev Burman's music is out and out Indian, his long association with Dev Anand not merely attracted him towards Western pop music and jazz but enthused him enough to try out the same in his compositions. The reason behind his incredible success and the fact that his music remains a part of public memory is that he was modern in his outlook to music, always on the move, never confining himself to one kind of music, unlike his peers Naushad or Madan Mohan. His experimentation with music itself proves that he had an unlimited power of assimilation. He was not biased over purity of ragas. His only yardstick was whether the music was lively or not, whether it spoke to its listeners, whatever be its origin, East or West. The icing on the cake was, of course, Lata's mesmerizing '*Megha chhaye aadhi raat*', where Sachin brings together the East and West in a remarkable fusion. The basic tune is based on a Tagore song. The mixing of Western music with Indian classical in the interludes enhances the beauty and brilliance of the composition. The song begins with a typically Western piece using guitar, accordion, bongo and drums before moving on to an assortment of Indian instruments like sitar and tabla with violin, flute and sarangi/esraj.

Lata and Kishore also sang the same song '*Khilte hain gul yahan, khilke bikharne ko'* separately. The difference between the two songs was that Lata sang it on a long measure but with a short strip in '*ko*' whereas Kishore sang the same in ghazal style. Both the songs are soothing to the ear. Lata and Kishore presented us a lovely duet *'Aaj madhosh huwa jaayere, mere man...'* The song *'Reshmi ujala hai, makhmali andhera'* sung by Asha reminds one of her *'Raat ekeli hai'*. Lastly, no one can escape the grief of being in love and that is what is depicted in the song *'Kaise kahein hum pyaar ne humko kya khel kya dikhaye'* sung by Kishore. Kishore was not only a comedian but also a tragedy master. How beautifully pathos conquered his voice!

Tere Mere Sapne continued the tradition of great music now associated with the Sachin—Dev Anand combination. Two songs, sung by Lata and Asha, deserve special mention. The kirtan is a devotional form of music typical of Bengal. Sachin had used the kirtan in many films in which he was the music director. In fact, he played a big role in popularizing this form in Hindi film music. In *Tere Mere Sapne*, he combined kirtan and bhajan for a masterpiece in Lata's voice *'Jaise Radha ne mala japi'*. Asha Bhonsle does a valiant job of the classical-based *'Ta thai ata thai'*, pictured as a dance scene on Hema Malini. It is difficult to judge which of the two songs is more attractive. But simply by dint of its sweetness, the one by Lata will probably score more points. Apart from these, Sachin gave Kishore and Lata two of the finest duets of their careers: *'Haan maine kasam li'* and *'Jeevan ki bagiya mahkegi'*. The melody and rhythm of these songs have become a thing of the past. One no longer hears such a fusion of beautiful lyrics and sweet music. Lata's song *'Mera antar ek mandir hai tera hai tera'* is a superb song of surrender to love. Lata almost turns this song into a devotional one. Apart from this, Asha's contribution is also laudable. Her songs *'Ud chala hawa banke'* is a frothy and smart number and the other one *'Mera sajan phool kamal ka'* is an instance of SD's experimentation with a fast thumri.

It is surprising that though Sachin has created music for some of the finest duets ever in Hindi cinema, in the early stages of his career, he felt that audiences do not quite like duets. In fact, in the 1950s, solo songs were invariably more popular than duets. Sachin once told lyricist Majrooh Sultanpuri, 'We spend so much time for making a duet successful, but as you see; no one likes it.' Majrooh replied, 'The fault is ours. We lyricists do not write duets that the hero and heroine can enact to entice audiences.' The outcome of the discussion can be seen in many hit songs of the 1950s. For example, '*Chhor do aanchal zamana kya kahega*', '*Haal kaisa hai janab ka*', '*Aankhon mein kya ji*', '*Arey yaar meri, tum bhi ho ghazab*', and so on. Kishore, Asha, Majrooh and Sachin took duets to the height of popularity in Hindi films.

Sachin also released two Bengali songs this year, both steeped in the folk and bhatiyali traditions. Both songs were written by Meera Dev Burman and both were extraordinary compositions. The first song was '*(Ami) takdum takdum bajai Bangladesher dhol*', and it is indeed serendipitous that this was the year Bangladesh was born. From the distant shore of the Arabian Sea came Sachin's voice and melody over the Padma and the Meghna, as if saluting his birthplace: '*Bangla! Janam dila amare/ Tomar paran amar paran / Ek narite bandha re/ Ma-puter ei bandhan chherar/ Sadhya karo nai/ Sab bhule jai, tao bhulina/ Bangla mayer kol*' (Bangla! You gave me birth. Your life is my life; both tied in the same vein. No one has the ability to sever this mother-son tie. I forget everything but never the lap of my mother Bangla). The tune reveals Sachin's passion for his native land. In an inspired voice, he sang the song in a folk tune. The structure of this song has been taken from a folk tune of rural Bengal, where it is known as 'baula gaan'. These songs are in two different beats: first in slow measure like bass music and then in fast measure, increasing the beat twofold to fourfold, which is locally known as *'chali'*. In *'chali'*, at the end of the song, only one word is to be sung at a high pitch, articulating the lyrics in the *rasa* of heroism (veer-rasa), in the tune of lamentation, in faster and faster tempo reaching the major E-scale (tara). The initial play of the tune (alaap) with *a-a-a* continues for long which can often seem irritating to the audience. Sachin Dev Burman transformed this old folk song from East Bengal, often looked upon as an outcast tune, to a high-standard, graceful folk song, acceptable to all. He did this in his own style, changing the beat and tempo, changing the rhythm and imparting an entirely new measure and a new tune to it. He had neither copied this folk tune nor followed it; he had only extracted its melancholy.

The other song was a bhatiyali: *'Tora ke jasre bhati gang baiya'*. A particular type of bhatiyali songs is called karun bhatiyali (sad or doleful bhatiyali). *'Tora ke jasre bhati gang baiya'* is an example of this category. Here, the wail of a village girl attains the level of an extraordinary creation through the magic of Sachin Dev's music. The same song (and perhaps the original that inspired Sachin) has been sung by Abbasuddin as well. But Abbasuddin's version is not half as lively as Sachin's. In comparison to Sachin, Abbasuddin sounded just ordinary with the evocative lyrics *'Aare o bhatiyal ganger naiya / Thakur bhaire kaiyo amay naiyor nito aiya / Oi na ghate baiya re kandi desher pare chaiya / Chokkher pani nadir jale jaitechhe mishiya* (Oh boatman of the bhatiyal river, ask Thakurbhai to take me to my parental home, sitting at that ghat I look at my land and weep, my tears mingle with the river water.)

Unless an appraisal is made of the silent contribution of Sachin-karta to the world of music, future generations will miss out on a legacy that is immortal. I wonder if Sachin himself knew that he had revolutionized the world of music. He might have been conscious of giving birth to his own style. But did he realize that he had established the common man's music, folk music, in the highest throne of the durbar of the world's music. Being of royal descent, reared in an atmosphere where classical music was considered superior, it was unthinkable for a man like him in the context of the time to have cultivated folk music, the songs and music of the low-born, of people without any social status, of the boatman, of the mendicant and the baul, of the fakir. Sachin picked the jewels of folk music in canals and marshes, in rivers and hills, in woodlands, in villages and marketplaces, in the assembly of Vaisnavas, in a fakir's dargah. He embraced with honour what was considered the outcast culture of the lowliest of society. For this he had to suffer not a little slight and neglect. Unlike today, folk songs were not fashionable in those days and were not a part of the urbanized musical experience; such songs of the unlettered and the rustic were looked down upon even by the middle class. And to think that a prince in such an environment, well versed in classical music, sang and spread folk songs the world over! In films and outside of it, a majority of his well-adored songs are based on the folk tradition. In a way it was for the best that he took the decision to come to Bombay. Had he succeeded in becoming a music director in Calcutta, could we have this Sachin Dev Burman of multifaceted talent? Perhaps he would not have attained this worldwide fame. And perhaps the folk song of Bengal wouldn't have had the reach it attained thanks to Sachin popularizing it through his Hindi film songs.

Three films under Sachin Dev's music were released in 1972: *Anurag* directed by Shakti Samanta, *Yeh Gulistan Hamara* by Guru Dutt's brother Atmaram, and Tapan Sinha's *Zindagi Zindagi*. Any Bengali must be acquainted with two Lata songs from *Anurag*. If

'*Sunari pawan, pawan purbaiya*' echoes Sachin's Bengali number '*Tora ke jasre*', '*Neend churaye chain churaye*' brings to mind his '*Banshi shune aar kaj nai*'. These two songs show how pleasing to the ear it becomes when Bengali songs are adapted to Hindi films. I have heard many people say that Bengali songs do not have the 'enthu' or vigour of Hindi songs. Sachin proved them wrong over and over again. Another hit number in *Anurag* was rendered by Kishore in typical Bihari style: '*Ram kare babua*'.

The 1970s witnessed a gradual change in the formula of songs and in the use of musical instruments. Old masters like Shankar-Jaikishan and Naushad were slowly making way for a new breed of musicians who were more aggressive in their style of music. Leading this pack was Sachin's son, Rahul, who was growing in stature as a musician with each passing day. He had in fact sounded the future course of music with the score for the Shammi Kapoor thriller *Teesri Manzil* in 1966. Shammi Kapoor had always had stalwarts like O. P. Nayyar and Shankar-Jaikishan as music directors for the string of musical hits he had given in the 1960s. Yet it was Rahul who was chosen for *Teesri Manzil* and what enormous hits the songs turned out to be! Even today, people hum its songs '*Aaja aaja main hun pyar tera*', '*Deewana mujhsa nahin*' and '*O mere sona re*'. Rahul was a votary of extensive use of the orchestra. Not for him the soil of Bengal as inspiration, nor the serenity of a boat plying over the tranquil river or the longing of a sunset over the banks. His inspiration lay in the music of Elvis Presley, the Beatles and Henry Mancini's jazz composition. There was a gulf of difference between his and his father's thoughts on music. Till his last days, Sachin Dev Burman gave pride of place to Indian music in his compositions. For him, orchestra meant an amalgamation of the flute, sitar, sarod, violin, dilruba, ektara, dhol, kansa, jaltarang, santoor, etc. At best, Western instruments included the mouth organ, clarinet, piano, accordion, and guitar. Rahul chose Western music and Western instruments. Sachin had come to Bombay with a stock of folk music which he had gradually embellished and incorporated in his film music. This stock had taken him to the zenith of success. So Sachin Dev Burman remained Sachin Dev Burman. And because he remained so, in 1972, he received the national award for the best music director for *Zindagi Zindagi*.

Having mentioned Rahul and the duel of Western and Oriental music, let us look at the relationship between the father and son. Needless to say, Sachin Dev was very fond of his son. He often advised his competitor composer, 'Give due importance to the tune of the song.' The son understood his father and put his advice to good use. He earned a lot of fame by drawing upon his father's tunes in many of his own songs. Rahul realized that a tune devoid of the feel of the soil was bound to be short-lived. So later in life he sought refuge in his father's tunes. Finally he regained his throne with the support of his departed father's tunes. The music in *1942—A Love Story*, reflects his father's earthy tunes. Sachin Dev Burman proved through Rahul that his music transcends the limits of time, it is eternal. His songs rejuvenate people even today and will continue to do so in future too.

Let me recount an incident about the relationship between this father and son duo:

> The elder Karta was out on a morning walk. Suddenly he overheard some people saying, 'Look, R. D. Burman's father.' Abruptly ending his stroll he returned home and bristled at his wife: 'What a big shot your lad has become, eh! What music is he producing?' The proud mother handed over the son's new record to the father. The film: *Amar Prem*. '*Chingari koi bhadke*', '*Kuch toh log kahenge*', '*Yeh*

kya hua'...the sixty-five-year-old father listened to the songs and all his rancour at being described as his son's father drained out of him. The boy had practised under him right from the age of four. And what better gurudakshina (gift given to a teacher as fees) could there be.' (*Anandlok*, 22nd May 2001)

Pancham talked about the reaction of his father in this context:

> My father was at last proud of me. One day returning from his morning walk he said, 'Today I'm very happy with you. Till now I was recognised as S. D. Burman but today someone pointed me out and said 'There goes R. D. Burman's father.' (*Filmfare*, 22 May 2001)

The songs of *Amar Prem* relieved Sachin. That the son had outgrown the father made him happy. But soon there was disappointment. In acknowledgement of the changing times, Dev Anand looked beyond the age-old relationship with Sachin and chose Rahul for his film *Hare Rama Hare Krishna*. This in itself did not make him as sad as he felt when he listened to '*Dum maro dum*' in the studio. He might well have wondered at what lessons he had given his son, who had learnt music right from the foundation from him! Far from carrying on his tradition it seemed a deliberate attempt to forego tradition, an utmost effort to defy the father and his legacy! Rahul could see his father walking slowly out of the studio with his head lowered. No more of that spirited countenance, but a stooping figure, as if a vanquished prince was returning.

That day Sachin Dev Burman might have reminisced with a heart full of sorrow. Right from Rahul's infancy, Sachin had always given in to his son's desires even at the cost of his own. He always encouraged his son in the pursuit of music. His son was not attentive about his general education, but that did not bother his father. Even when Rahul failed in his annual examination, Sachin had presented him with a bicycle and a badminton racket. He was always positive; he hated negativity. He left the boy behind with his maternal grandmother in Calcutta for his studies before leaving for Bombay. But, like father like son! Just as Sachin gave up his studies in Calcutta against the wishes of his father and got immersed in music, so did Rahul. Pancham's early expertise with the mouth organ demonstrated that Sachin had passed on more than his blood to his son. Sachin realized that it would not be possible to keep Rahul away from the world of music. Since an understanding of beat is the first step in music, Sachin arranged with his favourite tabla player, Brajen Biswas, to train Rahul on the tabla. Later, Rahul learnt percussion instruments from Shamtaprasad and sarod from Ustad Ali Akbar Khan, all as per the wishes of his father. But all along he demonstrated an irresistible desire to learn Western music. But thanks to Ali Akbar Khan, the foundation of classical music was also laid in him.

Sprightly, utterly devoted to music, disinterested in general studies, such was the nature of Rahul. Sachin Dev thought it better not to keep him for long at Calcutta and brought him over to Bombay in 1955. Immediately on reaching Bombay, the boy started insisting on composing music. But what sort of music can a sixteen-year-old create? And even if he does, who will believe that it is his? The boy composed tunes on his mouth organ and presented these to his father. His tunes gave a clear indication of a morning leading to the day. But could a mere boy be taken as an assistant music director? Rahul was also not the type to give up. Finally, the father had to relent before the son's indomitable desire. In 1955, Rahul, sixteen years old at the time, worked for the first time with his father on *Pyaasa*. Observing his talent in music, Guru Dutt bestowed on him the responsibility of scoring the music for his film *Raaz* the very next year. Unfortunately, the film got abandoned after only two songs had been recorded.

In the year 1956, *Funtoosh* was released. Rahul found his tune had been lifted by his father. The song 'Ae meri topi palat ke aa' had already been stamped in print as S. D. Burman's creation as a music director of *Funtoosh*. The son did not take it favourably and asked him, 'Why have you lifted my tune without my permission?' Rahul's creative fervour satisfied his father greatly. The son was puffed with pride seeing his illustrious father borrowing his tune. He said, 'Don't ever think I can't make a good tune'. Appreciating the sensitiveness of his son, SD replied, 'Tell me who has borrowed your tune? It's me, S. D. Burman, your father. Don't you consider yourself fortunate?' Pancham was not a boy to give up ground without a fight. He said, 'It's alright. But please admit that I too am a good composer'. Father hugged his son affectionately and said, 'This is what I expect from you.'

Pancham has quoted SD as saying: 'I was testing your tune on the public! Now that 'Ae meri topi' has proved a hit, I know you'll make it as a composer when your time comes'.

A friendly competition between father and son began. Pancham benefited greatly from this competition. He wanted to carve a different path to get out of the shadow of his father. He wanted to make his own gharana, his own tradition. He was attracted to Western tunes to create unconventional tunes. It was not in *Junglee* or *Teesri Manzil* that we heard rock-n-roll for the first time. It was in *Pyaasa* (1957) under the music direction of S. D. Burman that Pancham set to music the tune of rock-n-roll in the song 'Sar jo tera chakraye'. It is unimaginable for a boy of fifteen to give such a rhythmic, breezy tune to a song. This tune had not been heard before in Hindi film music. The way father Sachin gathered like bee the honey hidden in folk music, Pancham also stored in his soundtrack gems of music from all over the world like jazz, rock, swing, circus music, Mexican mariachi, Brazillian bossa nova etc.

In the year 1958, SD created a wonder in *Chalti Ka Naam Gaadi*. Remember the duet sung by Kishore Kumar and Manna Dey '*Babu, babu samjho ishare horn pukare*', Kishore's solo and chorus respectively '*Ek ladki bhigi bhagi sei*', '*In haathon se sabki gadi chaal rahi hai*'? Can you compare any of these songs with earlier songs composed by SD? Can you guess whose invisible hand had brought to life the tunes loved by the new generation? A singer like Manna Dey danced while singing the song. That was not the handiwork of a single person. It was the combined effort of father and son. In the later stage, following his father, Pancham created musical sounds from all sorts of things used in our day-to-day life and showed his ability for improvisation.

The word about a wonder boy's arrival in filmdom had already spread. Director Guru Dutt could not believe even in his dream that the song '*Sar jo tera chakraye*' composed by Pancham would be a great hit. He wanted to play a game of speculation. RD's first break as a music director came through Guru Dutt. RD was excited. Guru Dutt signed him as a music director for *Raaz*. RD remembered the reaction of his father:

> My father wasn't in favour of this. He feared that since I'd only put in two years in the industry, a successful film would go to my head. But Guru Dutt was adamant. Unfortunately, after two songs were recorded, the film was shelved. I was thoroughly dejected. I pleaded with the director that it was my first film but he said, '*Sorry apne ko jum nahin raha*'.' (*Filmfare*, June 16-30,1984)

At this time, Mehmood came to S. D. Burman. He requested him to take up the music direction of his film *Bhoot Bungla*. SD told him, 'What do you think of me? I don't score music for ghost films.' Mehmood had earned some reputation as a comedian by then. Johnny Walker was losing ground to him. To speak the truth, SD did not like to take the risk of scoring music for a film directed by a brand new director. Sitting in a corner, Pancham was playing the tabla. What Mehmood did was to cut 'SD' and put 'RD' before the surname Burman and signed a contract with Rahul as a music director. Although Rahul had entered into an agreement with Mehmood for the film *Bhoot Bungla*; officially the first movie for which he scored the music was *Chhote Nawab* (1961). Akbar was the director of this film. This was also Mehmood's film. The journey of R. D. Burman as a music director began from here.

The probationary period of Pancham under the supervision of father S. D. Burman was going on and at the same time an independent score as music director began. Pancham thought he should not be typecast like other music directors. He did not want to score conventional music. He was constantly in search of exceptional tunes. Ultimately he made it. Father S. D. Burman tried his best to bring him back from the clutch of western music but failed. Pancham by then established his gharana by 'Indianising' Western music.

The West at that time was rocking with the likes of Black Sabbath, Led Zeppelin, the Beatles and jazz music. The rest of the world was slowly waking up to the new music and Pancham was no exception. He realized the potential of the genre. He cultivated it and infused it into his music, though with a difference, retaining his own stamp of identity. He firmly believed that every composer must have knowledge of all kinds of music before he can dream of becoming a creator in his field.

Rahul composed music for a few more films like: *Chandan*

Ka Palna, Bhoot Bungla and *Pati Patni*. Though *Bhoot Bungla* brought limited success, the ground was steadily shifting from under Rahul's feet. He desperately wanted to be an independent music director. He was no longer content with being an assistant to his father. On the recommendation of the music director duo Shankar-Jaikishan, he composed the music for *Teesri Manzil*. The huge success of the film erased the pain of failure of the previous years. Never did he have to look back ever again.

In the unrestrained storm generated by songs like '*Aaja, aaja, main hun pyar tera*', '*Dum maro dum*' and other popular chartbusters, his son might well have appeared as an unknown identity to Sachin. He may have wondered as to whom to hand over the legacy of the world of music he had nurtured bit by bit over years of arduous practice of Indian classical music and the pursuit of folk music. He knew that music, the roots of which have not sprouted in Indian soil, which lacked its earthy feel, is but transitory, though it might flower for a while. Sachin was a worshipper of the eternal. He knew well that skilful presentation could dazzle the eyes for a while but could never wet the eyelids. Such music that depends on snazzy presentation changes with time. But Indian classical music in its splendid glory and folk music with its graceful earthy appeal have made their place in the heart of humanity for eternity.

In his lifetime itself Sachin witnessed the mighty rise of his son. He felt pride for his successful son. He felt sad at '*Dum maro dum*' but had he lived for a few years more his pride and joy would have known no bounds. In later years, RD realized how correct his father's assessment was. He savoured the earthiness of Sachin's music. He understood how through his experimentation, Sachin had created a captivating fusion of classical, Western and folk music. Likewise, the son also imparted Indianness to Western music using his wonderful talent. In this context, Salil Chowdhury says:

Pancham was then at the crest of the mighty wave. His stars were, so to say, in an auspicious conjunction. Who could touch him? What extraordinary tunes he created, some with the nectar of classical music, some with the earthy flavour of folk music and others with the intoxication of the *Arabian Nights*. And of rhythm, he was a magician. Using a madal [a kind of tom-tom] he created a beat which became well-known as 'Pancham's beat' in the world of Hindi songs. (*Aajkaal*, 6th Feb,1994)

Had he been alive, Sachin would have revelled in what Pancham achieved in the years between 1975 and 1984. He would have been happy, would have felt real pride, had he listened to RD's subsequent romantic songs like '*Chura liya hai tumne jo dil ko*' (*Yaadon Ki Baraat*) or '*Tere bina zindagi se koi*' (*Aandhi*). He would have been further relieved to hear the gems that the Gulzar—Pancham combination gave to the world of music: '*Musafir hun yaaron*' (*Parichay*), '*O majhi re*' (*Khushboo*), '*Naam gum jayega*' (*Kinara*), '*Tum aa gaye ho*' (*Aandhi*) and so many other beautiful songs.

After 1984 came the catastrophe. There was a marked change in the kind of music being produced. RD could not quite recreate the magic that he had demonstrated for over a decade. Film producers also fell for copycats, leaving RD behind. He had his first heart attack soon after he learnt that Subhash Ghai had dropped him from his film *Ram Lakhan*. He underwent a bypass surgery in London. It is now known that during the next five years Rahul had little work. The industry which had once danced to his rhythm now had no time for him. Pancham spent the last few years of his life in utter loneliness. There was no question of finding comfort with his mother, because by then she was already suffering from mental ailments. He spent these years remembering his father, listening to his father's songs, besides listening to Rabindra sangeet. He almost gave up his musical practice. The end would perhaps have been as tragic had Vidhu Vinod Chopra not made *1942—A Love Story*. Rahul dipped into the treasure trove of his father's world of music to create some of his most brilliant compositions. In deep reverence, the son admitted defeat before the father. At dawn on 4 January 1994, he saw in his dream a royal personality come to take him away, sitting on the deck of a boat, singing an earthy tune at the crest of the waves of the river.

It is a matter of conjecture what more RD would have achieved and what treasures we would have had in the world of Hindi songs and music but for his untimely death. But the fact remains that Rahul attained his last success sheltered under the canopy of father Sachin Dev Burman's music.

It is undeniable that Rahul was not only Sachin's son but also his rival music composer. A lot has been said on the merits of the two as composers. Discussions on who is a better musician are also not difficult to find. Let us have a few samples:

Two of two different types: Shakti Samanta:

> The two are different. Instead of going into who is more and who is less (talented) I would say that both were born with their individual talents. Both had their inherent talents. I have worked with Sachin-da as well as with Pancham. Sachin-da's tunes had an earthy attraction. He was more influenced by folk music which formed an inalienable part of his music. His thoughts on folk (songs) and his attempt to modernize them are unmatched. On the other hand, Pancham Indianized Western music in such a way that he alone is his comparison. In my film *Aradhana,* Sachin-da was the music director. Pancham was

then Sachin-da's assistant. It is only natural for the son to be influenced by the father. So Pancham delved into some of the good things of his father and elevated them to a different level.

What is better—Sandesh or Rasogolla: Hrishikesh Mukherjee:

> What is the point of this comparison? It is like asking a Bengali which is better of the two: sandesh or rasogolla. Sachin-karta has worked in four or five of my films and Pancham in eleven or twelve. Working with the two of them I have seen that they are differently talented in their own individual fields. Sachin-da was like one born in an exceptionally auspicious moment, and Pancham was a genius, unbelievably talented and an able son of an able father. Pancham inherited all the qualities of his father and would again and again refine them through his own experimentation. The rest is for you to understand.

They themselves are their comparison: Dev Anand:

> Sachin-da was a genius. I cannot recollect anyone before him coming to Hindi film industry with such a stock of tunes as his. He was one of the chief architects of our banner. I have no hesitation in declaring now that at the zenith of my career, Sachin-da's music in our films was one of the main attractions of the films. And I have know Pancham for so long. He used to work with his father, an able assistant. And he emerged from the shadow of his father on his own strength. Thereafter, the extraordinary music he imparted to my films is history. Both are unique. Not only I but anybody from the Indian film industry will admit this. They cannot be compared with each other.

Genius, genius both: Rajesh Khanna:

> What can I say? Both are geniuses, both extraordinarily talented. I shall make a mess if I want to judge, because I do not have the capacity to judge them. Some of my most famous films had music by either Sachin-da or Pancham. Their songs made my roles come alive. Even today, whenever I get nostalgic, I am reminded of Kishore's songs in my old films. Which one should I cite '*Mere sapnon ki rani*', '*Chingari koi bhadke*', '*Yeh lal rang*'? Both created history. Genius, genius both.

Two sides of the moon: Gulzar:

> Extraordinary talent. Like two sides of the moon. How do I compare? There is no doubt that Pancham was an able successor. Since I was influenced by Sachin Dev Burman, I could judge Pancham also. In order to understand Pancham one has to understand Sachin-da first. Only when one is able to understand the father does the question of understanding Pancham arise. Pancham covers much of my career as a director. He had an uncanny understanding of tune, beat and tempo. And he had no parallel in matching the tune to the character in the film. This very quality, this very personality is derived from tradition. Whatever more he achieved is entirely from his own understanding. This is incredible! There cannot be any debate on their individuality, on their talent. The question should never be raised.

A delicate question: Kavita Krishnamurthy:

> It is a delicate question, you know. Still, I would say Sachin-da was the main character of his time, and Pancham-da

an exceptional music composer of his time. In Sachin-da's songs the melody was so sweet, even though local intonation was well marked in it. And Pancham-da's 'orchestrization' was simply superb, inimitable. No one could do it the way Pancham-da assimilated so many musical influences in his own style. And individuality comes from talent, it is inborn. I sang for Pancham-da in *1942—A Love Story*. To me it remains an extraordinary experience. (*Anandlok*, 22nd May 2001)

The reader must condone my digression. If I write about Rahul it is both to convey that Sachin Dev Burman never compromised on music and to give an idea of the transition from one generation to another. Returning to Sachin and his delightful music in *Zindagi Zindagi*, he had two songs in the background. '*Zindagi ye zindagi*', a modern song in slow measure, and the folk-inspired '*Piya tu ne kya kiya re*', where he surpassed himself. Unless one listens to the song, it is difficult to understand that it is possible to accomplish in a folk tune what he managed to with it. As Ameen Sayani pointed out, even at the age of sixty-six, Sachin Dev Burman could conjure up a tune steeped in child-like simplicity and youthful vigour. The other songs Manna Dey's '*Mera sab kuchh mere geet re*' and Kishore's '*Khush raho sathiyon*' and '*Tu ne hamein kya diya ri*' also became very popular.

I have often mentioned how Sachin's compositions capture Nature in all its pristine, unblemished glory. No one managed to bring to life the murmuring stream and the echoes of the mountain as well as he did. His score for *Yeh Gulistan Hamara*, a film based on the Northeast, is another proof of that. The film's music is a triumph of Northeastern music brought to the world of Hindi films. Though the film was not very popular, its songs have remained in the hearts of those who follow Hindi film music. These songs include Kishore's *'Suno meri baat, chalo mere saath'* and the unforgettable Kishore-Lata duet *'Sun sun gaon ki gori re'*. Incidentally, character actor Danny too lent his voice to a song in the film: *'Mera naam Aao, mere paas aao'*.

It is quite interesting to note that despite the fact that Lata had sung innumerable popular songs under his music, Sachin chose *'Kya ye zindagi hai, kaisi bebasi hai'* from *Yeh Gulistan Hamara* as Lata's best with him. He commented on this song:

> Till 1971, *'Kya ye zindagi hai'* is my best song in Lata's voice. In this song Lata captures in her dew-fresh voice the struggle for life, a life full of pain and suffering. Anand Bakshi's words convey the sufferings of life like very few songs. So far, this song has given me the maximum creative satisfaction.

Sachin sang two Bengali songs in 1972: *'Radhar bhabe kala haila gora'* and *'Na amare shashi cheyona'*. The first is a devotional song in praise of Gaur, composed in the tune of East Bengal's Gaurvandana. Sachin articulates the words *'Radhar bhabe kala haila'*, stopping at this stage to emphasize 'Gora' to make it prominent and stops again. The beauty of the song lies in the tune of 'O bondhu'. It is not bhatiyali in the seventh scale, neither is it a movement from the scale of the deepest tone (udara) to the major E (tara). He simply expresses the tune with passion, maintaining the tempo and the rhythm. *'Na amare shashi cheyona'* is a famous song, which lovers of Hindi films songs will recognize as *'Ja mujhe na ab yaad aa'* in Kishore's unforgettable voice in the 1974 Rajesh Khanna film *Prem Nagar*. Sachin used to introduce small swings in composing his music. He liked the raga Komal Gandhar. This song also demonstrates komal 'dha' in raga Bhairavi. Right at the beginning, he startles the listener with his melodious *'na-na'*. On this *'na'* itself he moves from antara to antara and then returns to sthayi. The refrain *'na'* is the lifeline of the song and demonstrates his ability to play with words fulfilling the demands of the tune and rhythm. It is this that enables him to convert even a prosaic line into a song.

When I think of Sachin Dev Burman's music, the extraordinary, unpredictable nature of his compositions and his singing style, it reminds me of an enfant terrible, a mind that was to subvert, to radically change the texture of popular music with musical idioms, rhythm, total inflexions, much of which was weaned from his great repertoire of East Bengal folk music.

By now, age had begun to impact Sachin's health adversely. He somehow managed to continue working with his indomitable mental strength. Music was his life and he continued working tirelessly in pursuit of his muse. The result was the release of four films in 1973 with him as the music director—Hrishikesh Mukherjee's *Abhimaan*, Vijay Anand's *Chhupa Rustam*, Pramod Chakrabarty's *Jugnu*, and Rajendra Singh Bedi's *Phagun*.

Abhimaan is an extraordinary film with extraordinary songs and exceptional acting by Amitabh Bachchan and Jaya Bhaduri. The film's music had to be composed keeping in mind the fact that music plays the most important role in the story. It is the story of professional jealousy and tension between a husband and wife when the latter begins to overshadow the former as a singer. Since the husband and wife are competitors in the world of music, the songs had to be of a high standard in order to sustain the film and lead it to success. Sachin-karta accepted the challenge. Thus were born such wonderful songs as audiences would remember forever. Karta told Pulak Bandyopadhyay:

I can create four '*Ami chhinu eka*' in a week, but these songs will take four months. Remember, those who buy records range from seventeen to twenty-seven. Only if they like the song will they buy and take the record home. Then their parents will listen to it. This is how it becomes popular. (*Kathay Kathay Raat Hoye Jay*)

In *Abhimaan*, Sachin achieved a perfect blend of music that was both artistically and commercially successful, superimposing a popular tune on a classical base. Above all, the engrossing rapture created by the flute fills the mind with the soft glow of moonlight. Lata sang three songs, '*Nadiya kinare*', '*Ab to hai tumse*', and '*Piya bina piya bina*' for this film. All are unforgettable melodies. Who else but Lata, with her divine voice, could have been chosen to sing the songs which were meant to overshadow the hero's voice? Whatever it may be, whatever might have happened on screen, the melody of Kishore's solo '*Meet na mila re man ka*' was unforgettable. Then there are the duets—the effervescence of Lata and Rafi's '*Teri bindiya re*' and the poignancy of Kishore and Lata's memorable '*Tere mere milan ki*' based on the classic Tagore song '*Jodi tare nai chini go*'. Suffice it to say that even thirty-eight years later they remain the benchmark against which duets are measured. In one fell stroke, at an age when people retire from active life and rest on their laurels, Sachin Dev vanquished his competitors once again with his only ammunition—the classico-modern song.

More importantly, Sachin Dev Burman's continuous experimentation shattered existing systems and customs of the world of Hindi film music. We have already talked about how he breached the 'tune first, lyrics next' convention. Let me now turn to another custom that still held firm. It had been the custom in Hindi films that only one playback singer would sing for the hero in one particular film—Mukesh for Raj Kapoor, Kishore for Rajesh Khanna, Mohammad Rafi for Shammi Kapoor and Dilip Kumar. Sachin broke this convention right at the beginning. In many of his films he made the same artist lip-sync to the voice of several singers in the same film. He was never concerned with which playback singer's voice matches the hero's. He used to decide his singers (both male and female) depending upon the situation of the film and the mood of the song. In *Abhimaan*, Kishore and Rafi sang for Amitabh; likewise, in *Manzil*, Rafi and Manna Dey sang for Dev Anand. In *Sagina*, Dilip Kumar lip-synced for Kishore. Given the strong support the custom had in those days, Sachin's experiment was nothing short of miraculous.

Abhimaan fetched Sachin Dev his second Filmfare Award, almost twenty years after his first in *Taxi Driver*!

It is quite strange that S. D. Burman won only two Filmfare awards. He also got the National Award twice apart from the BFJA and other awards.

As far as winning awards go, neither father nor son got a fair deal. Though they delivered umpteen hits in the three decades that they made music, their contemporaries walked away with more awards than they did. One cannot judge their talent in terms of awards.

I have already said that both of them are inimitable geniuses with distinctive styles. Drawing upon the vast store of folk music forms and from the classical heritage, S. D. Burman produced music which is at once vibrant and unorthodox both in form and substance. Similarly, RD's music is a melting pot of all forms of music of the world, be it Indian classical, folk, modern or Asian, African, European and American. He drew inspiration from all of them and by innovation and improvisation made them his own.

However, it seems that the father was marginally luckier with awards than the son. S. D. Burman got National Awards and also the Padma Shri from the Government of India. Let us look at the award-chart of S. D. and R. D. Burman.

SD's chart looks as under:
- 1934: Gold Medal, All India Music Conference, Allahabad.
- 1958: Sangeet Natak Academy Award
- 1959: Asia Film Society Award
- 1964: Sant Haridas Award

National Film Awards

- 1969: Padma Shri
- 1970: National Film Award for Best Male Playback Singer: Aradhana: *Safal hogi teri aradhana.*
- 1972: National Film Award for Best Music Direction: *Zindagi Zindagi.*

Filmfare Award's

- 1954: Filmfare Best Music Director Award: *Taxi Driver*
- 1973: Filmfare Best Music Director Award: *Abhimaan*

BFJA Awards

- 1965: Best Music (Hindi section) *Teen Deviyan*
- 1966: Best Music (Hindi section): *Guide*
- 1966: Best Male Playback Singer (Hindi section): *Guide*
- 1969: Best Music (Hindi section): *Aradhana*
- 1973: Best Music (Hindi section): *Abhimaan*

I have already discussed how unfortunate R. D. Burman was with respect to awards. He was not even nominated for a National Award though the singers and lyricists of his films had won them. It is literally a shame that we failed to give due recognition to this genius of a composer when he was alive. The chart of awards for his films would reveal how intrigue deprived him of richly-deserved awards.

Filmfare Awards

- 1982: Filmfare Best Music Director Award: *Sanam Teri Kasam*
- 1983: Filmfare Best Music Director Award: *Masoom*
- 1994: Filmfare Best Music Director Award (posthumous): *1942—A Love Story*

BFJA Awards

- 1977: Best Music (Hindi section): *Hum Kisise Kam Nahin*
- 1989: Best Music (Hindi section): *Parinda*
- 1993: Lata Mangeshkar Award: Govt. of Madhya Pradesh

Continuing with the tradition of popular music for films starring Dev Anand, *Chhupa Rustam* had a string of peppy numbers. Ever since *Aradhana*, Kishore had not only become a constant in Sachin's plan of things, he was also the reigning king of playback in the world of Hindi films. Unsurprisingly then, it was Kishore all over in *Chhupa Rustam*, in his trademark fun avatar with songs like '*Dhire se jana khatiyan mein*' (echoing Sachin's Bengali hit '*Nishite jeiyo phulabane re bhramara*'), '*Hum chhupe rustam hain*', and the tap-beat-inspired duet with Asha '*Jo main hota ek tuta taaj*'. Another romantic song by Kishore and Lata was also highly popular: '*Bolo kya humko dogey*'. Then there was Asha rendering a vampish number, '*Janu main jale mera dil*'. Talking of which, I recall Bhishmadeb Chattopadhyay writing a memorial piece on Sachin:

> Some people came to me from Bombay, complaining against Sachin for taking recourse to light music in a few films. I told them that his experiments have borne fruit. I

explained that they had to remember that in a film, songs and music are dependent on the narrative, the course of events. If a music director uses a sarod or employs raga Jayjayanti for a cabaret dance, will the audience accept it? (*Gaaner Kagaz*)

Though Sachin was nearing his seventieth year, the youthful fire in his heart seemed to be burning brighter as is evident in the sprightly numbers he composed for *Jugnu* in the same year as *Abhimaan*. If the latter was vintage classical Sachin, steeped in ragas, Jugnu was a reminder of his versatility, an example of how good he was with modern, romantic and playful numbers. An example is the super-hit Lata—Kishore duet '*Gir gaya jhumka*' with its naughty playfulness. Just as in his own Bengali songs he uses the indeclinable—*ah, o-ho, a-ha, o-o-o*—to bring the requisite effect, here too he had Lata and Kishore articulate an odd phrase of longing and mischievousness, conveying the playful nature of the romantic relationship between the hero and the heroine. Another example is Lata's '*Jane kya pilaya tu ne bada maza aaya*'. Kishore's song '*Tera peechha na main chhodunga*' shows Sachin's in creating a efficiency chartbuster in keeping with the demands of the era. Hearing the bubbling effervescence of these songs it is difficult to imagine that the composer was nearing seventy years of age. It was as if Sachin-karta had just stepped into his youth.

Noticing the youthful vigour in his songs, Asha Bhonsle asked Sachin Dev:

'Dada, please tell me how is it that your songs are so full of youthful vigour even now?' Karta replied, 'Look Asha, songs are my life, my religion, everything I have. Just remember one thing. Whenever you sing a song, you must merge yourself with its meaning, with its character. You must become the character singing the song, that is, when you are singing a cabaret song, imagine you are Helen.' Asha started laughing loudly at these words. Sachin Dev continued, 'Do not laugh. Look, as long as you cannot cultivate the song in your heart, you will not be able to sing it properly.' (*Bhati Gang Baiya*)

In *Phagun*, Sachin paid a tribute to his memory of the celebration of Holi in Tripura in his younger days, when he would visit Agartala, compose songs for Holi, and walk through the streets in a group, singing with joy as if drunk with the colours of his beloved 'phagua'. He composed a brilliant Holi number '*Piya sang khelo holi*', intoxicatingly rendered by Lata Mangeshkar. With youthful exhilaration in their voices, Kishore and Asha sang '*Kab maney o dil ke mastane*'. And there was the exquisite Mira bhajan '*Mere to Giridhar Gopal*' in Lata's honey-oozing voice, which almost imparts life to the stone idol of Gopal.

Though increasingly frail, Sachin Dev did not deprive his fans of Puja songs that year. He came out with one record which had what turned out to be the last songs he sang, '*Se ki amar dushman dushman*' and '*Ki kari ami ki kari*'. But the voice gives away his illness. In place of the openness for which his voice is famed, one finds a touch of fatigue. The weariness is clear to anyone who listens to the songs. The hoarse voice that scaled E-major with such ease for so long now betrayed his breathlessness. And yet, '*Ki kari ami ki kari? Bol re Subal bol dada*' is a heart-rending classic. This wonderful song of separation was his last gift as a singer to us.

In 1974, three films were released under Sachin Dev Burman's music direction—K. S. Rao's *Prem Nagar*, Tapan Sinha's *Sagina* and Basu Chatterjee's *Us Paar*. The songs of *Prem Nagar* became a rage, particularly two Kishore Kumar numbers, *'Bye bye miss good night'*, which once again demonstrated how wonderfully youthful Sachin could be despite his illness and age, and the classic 'drunk' number *'Yeh lal rang kab mujhe'*, where Kishore effortlessly conveys the agony of an alcoholic. Another solo by Kishore *'Jaa jaa jaa mujhe na ab'* is somewhat similar to SD's Bengali song *'Na aamare sashi cheyo na'*. In *Sagina*, Sachin dipped into his repertoire of Bihari folk tunes which he had collected during his tour of Bihar and Uttar Pradesh after the All-India Music Conference of 1934. How lively it turned out in Kishore's *'Aag lagi hamari jhopariya mein hum gaaye malhar'*. Another Kishore song from the film still lives in one's memory. This song proves what an expert Sachin Dev was in creating a tune suited to a given situation. I am referring to *'Sala main to sahab ban gaya'*, Sagina Mahato's mocking self-appraisal after becoming a leader after one peg too many. Some say it is inspired from the Italian song 'Chella Lla' by Renato Carosone. Also, perhaps this is the first Hindi film in which Anup Ghoshal sang. The song was *'Chhote chhote sapne hamar'*. *Us Paar* boasts only five songs of which two deserve mention. Lata's solo *'Yeh jabse huyi jiya ki chori patang sa ude'* starts with a romantic dialogue between the hero and heroine. Moushumi Chatterjee's laughter creates an erotic ambience along with the flute which played a vital role. S. D. Burman would definitely have sung this song if he was not unwell. He had chosen Manna Dey to sing *'Piya maine kya kiya mujhe chhod ke jaiyo naa'*. Manna Dey took the challenge in right spirit and sang this song imitating the singing style of S. D. Burman. How far he succeeded is anybody's guess. But it is a marvellous song indeed!

The next year, 1975, saw two of his films being released, which were, in effect his swansong—*Chupke Chupke* and *Mili*, both directed by Hrishikesh Mukherjee. Well, what music he created in these films! With age, his compositions seemed to have reached an unsurpassable height. In an era that was becoming more and more inclined towards son Rahul's *'Dum maro dum'* and *'Mehbooba mehbooba'*, Sachin stayed true, with absolute devotion, to Indian tradition and culture in his music.

The songs from both these films became very popular. Lata had a field day with gems like *'Chupke chupke chal ri purvaiya'* and *'Ab ke sajan sawan mein'*, the former pensive, moody, conveying the lilt of the yesteryears that soothes one and makes one long for one's beloved; the latter naughty, playful, like the monsoon rain drenching one's courtyard while one waits for one's love to come home. And Sachin also brought together the two rivals Kishore Kumar and Mohammad Rafi in what is probably their most popular duet ever: *'Sa re ga ma, ma sa re ga'*. What a powerful song it is! This is what a duet should be like. Though popularly thought of as a fun song, given the situation in which it is sung, the seeds of classical music are hidden in it.

Mili had three immensely popular songs. Lata's *'Maine kaha phoolon se'* conveys the wonder of creation and it is no longer surprising that something as young at heart was composed by someone in his seventieth year. Kishore's *'Aaye tum yaad mujhe'* and *'Badi sooni sooni hai'* were in keeping with the serious and mature nature of the hero, played by Amitabh Bachchan, and remain two of the singer's finest songs. *'Badi sooni sooni hai'* is generally credited as Kumar Sachin Dev Burman's last composition.

Streaming through the windows of his Bandra home, 'Jet', the setting sun hovered on the horizon, on the verge of dipping into the sea for its ritual evening bath. Watching the sunset was a childhood fascination Sachin had nurtured even in the concrete jungle of Bombay. And now in the evening of his own life, the memories of those baul-bhatiyali days haunted him more and more—sailing on a boat over the Gomti, its waters sparkling in the midday sun, puffing on his hookah in the company of the boatmen, the strains of the bhatiyali harmonizing with the beat of the boat's oars in the calm water. The past beckoned him. He could hear the call of his innermost self. Success, fame, honour counted for little any more. Rabindranath expressed the innate truth in the following words: *'Jaha chai taha bhul kare chai/ Jaha pai taha chai na'* (Whatever I want, I want by mistake/ whatever I get I do not need). Increasingly, Sachin-karta's mind travelled to his country home. Those days of peaceful leisure, those days of playing the flute, beckoned him; the bend in the river, the palm and betel-nut orchards played hide-n-seek with him. The call of the past: 'Whither has gone the smell of mother earth, whither my mother's lap? Where is that smile, that play and the days?'

Right from 1930, it had been a difficult struggle for SD. He did not have a foothold and he made a name for himself in the musical world without the help of any godfather. Forty-five long years of disappointments, humiliations and rejections, of continuous hard work, incessant practice and constant experimentation with his art led to victory, the sweet smell of success and international fame. Sachin Dev Burman was truly a wizard of music. The magic of music oozed out of his storehouse of talent like P. C. Sarkar's 'Water of India', limitless, seemingly unending, casting a spell and mesmerizing the listener. Personally speaking, his music electrifies my body and mind. Listening to him I feel his presence. I feel as if some mendicant is playing on his ektara and singing *'Rangila, rangila, rangila re'* or a boatman on the Gomti is singing the heart-rending bhatiyali, *'Mere sajan hain us paar'*.

Sachin Dev Burman's greatness lay in his ability to strike a delicate balance between the classical and the popular. His songs are plain and simple, bereft of complexities and full of grace. His songs hum in one's mind. He was always mindful that his compositions had to be accessible to the common man. The world of film songs has never been a field for exhibiting one's expertise in classical music. Yet, without abandoning the traditions of Indian music, he simplified the rigours of classical music for the benefit of the common listener. At times he had to create classical tunes too. And he did so with such delicate grace as would make the listener hold his breath. To me it appears that even though Sachin Dev's target audience had always been the common folk, his songs never failed to attract the connoisseur. Such a synthesis is rare in music makers.

Sachin Dev suffered from a paralytic attack during the recording of the songs for *Mili*. Rahul took the responsibility of completing the recording. Even as Kishore sang '*Badi sooni sooni hai*', Sachin-karta was in deep coma. Karta lived for another five months. Meera and Rahul made every possible effort to revive him. Day in and day out they would tell him old anecdotes from their days in Tripura, remind him of close friends from Calcutta and narrate countless other stories from the past. But to no avail. It was only once that he is reported to have opened his eyes. The day East Bengal defeated Mohan Bagan in a league match by 5-0; Rahul shouted the news for the benefit of his father. A die hard supporter of East Bengal, an out-and-out Bangaal, the prince opened his eyes for one last time and never thereafter. On 31 October 1975, the Prince of Music, King of Kings, Kumar Bahadur Sachindra Chandra Dev Burman breathed his last.

Posthumous movies:

Hrishikesh Mukherjee's *Arjun*, Pramod Chakraborty's *Barud* and Samir Ganguly's *Deewangi* were released in 1976.

The Bengali version of the Hindi film *Aradhana* was released in 1976.

Din Dayal Sharma's *Tyaag* was released in 1977.

Epilogue

Reverence is a cascade of never-ending devotion. However, in present times, it surfaces as transient popular excitement in the birth and death centenary years of late celebrities. A flood of assurances and pledges comes from public and private bodies but after some time they die a natural death. The memory of the masses is short-lived. Pledges peep in from the grave again on the next birth or death anniversary. Truly, the present times are very cruel. Nothing is actuated without a selfish motive.

It is not true that the neglect and indifference of the royal family of Tripura and the narrow mentality of Tripura forced Sachin to stay in a different state. Even the present generation of Tripura has failed to appraise the musical talent of the great maestro. They ask without thinking, 'What is his contribution to his Tripura?' They forget that contribution is of two types—visible and invisible. Monetary contribution is visible whereas the contribution of creative talent is invisible. It is limitless, uncountable—the whole world gets enlightened by the radiation of creative faculty.

The unconcerned prince tolerated the disregard of Tripura in his lifetime, but the posthumous neglect of his contribution is heart-rending. I am not only a devotee of Rabindranath Tagore, but also a child to him. His talent, like the sun, illuminated all the lanes and by-lanes of literature. He was an extraordinary painter and a fascinating wizard of music. Others are mere pygmies before his multifarious talent. He is incomparable and single-handedly pushed Bengali literature and music ahead by a few hundred years. People worship him rightly.

There is no denying of the fact that such a person deserves a 'Rabindra Bhawan' in his honour. My objection lies elsewhere. In the year 1961, Acharya Suniti Kumar Chattopadhyay laid the foundation of 'Rabindra Bhawan' in some other place. In that case, what cultural inspiration provoked the Government of Tripura to build 'Rabindra Bhawan' in the premises of the house of Kumar Sachin Dev Burman? Had this shameful incident occurred in his lifetime, Rabindranath Tagore, would have objected to this because he never hesitated to bestow honour and respect upon deserving talent. The most painful fact is that the premises of the house of S. D. Burman were acquisitioned by Tripura government when he was alive and 'Rabindra Bhawan' was also inaugurated during his lifetime even when there was no dearth of land in Tripura, particularly at Agartala, the capital town.

For lack of proper conservation, so many memorable institutions and talents have been lost in the abyss of oblivion. The responsibility of conservation does not lie only with the government; it is a part of the duty of vigilant people. Nobody raised their voice for the preservation of Sachin-karta's house as a memorial. A separate 'Sachindra Bhawan' did not come up. The Tripura government, in order to ventilate its cultural urge, made an announcement that the Government Music College would be named 'Sachin Dev Burman Music College'. Let me tell you the history of the birth of this music college. Sangeetacharya Pulin Thakur aka Pulin Dev Burman established this college bit by bit using his savings, fighting hand to mouth with poverty. I have already discussed the relationship between the two. Pulin Thakur was not only a relative of Sachin-karta; he was his soul's kith and kin. Whenever Sachin visited Agartala, he made it a point to spend hours with Pulin Thakur discussing the nuances of classical music. Pulin Thakur held the degree of Sangeet Bisharad from Lucknow's Bhatkhande Music Institute University. He got the nomination of this university for this college. There was a lack of space for the institution. The classes were held in a room of Umakanta Academy in the evening. Pulin Thakur was the only teacher. Even in that precarious condition, his students Rabi Nag and Aswin Dutt (tabla player) were crowned with the degree of Sangeet Bisharad. This was not a mean achievement.

At present, the music college is in a deadlock. It does not have many students and the teachers are of very ordinary calibre. I don't know what glorious achievement it would be to name a defunct institution in the name of S. D. Burman! The Tripura government first disgraced Rabindranath Tagore by establishing 'Rabindra Bhawan' at the premises of S. D. Burman's house, the person who had the rightful claim over it as his memorial. They made the same mistake with the music college. Sachin-karta would have died of shame if he was alive. He could not have shown his face to Pulin Thakur for this shameless act.

Tripura is known by SD's name. What a shame that we have driven him out of his own house! In fact, Sachin Dev Burman is a refugee in reality. After the Partition, he lost the palace in Comilla's Chartha. This house was used as a military godown by Pakistan for some years. After that, it became a centre of animal husbandry. As if that was not enough, at present it is Bangladesh government's poultry farm house. The palace of Sachin-karta has lost its beautiful ambience. The original house is not visible any more. It is completely hidden by the new building erected in front of it. The three big tanks are being used for pisciculture. It is a matter of regret that Bengalis who boast of Bengali culture have failed to realize the importance of the preservation of this house. The West Bengal or Tripura governments did not request the Government of Bangladesh to preserve this house as a memorial of Sachin-karta. The Bangladesh government, too, cannot avoid its responsibility as a bearer and upholder of Bengali culture.

Sachin Dev Burman established a private music school named 'Suramandir' at 1A, Basanta Roy Road, Calcutta in the year 1936. Music lovers would remain ever grateful to the Government of West Bengal if it takes over the house of S. D. Burman at South End Park, Calcutta to restore the immortal memories of the great maestro. The houses at 1A, Basanta Roy Road and at South End Park solicit governmental interference for preservation.

However, the story of Sachin's life will remain incomplete if we do not acknowledge the contributions of Meera Dev Burman to Sachin-karta's life. She was not only the wife of a celebrated musician but also witnessed his rise and fall, she was his companion in happiness and sorrow, a connoisseur of music and above all a lyricist-friend. She was an expert in music and dance. She had learnt classical music from Bhishmadev Chattopadhyay, thumri and kirtan from Sri Dhirendra Chandra Mitra and Rabindra Sangeet from Sri Anadi Dastidar. Srimati Ameeta Sen of Santiniketan, mother of Nobel laureate Amartya Sen, gave Meera lessons in dance. In the year 1944, at the wishes of her husband, she took instructions of classical music from Ustad Fayyaz Khan after coming to Bombay. It was music which tied them together to love and marriage. She had learnt music before her marriage from Sachin-karta. Meera felt an amorous attraction towards Sachin even before her acquaintance with him. A glimpse of it can be highlighted from a letter of Ameeta Sen. After the death of Sachin-karta and Rahul, she wrote a letter to depressed Meera; I quote a part of it:

Beloved Meera,

Even today you are that very little Meera to me. I still vividly remember your beautiful, vibrant face. You all stayed at Racking Street, Waari, Dacca and we were in Larmini Street. You used to come running to me to learn dance in the morning and evening. After some time, people started applauding your dance performances. You used to get invitations from so many institutions. In the mean time, I went abroad with my husband. I remember the day I returned—you came running to me. In an excited voice you told me, 'Aunty, do you know—one Sachin Dev Burman is singing superbly?' I can't forget that face of yours even today, madly and deeply in love with music. After that you couldn't be enchained. You used to buy whatever records of Sachin Dev Burman come out in the market and forgetting everything, even food and bath, you listened to his songs. Once you invited Sachin Dev Burman to your house. That was enough! The forceful love of Sri Radhika Meera drew Krishna Sachin Dev Burman nearer to her. There was so much dispute about your marriage, but ultimately you won—your turbulent love won unmistakably. Meera, your love episode will entail the birth of poetics...

This letter of Smt Ameeta Sen proves beyond doubt that Sachin and Meera had deep, unyielding love for each other.

Talent has a devastating character. Keen talent overshadows talents with probabilities. In the grip of Rabindranath Tagore's all-pervading talent, other talents of the Tagore family got eclipsed and could not flourish the way they should have. It was fortunate that Rahul Dev Burman was saved from this disaster as he cut a path of music very different from his father's for himself. Even then he couldn't escape the influence of his father. Both of them are instances of incomparable talent.

Although the talent of her husband and son had overshadowed Meera's talent, yet connoisseurs of music admit in no uncertain terms that she was a real genius. Otherwise, how could she have participated on invitation in the Allahabad Music Conference in 1937? She sang a few songs under the baton of S. D. Burman—three solos and five duets with SD. She couldn't find time to practise music. She was extremely busy as a housewife. In the words of Salil Ghosh:

> Once I asked Sachin da, 'Doesn't boudi sing? I want to organize a solo performance of hers.' Sachin da smiled and replied, 'Where does Meera get the time for the pursuit of music? She spends all her time keeping my income tax account.' This was absolutely true. It was only because of Meera Devi that Sachin da could forget everything else in the pursuit of music for thirty long years, with absolute attention and without any distractions. Meera Devi took over all his other responsibilities and performed her duties to perfection. Ever smiling and deeply immersed in music, Meera Devi was also an extraordinary character with varied talents.

Now let us listen to Sachin Dev Burman:

> Meera not only writes lyrics, she is also a competent music composer. I have composed the tune of many of my popular songs with her help and in her company. The mukhdas of many of my popular songs have been composed by Meera. It often happened that I would compose a tune based on which Meera would write a song in Bengali matching the

metre and prosody of my tune, just in order to explain it to the lyricist of the Hindi songs, who would then write the song in Hindi [...] HMV has recorded six songs [In fact, by 1973, the number was eighteen] written by her which I have sung. Meera's contribution to my successful career in music is undeniable. It is her help, inspiration, encouragement and selflessness which laid the foundation of my success as a music director and singer. I have always considered myself extremely fortunate in having a wife like Meera.

Even if we don't remember Meera Dev Burman for her music, her lyrics are immortal. As she was a natural poet; the lyrics she penned bore her artistic workmanship, romantic thought, glorious blending of words, melancholy of a painful heart, similes and pictograms which rouse one's curiosity to know why she confined herself to writing lyrics. Why didn't she write poetry independent of lyrics? She was equally good at writing rhymed and unrhymed verses. All her lyrics were written in Bengali, particularly the language of East Bengal.

Meera Dev Burman was very sensitive, moved by love alone. Sachin's songs, even before they had met, had given birth to an amorous attraction, acquaintance led to attachment and attachment to marriage. They were an inseparable couple. In the introduction to *Sargamer Nikhad*, Salil Ghosh specifically mentioned them as an 'ideal couple'. Some people, taking advantage of the inadvertence of the readers, are ever-ready to assassinate the characters of celebrities and all the negative things that have been written about the relationship of Sachin and Meera are a result of a misreading of the same.

All of us look at things from our own perspective. There was no bone of contention between Sachin and Rahul as such but certain writers tried to depict them as contenders with feelings of mutual hostility for the sake of cheap publicity.

Both Sachin and Rahul respected each other's work. It is difficult to find an instance of a son following in the footsteps of an illustrious father into fame! However, there are positive and negative aspects of being the son of a famous father. After being in his father's shadow for several years and having ghost-composed some of the senior Burman's popular compositions in the late fifties and sixties, junior Burman definitely went on to prove his mettle. But how can you stop people from speaking ill of them? Rahul's jealous contemporaries spread the rumour that the soundtrack of *Amar Prem* was his father's handiwork.

It was not as if there were no ego clashes or differences of opinion between the father and son, but his father was Pancham's idol. SD groomed him as a composer and encouraged him to learn to play different instruments. Rahul saw how his father carved out his own gharana slowly but gradually and established it resolutely.

Like father, like son. The way Sachin Dev Burman gave Hindi and Bengali music his own stamp by mixing folk song with modern and classical music; Rahul also devised his own style and went on to be the first to bring about a fusion of Western rock and jazz with Indian classical music. He Indianized Western, African and Arabian music.

There are misconceptions among people that RD's moving away from S. D. Burman's team created a rift between father and son. This is utterly untrue. There are indeed some stories about the passing of the baton of music direction from father to son. Dev Anand was in a fix on how to drop Dada Burman who had come to symbolize the Navketan banner. He shrewdly suggested to him that he may compose the traditional tunes for *Hare Rama*

Hare Krishna leaving his son to do the modern songs. S. D. Burman refused to go along with Dev Anand's idea. 'Never mix our musical identities,' S. D. Burman told Dev Anand, 'Leave *Hare Rama Hare Krishna* to be wholly scored by Pancham. I have trained my son to do both traditional and modern music.' He further said emphatically, 'No way, let Pancham do the film all by himself. Pancham is now a full-fledged music director, Dev. My coming together with him, for the first time in our careers, will help neither me nor him.'

Do these comments reveal mutual rivalry between father and son? There might have been a competition between them but it was fair enough.

Yes, S. D. Burman was terribly upset and hurt after listening to his son's music in *Hare Rama Hare Krishna*. He was not hurt because he had to pave the way for his son when Dev Anand, in spite of their long association, ignored him and appointed RD as music director in his place. He was dismayed when he heard the recording of the song *'Dum maro dum'* in the studio. He was upset; he thought his son who carried his flag, whom he had taught music from childhood, had forsaken him. Was it a repudiation of inherited culture? Was it an attempt to disown his father? Rahul saw his father slowly walking out of the studio with his head bowed down. It looked as if a defeated king was retreating from battle.

This is one of the passing phases of life. Rahul's parents still remained justifiably proud of him. 'Tell me,' said his mother Meera, 'Is there a composer in our films today who could have done the classy music of *Amar Prem* along with the jazzy music of *Hare Rama Hare Krishna?'*

Whether people like it or not, creative achievements are always remembered even after the death of the creator. As long as people do not understand that talent is far above and cannot be equated with personal character; character-assassination will continue.

In those days, people who embraced music as a livelihood were considered outcastes in society. Gentlemen and ladies belonging to middle and high classes who recorded music with record companies used to write 'amateur' within brackets beside their names, suggesting that no money had been passed in the deal. Being a prince, SD had shown the courage to accept music as livelihood breaking all barriers, customs and norms of royal aristocracy. It was, in a word, 'revolutionary'. He had to sacrifice and sever all ties with the royal family of Tripura to which he belonged. Where an ordinary person was scared of his reputation to take up music as livelihood, S. D. had not only taken to music but also propagated and brought to light the disdained, unheard folk music of the then East Bengal and Tripura in the circumference of urban society. The songs of boatmen, murshids, darbeshs, minstrels and kirtanias which are considered the songs of low-caste, poor people became the rage of the day.

S. D. Burman proved that age is no impediment to creativity. If we are to dwell on his versatility, we would find an endless patchwork of ideas on the canvas. S. D. Burman composed music for eighty-nine Hindi movies. His record of highest average of hit songs (movie-wise) remains unbroken. He was the only great composer who remained in demand till the end of his life, unlike his contemporaries who gradually faded away. His greatest gift lay in the fact that he could be equally jazzy and trendy in a dhoti. His grip on Indian folklore, his sound classical base, his capacity to absorb from the scene around him made him the greatest all-rounder in Indian film music.

S. D. Burman left for his heavenly abode on 31 October, 1975 after suffering a paralytic stroke a few months earlier. There was a time when the royal family of Tripura criticized him for making a living out of music as it brought down the image of royalty. Sachin Dev Burman was hurt and slowly he snapped his ties with Tripura. Today the Tripura royal family is known by his name.

Even if you get recognition from the whole world as a versatile talent, it does not fetch full satisfaction unless it comes from the soil of your own—the place of your birth. Tripura disowned him, but Tripura remained in his blood. S. D. Burman's comments deserve close attention. 'I am a son of the soil of that Tripura. Perhaps that is why I have spent my entire life singing and only singing. Music is my muse.'

Lastly, I repeat what he has said in the concluding part of his autobiography, *Sargamer Nikhad*:

'My only identity is that I am the child of mother Bengal; my music is the wealth of all Indians—my tune is a symbol of India. '

Then again he concluded, 'In the sunset of my life, I don't want anything—anymore—I only want to remain as lees in the seventh musical note.'

Appendix I
Chronology of Life

1906	1 October, born at Comilla, Tripura. Father—Nabadwip Chandra Dev Burman, son of Maharaja of Tripura, Ishan Chandra Manikya. Mother—Princess of Manipur, Nirupama Devi. Youngest of five brothers and four sisters.
1909	After a long gap of forty years, contact with Tripura was re-established. Father joins as minister in the royal ministry of Tripura at the invitation of King Birendra Kishore Manikya; Sachin Dev starts visiting Agartala regularly.
1911-12	Schooling at Kumar Boarding, Agartala. Teachers over-indulge princes. Nabadwip noticed it and took Sachin back to Comilla.
1913	Admittance in Yusuf School, Comilla.
1915	Admittance in Class V in Comilla District School; sang in a school function for the first time on the occasion of Saraswati puja. Headmaster wrote a letter of appreciation to Nabadwip Chandra.
1920	Passed Matriculation from the same school. Wanted to study in Calcutta. Father refused. Blessing in disguise.
1922	Passed Intermediate of Arts from Victoria College, Comilla. 1924 Passed Bachelor of Arts; Nabadwip Chandra accompanied him to Calcutta and got him admitted in M.A. (English), Calcutta University. Stayed in Tripura Palace, Ballygunj, Calcutta.
1925	Started training in music under Krishna Chandra Dey giving

	up studies. Later started training under Krishna Chandra's guru, Badal Khan, with his permission. For some time trained under Bhishmadeb Chattopadhyay. Training continued.
1926	Father Nabadwip Chandra got him admitted to Law College, Calcutta. After a few months left studies altogether and got immersed full time in learning music.
1927	First radio performance at the Indian Broadcasting Company, Calcutta. Sang East Bengal folk songs.
1928-30	All the artist-friends of Comilla came to Calcutta in pursuit of livelihood. *Sursagar* Himanghu Dutta, lyricist Ajay Bhattacharya and film director Sushil Mazumder were famous among them. S. D. Burman was bent on specialization.
1931	Death of father. King of Tripura offered him the charge of education department, but he declined. Shifted from Tripura palace to a one-room tenement of Palit Street.
1932	Failed in audition test by H.M.V. First gramophone recording from Chandi Charan Saha's Hindustan Musical products and this opened the gates of Chandi Babu's fortune. It became a major success story. The songs were 'Dakle kokil roj bihane' and 'E pathe aj esho priya'.
1933	Disappointment soon after major success. Sang for the first time for the film *Yahudi ki Ladki* which had music by Pankaj Mallick. But the song was rejected by the director and re-recorded by Pahari Sanyal. Two records of Bengali songs were released.
1934	Participation on invitation to All-India Music Conference organized by Allahabad University. Awarded Gold medal. Four records were released boasting eight songs. All were great hits.
1935	First film song in Tinkari Chakrabarti's *Sanjher Pradip*; acting in Dhiren Ganguli's *Bidrohi*, also in Madhu Bose's *Selima*. First music direction in *Sudurer Priya*; Attended Bengal Music Conference in Calcutta and presented thumris; conference inaugurated by Rabindranath Tagore with Maharaja Bir Bikram Manikya of Tripura as the chief guest; Fayyaz Khan also performed. Five records were released of which 'Nishithe jaiyo phula bane' was a masterpiece.

1936	Shifted to Basanta Roy Road; established music school 'Suramandir'. Recorded three albums; started experimenting and composing music in own style.
1937	Directed music jointly with Bhishmadeb Chattopadhyay in Sukumar Dasgupta's *Rajgi*; sang a few a songs himself with his own music; also played a role in it. Recorded five albums of which two were in Hindi.
1938	10 February—married Meera Dhar, a singer herself and granddaughter of the late Kamalnath Dasgupta, a retired judge; Meera was his student; shifted to 10 Hindustan Road. Three records were released.
1939	Only son Rahul was born on 27 June; the book *Surer Likhan* was published containing twenty-five of his songs with notations; membership of Progressive Writers Association (P. W. A); became president of its folk music branch; composed music for *Jakher Dhan* with Dhiren Das as assistant. Released three Bengali albums.
1940	Joint music direction with Hariprasanna Das for *Rajkumarer Nirbasan* and with Bhishmadeb Chattopadhyay for *Amargeeti*. Two records were released.
1941	Music direction for Sushil Majumdar's *Pratishod*. Five records were released of which '*Padmar dhew re*' is very famous. Sang in Hindi movie '*Tajmahal*'.
1942	Direction of music in Jyotish Banerjee's *Milan*, Sushil Majumdar's *Abhayer Biye*, Ajay Bhattacharya's *Ashok*; declined invitation from Chandulal Shah, owner of Ranjit Studio, to go to Bombay. Released four records.
1943	Performance in Bengal Music Conference, Calcutta, presided over by Tripura Maharaja Bir Bikram Manikya. Music direction *Jajsaheber Natni*. Released three records.
1944	Music direction in Hari Bhanja's *Matir Ghar,* Ajoy Bhattacharya's *Chhadmabeshi* and Chhabi Biswas's *Pratikar*; left for Bombay on invitation from Filmistan by its owners Chandulal Shah and Shashadhar Mukherjee. Released three records before leaving Calcutta.
1945	Jyotish Banerjee's *Kalankini* under his music direction was

	released. Three records were released of which one was in Hindi.
1946	Bengali film *Matrihara* with his music was released; in Bombay, the first Hindi film *Shikari* under his music direction was released with Ashok Kumar in the lead role singing the first Hindi song by him; Filmistan's *Eight Days* was released with the first Hindi song in Sachin's voice, *Ummeed bhara panchhi*, under his music direction. Five records were released of which two songs were duets with Meera Dev Burman. The records also boasted two solos of Meera.
1947	Three Hindi films were released—*Do Bhai, Chittor Vijay* and *Dil Ki Rani*. 'Mera sundar sapna beet gaya' (*Do Bhai*) became a super hit and made a star of Geeta Roy (Later Dutta). Released four non-film (except one) Hindi records. All were popular numbers. HMV's management persuaded him to join them and he responded politely to their request. Introduced the concept of 'music first, words next' in Hindi cinema.
1948	Only one film *Vidya* with his music was released. It boasts ten songs. Gouri Prasanna Majumder penned lyrics for S. D. Burman for the first time. Seven records included three in Hindi comprising five songs, in one of which he sang a duet with Meera Dev Burman (the reverse side of this album contained Meera's solo '*Dali dali phul*'). Acquaintance with Dev Anand and his brothers.
1949	Two films *Kamal* and *Shabnam* were released. Major success attained with B. Mitra's *Shabnam* but he was not happy and wanted to return to Calcutta. Ashok Kumar persuaded him to direct the music for his film *Mashal* before leaving Bombay. Three records were released.
1950	At last fortune smiled on him. Three films—*Afsar, Mashal* and *Pyaar* were released. With the super success of *Mashal* the demand for SD soared. He had to abandon the idea of returning to Calcutta. All the songs of *Mashal* became big hits. Manna Dey's rendition of '*Upar gagan vishal*' set new standards for success in Hindi film music. Manna Dey admitted: 'my successful march began with that song'. This film established

Manna Dey as a singer.
Samar, the Bengali version of Hindi film *Mashal* was also released this year. Two records of his Bengali songs were released.

1951 Six films—*Buzdil, Ek Nazar, Naujawan, Bahaar, Sazaa* and *Baazi* were released. *Baazi* marked the beginning of one of Hindi cinema's most celebrated lyricist-music director combinations. An unknown entity, Sahir Ludhianvi, was brought in by S. D. Burman as lyricist for *Baazi*. In *Baazi*, SD showed his extraordinary creativity by turning Sahir's ghazal *'Tadbeer se bigdi hui taqdeer bana le'* into a fast-paced, seductive number. It became a raging hit. Geeta Roy listed this song as one of her ten favourite songs from those she'd sung till 1957. The other big hits *'Saiyyan dil mein ana re'*, *'Qusoor aap ka huzoor aap ka'* (*Bahar*), *'Jhan jhan payal baje'*, *'Rote rote guzar gayi raat re'* (*Buzdil*), *'Mujhe preet nagariya jana hai'* (*Ek Nazar*), *'Thandi hawayein lehra ke aaye'* (*Naujawan*) and *'Tum na jane kis jahan mein kho gaye'* (*Sazaa*) gave a glimpse of Sachin's equally strong hold on melody.

Only one record of Bengali songs was released.

1952 *Jaal* and *Lal Kunwar* were released this year. Hemant Kumar became famous overnight in the world of Hindi film with his song in *Jaal*—*'Sun ja dil ki dastaan'*. *Jaal* was a milestone in the careers of SD, Guru Dutt, Dev Anand and lyricist Sahir. The songs *'Raja jani laga mohe nayana ka baan re'* sung by Samsad Begum and Suraiya's *'Tum jo mile arzu ke dil'* in the film *Lal Kunwar* won the heart of millons.

During 1952-55 Sachin did not record any Bengali song.

1953 Composed music for *Babla, Arman, Jeevan Jyoti* and *Shahenshah*. The year was a moderate one.

1954 In a year when he came up with rather nondescript scores for films like *Angaare, Chalis Baba Ek Chor* and *Radha Krishna*, it was again a Navketan film, *Taxi Driver*, which brought Sachin glory, the Filmfare award for best music director. Talat's song *'Jaayein toh jaayein kahan'*, Lata's *'Dil se milaake dil pyaar kijiye'* are masterpieces.

1955	Five films—*Devdas, House No. 44, Munimji, Mad Bhare Nayan* and *Society* were released. The first three films saw the composer in great form with compositions ranging from Vaishnava kirtans to those based on Latin American beats.
1956	Only one film *Funtoosh* was released. Sachin gave Kishore another hit with *'Dukhi man mere sun mera kehna'*. The tune of another song *'Aye meri topi palat ke aa'* was lifted from son Rahul's compositions. Sachin came out with a Bengali record during the pujas after a gap of four years. The famous songs are *'Mano dilo na bondhu'* (Hindi version—*'Jaane kya tune kahi' Pyaasa* (1957) and *'Tumi ar nei she tumi'*.
1957	Four movies were released. Except I. S. Johar's *Miss India*, the music of all other three films, such as Vijay Anand's *Nau Do Gyarah*, Subodh Mukherjee's *Paying Guest* and Guru Dutt's *Pyaasa* dramatically different from each other became instant hits. The group of Sachin Dev, Kishore Kumar, Asha Bhonsle and Majrooh Sultanpuri reached the pinnacle of popularity. One record of Bengali songs was released.
1958	Received Sangeet Natak Academy Award. Five movies, *Chalti Ka Naam Gaadi, Lajwanti, Kala Pani, Sitaron Se Aage, Solva Saal* were released. Sachin revolutionized the world of Hindi songs with compositions as varied as those in *Chalti Ka Naam Gaadi* and *Kala Pani*, an intimate blend of Western music and Bengali folk music. Invisible hands of Rahul Dev Burman in his work. One record of Bengali songs was released.
1959	Shakti Samanta's *Insaan Jaag Utha*, Guru Dutt's *Kagaz Ke Phool* and Bimal Roy's *Sujata* were released. Asiad Film Award for *Pyaasa*. Sang the famous song *'Sun meray bandhu re'* in *Sujata*. One record of Hindi film songs was released during Durga Puja.
1960	Directed music in seven films including Mohan Saigal's *Apna Haath Jagannath*, Raj Khosla's *Bombai Ka Babu*, Vijay Anand's *Kala Bazaar*; first heart attack. One record of Bengali songs was released.
1961	Not much work owing to illness. A blank year. But his love

	for Calcutta knew no lit-up despite his illness. Released one record of Bengali songs. Except Dev Anand, all the directors and producers deserted him.
1962	Three films—*Baat Ek Raat Ki*, *Dr Vidya*, and *Naughty Boy* not of much importance were released. Selected as Jury member at the International Film Competition in Helsinki, Finland.
1963	Sachin returned to top form with three big hits which are still considered amongst the finest musicals ever in the history of Hindi films: *Bandini* directed by Bimal Roy, R. K. Rakhan's *Meri Surat Teri Aankhen* and Vijay Anand's *Tere Ghar Ke Samne*.
1964	Three movies, *Benazir*, *Kaise Kahun* and *Ziddi* were released. Awarded *Sant Haridas* Award by Surashinger Samsad for '*Kaise Kahun*'.
	Sachin did not record any Bengali song in 1964.
1965	*Guide* directed by Vijay Anand and *Teen Deviyan* directed by Amarjit were released. A new horizon opened for Hindi film music with the songs of these films. Adjudged the best music director by BFJA (Bengal Film Journalists' Association) for *Teen Deviyan*. Sang two background songs in *Guide*: '*Wahan kaun hai tera musafir*' and '*Megh de, pani de*'. *Teen Deviyan* is a glaring example of a most ordinary film becoming a box office hit only by virtue of its music.
	Sachin recorded two Bengali albums.
1966	Illness prevented him from taking up any films. He did not record any Bengali songs. He picked up his pen. On 8 September 1966, film journal *Cine Advance* published his article 'The role and indispensability of music in Indian films'.
	BFJA awards for best music and best playback singer in *Guide*.
1967	Only one film Vijay Anand's *Jewel Thief* to his credit. Kishore Kumar, Lata and Asha kept the audience enchanted. The hit songs are: '*Yeh did na hote bechara*', '*Aasman ke neeche*', '*Raat akeli hai*', '*Rulake gaya sapna mere*' etc.
	Sang two Bengali songs during Durga Puja.
1968	No Hindi films to his name due to frail health. Recorded two Bengali albums. With age his voice was becoming more and more youthful.

1969	Three films were released—Shakti Samanta's *Aradhana*, Dulal Guha's *Jyoti* and O. P. Ralhan's *Talash*. Trailing behind Mohammad Rafi for long, Kishore Kumar leaped ahead with his chartbusters in *Aradhana*. Sachin was awarded National Film Award for best male playback singer for his passionate background song—'*Safal hogi teri aradhana*'. In *Talash*, the most remarkable song is Manna Dey's '*Tere naina talaash kaer jise*' in raga Misra Khambaj. Awarded Padma Shree by Government of India. Sachin sang three Hindi and four Bengali songs. Adjudged best music director by BFJA for *Aradhana*.
1970	Ramesh Saigal's *Ishq Par Zor Nahin* and Dev Anand's *Prem Pujari* were released. Yet another brilliant score in *Prem Pujari*. Started writing *Sargamer Nikhad*, his autobiography, serially in *Desh*, a Bengali magazine published from Calcutta. Sang four Bengali songs for Durga Puja.
1971	Four films, *Gambler* directed by Amarjit, Pramod Chakraborty's *Naya Zamana*, Samir Ganguly's *Sharmilee* and *Tere Mere Sapne* by Vijay Anand were released. Composed music for a Bengali film *Chaitali* after twenty-five years. Sang two Bengali songs and one Hindi during the puja.
1972	Directed music in Shakti Samanta's *Anurag*, Atmaram's *Yeh Gulistan Hamara* and Tapan Sinha's *Zindagi Zindagi*; National Award as Best Music Director for *Zindagi Zindagi* in which he sang two songs. Released one record of Bengali songs.
1973	Filmfare Award for the second time for *Abhimaan*. *Chhupa Rustam*, *Jugnu*, *Phagun* were also released. BFJA award for *Abhimaan*. Released one record of Bengali songs.
1974	*Prem Nagar*, *Us Paar* and Tapan Sinha's *Sagina* were released. The songs of *Prem Nagar* became a rage.
1975	Directed music in Hrishikesh Mukherjee's *Chupke Chupke* and *Mili*; *Mili*'s music was completed by son Rahul after SD's death in Bombay on 31 October, at the age of sixty-nine.
1976	Posthumously released films *Arjun Pandit*, *Barood*, *Deewangi*,

Tyaag; for *Deewangi* he composed the music for only one song 'Chal sapno ke shahar mein tujhe le jata hun'. Bengali version of Hindi movie *Aradhana* released.

In his musical career spanning about forty-three years, S. D. Burman composed music for nineteen Bengali and eighty-nine Hindi films. Two other films—*Saaz* in Hindi and *Gauri* in Bengali—for which he directed music were never released. He recorded approximately two hundred Bengali and Hindi modern songs, folk songs and bhajans. In this, records for his Bengali songs number one hundred and twenty-seven solos and five with wife Meera Devi; seventeen songs were recorded in tunes composed by others.

Appendix II
List of Songs of S. D. Burman as Singer

Year	First Line	Lyrics by	Record
1932	Dakle kokil roj bihane	Hemendra Kumar Ray	Hindustan Records H-11
	Ei pathe aaj esho priyo	Shailen Ray	
1933	Bondhu elo modhu rate	Ajay Bhattacharya	Hindustan Records H-21
	Tumi to bondhu jaano	Ajay Bhattacharya (Himangshu Dutta)	-do-
	O kalo megh bolte paro	Hemendra Kumar Ray	H-51
	Ei kananer phool niye	Hemendra Kumar Ray	-do-
1934	Sapan na bhange jadi	Ajay Bhattacharya	H-120
	Aaji rate ke	Ajay Bhattacharya	-do-
	Jadi dakhina paban	Ajay Bhattacharya (Himangshu Dutta)	H-137
	Alo-chhaya dola	Ajay Bhattacharya	-do-
	Jhulaney jhulichhe shyamaray	Jatindra Mohan Bagchi	H-179
	Raibo na aar ujan	Jatindra Mohan Bagchi	-do-

List of Songs of S. D. Burman as Singer ♪ 227

	Song	Lyricist	Record No.
	Praner prabhu rahe prane	Ajay Bhattacharya	H-198
	Manaduhkhe marire	Unknown	-do-
1935	Kanthe tomar dulbe	Ajay Bhattacharya	H-224
	Ei mohua bane	Ajay Bhattacharya	-do-
	Ore sujan naiya (Film *Sanjher Pradip*)	Ajay Bhattacharya	H-266
	Nishithe jaio	Jasimuddin	H-293
	Sapan dekhechhe girirani	Ajay Bhattacharya	-do-
	Biday dao go more	Ajay Bhattacharya	
	Tumi ni amaar bandhu (Film *Sudurer Priya*)	Ajay Bhattacharya	H-305
	Bandhu banshi dao mor	Unknown	-do-
1936	Balo balo balo bondhu Jaagar saathi go mama	Ajay Bhattacharya	H-335
	Mama mandire ele ke	Ajay Bhattacharya	-do-
	Natun phagun jabe	Ajay Bhattacharya (Himangshu Dutta)	H-412
	Tomari sathe sure	Binay Mukhopadhyay	-do-
	Paradeshe keno go	Binay Mukhopadhyay	H-525
1937	Ke jabi chal Brindabane	Ajay Bhattacharya	Hindustan Records H-11451
	Phuler bone thako bhramer	Ajay Bhattacharya	
	Nayan more darasa bhikhari	—	H-11461
	Pritme huye badnaam	—	
	Jhan jhan jhan jhan manjeer	Ajay Bhattacharya	H-11494
	Pohalo raati jagiya	Ajay Bhattacharya	H-11548
	Ab main sharan tumhari	—	

Year	Song	Lyricist	Ref
	Mere pritam pyare	—	
	Gaurarup dekhiya hoyechhi	Kanailal Shil (Mukundalal De)	H-11553
	Pinjrar pakhir mato	Unknown	
1938	Tumi je chhile mor	Ajay Bhattacharya	H-614
	Jago mama saheli go	-do-	
	Tumi je giyachho	-do-	
	Prem jamunari pare	-do-	H-658
	Ore bandhure maner katha	-do-	
	Saaje nawal kishore (Film *Rajgi*)	-do-	H-558
1939	Champak jago jago	Ajay Bhattacharya	H-706
	Kandibona phagun gele	-do-	
	Megh jhore jay	-do-	
	Chhilo madhabi raati go	-do-	H-730
	Bujhi amaar pran jay	Kanailal Shil (collected by)	H-750
	Amaar Milan malati	Ajay Bhattacharya	
1940	Premer samadhi teere (Film *Tajmahal*)	Shailen Ray (Himangshu Dutta)	H-831
	Ami chhinu eka	Ajay Bhattacharya	
	Kuhu kuhu kuhu kuhu koelia	Kazi Nazrul Islam (Kazi Nazrul Islam)	H-857
	Meghla nishi bhore	-do-	
1941	Ore abodh neye (Film *Pratishodh*)	Premendra Mitra	H-930
	Ki maya laglo chokhe	–do–	
	Banshariyare, kothay shikhechho (Film *Rajkumarer Nirbasan*)	Ajay Bhattacharya	H-946
	Amaar ki holo go	Collected	H-889
	Priyo aajo nay, aajo nay	Ajay Bhattacharya (Shailen Dasgupta)	

List of Songs of S. D. Burman as Singer ♪ 229

	Godhulir chhayapathe	–do–	H-922
	Prem ko pyaro nishano (From *Premer Samadhi Teere*)	Munsi Zakir Hussain	
	Chalo chalo prem ki saathi	-do-	H-969
	Chokh gelo, chokh gelo (Film *Nandini*)	Kazi Nazrul Islam (Kazi Nazrul Islam)	
	Padmar dheu re	-do-	
1942	Malaya chalo dheere	Shishir Sen	H-11997
	Kokilare geyona gaan	Shailen Ray	
	Bideshire udasire phire (Film *Epar Opar*)	Ajay Bhattacharya	
	Ke jeno kandichhe akash (Film *Nari*)	Pranab Ray (Rai Chand Boral)	H-11998
	Dhire se jana bagiyan	—	
	Kaun nagaria jaore	—	H-1001
	Janam dukhini Sita	Shailen Ray (Himangshu Dutta)-	
	Banglar meye, banglari tumi (Film *Jiban Sangini*)	do-	H-1015
1943	Katha kao dao sara	Ajay Bhattacharya (Subal Dasgupta	H-1046G
	Madhu brindabane dole Radha	Robin Majumdar	
	Jabe alaker phul	Ajay Bhattacharya	H-1055G
	Phire gechhi bare bare	-do-	
	Bandar chharo jatrira sabe (Film *Chhadmabeshi*)	-do-	H-1068
	Nutan ushar sainik		
1944	Kal sagarer maran dolay	Shailen Ray	H-1086

	Shyamrup dharia esechhe maran	-do-	
	Pile pile harinaam ka pyala	Pandit Bhushan	H-1094G
	Shyam suno meri	-do-	
	Lalita marami sakhi	Shankar Gupta	H-1099G
	Piya sane milan piyas	Mohini Chaudhuri	
1945	Rangila re	Dukhai Khondakar and Jasimuddin	H-1221G
	Tui ki shyamer banshi re	Jasimuddin	
	Priyo rajanigandha bane	Kamal Ghosh	H-1160
	Dhik dhik amaar e jibane	Girin Chakrabarti (collected by)	
	Balam mujhse ruthke	—	H-1179
	Mere jauban ke phoolwaari	—	
1946	Bhulaye amay dudin	Mohini Chaudhuri	H-1201
	Ke amare pichhu dake	-do-	
	Rimjhim rimjhim (Film *Kalankini*)	Pranab Ray	H-1211
	Naina ko samjhake	—	
	Gay je papiya (with Meera Dev Burman)	Mohini Chaudhuri	H-1216
	Aaj dol dilo ke (solo by Meera Dev Burman)	-do-	
	Phul gendua na maro (with Meera Dev Burman)	—	H-1231

	Tum ho bade chit chor (solo by Meera Dev Burman)	—	
1947	Babu babu re (Film *Eight Days*, with S.L. Puri)	G.S. Nepali and Qamar Jalabadi	HMV N-26915
	Umeed bhara panchi (Film *Eight Days*)	G. S. Nepali and Qamar Jalallabadi	HMV N-26914
	Suni suni lage	—	HMV N-26951
	O mere raja	—	
	Jane wale sunta ja	—	HMV N-35123
	Kaun aya sapne mein	—	
	Prem kiye bin raha na jay	—	HMV N-35128
	In dino	—	
1948	Keno aleyare bandhu bhabi	Gouriprasanna Majumdar	Hindustan Records H-1299
	Bondhu go ei madhumas	-do-	
	Gunadham amader Gandhiji	-do-	
	Nirabe aankhi jale bhare keno	-do-	
	Gunadham hamare Gandhiji	Munsi Zakir Hussain	Hindustan Records H-1320

	Deshki janta tumhe	-do-	
	Ei chaiti sandhya jay britha	Mohini Chaudhuri	Hindustan Records H-1321
	Keno hai sapan bhangar agei (Solo by Meera Dev Burman)	-do-	Hindustan Records H-1328
	Kali badariya chha gayee (with Meera Dev Burman)	—	HMV N-35331
	Dali dali phool (Solo by Meera Dev Burman)	—	
	Prem jamunay haito keu	Mohini Chaudhuri	Hindustan Records H-1340
	Hai kije kari e mana niya	-do-	
	Ud gaya bhanwara	—	HMV N-35503
	Prem ka pinjra	—	
1949	Banshi tomar hathe dilam	Mohini Chaudhuri	Hindustan Records H-1384
	Ke dilo ghum bhangaye (with Meera Dev Burman)	-do-	
	Ami path cheye rabo	Gouriprasanna Majumdar	HMV P-11904
	Baje na banshi go	-do-	

List of Songs of S. D. Burman as Singer ♪ 233

	Maramiya re ei udas madhumase	-do-	
	Basarer phool gelo je shukaye	-do-	Hindustan Records H-1437
1950	Aankhi duti jhare hai	Gouriprasanna Majumdar	HMV P-11908
	Malakhani chhilo hathe	-do-	
	Aajo akasher path bahi	-do-	HMV P-11910
	Khulia kusum saaj srimati je	-do-	
1951	Sei je dinguli	Mohini Chaudhuri	HMV P-11915
	Jhilmil jhilmil jhiler jale	-do-	
1956	Mana dilo na bondhu	Rabi Guha Majumdar	HMV P-11931
	Tumi ar nei se tumi	-do-	
1957	Ghum bhulechhi nijhum	Gouriprasanna Majumdar	HMV P-11932
	O jani bhomra keno katha	-do-	
1958	Na na na phutonare phul	Gouriprasanna Majumdar	HMV P-11933
	Katha diye ele na	-do-	
1959	Suno mere bandhu re (Film *Sujata*)	Majrooh Sultanpuri	HMV N-52983
	Nanhi kali sone chali (solo by Geeta Dutt)	-do-	
1960	Dur kono parabase	Gouriprasanna Majumdar	HMV P-11934
	Banshi shune ar kaj nai	--	
1961	Saite pari 'na' bala	Rabi Guha Majumdar	HMV P-11948
	Bane phagun mane agun	-do-	

1963	Ore majhi, mere saajan (Film *Bandini*) O janewala ho sake (Film *Bandini*, singer Mukesh)	Shailendra -do-	HMV N-54136
1965	Je na jane biraher mane Keno se je hai Waha kaun hai tera (Film *Guide*) Piya tose naina lage (Film *Guide*, singer Lata Mangeshkar)	Rabi Guha Majumdar -do- Shailendra -do-	HMV N-83142 HMV N-84948
1967	Asamaye bajao banshi Jodi dako akarane	Rabi Guha Majumdar -do-	HMV N-83248
1968	Tumi esechhile parshu Koi koi re ghungur Bhongite taba nesha Chander aloy kalo	Rabi Guha Majumdar -do- Meera Dev Burman -do-	HMV 7-EPE-1071
1969	Meri duniya hai ma (Film *Talash*) (with three other songs from the same film by others)	Majrooh Sultanpuri	Angel Records 45 AE 1061
	Safal hogi teri aradhana (Film *Aradhana*) (with another song from the same film)	Anand Bakshi	Angel Records 45 AE 1316
	Prem ke pujari hum hai (Film *Prem Pujari*) (with other songs from the same film)	Neeraj	Angel Records 45 AE 1271
	Ganer kali surer durite Subal re bolo bolo	Meera Dev Burman -do-	HMV 7-EPE-1087

List of Songs of S. D. Burman as Singer ♪ 235

	Shono go dakhina hawa	-do-	
	Barne gandhe chhande gitite	-do-	
1970	Biraha bado bhalo lage	Meera Dev Burman	HMV 7-EPE-1128
	Ghate lagaiya dinga	-do-	
	Raater atare bhijaiya adore	-do-	
	Kalsape dangshe amay	-do-	
1971	Takdum takdum bajai	Meera Dev Burman	HMV 45-N-83441
	Ke jas re bhati gang baiya	-do-	
	Doli me bithai ke (Film *Amar Prem*)	Anand Bakshi (Rahul Dev Burman)	
1972	Radhar bhabe kala hoila gora	Meera Dev Burman	HMV 45-N-83496
	Na amare shashi cheyona	-do-	
1973	Se ki amaar dushman dushman	Meera Dev Burman	HMV 45-N-83543
	Ki kori ami ki kori	-do-	
1976	Safal hogi teri aradhana (Bengali film *Aradhana*) (with six more songs from the same film)	Anand Bakshi	HMV ECLP-3404

This list has been prepared with details from Kalyanbandhu Bhattacharya's article 'Sachinkantha', published in *Desh*, Entertainment Number 1385, Bengali Era.

Appendix III
List of Songs of S. D. Burman as Music Director (Bengali films)

1935

Sanjher Pradip
Director: Tinkari Chakraborti
Cast:—
Lyrics:—
Songs:
1. Ore Sujan naiya—S. D. Burman
2. Nishithe jaiyo phulabane—S.D.B.
Record No. Hindustan Records H-266
(It was a short film released along with *Biraha*.)

Sudurer Priya
Director:—
Cast:—
Lyrics: Ajay Bhattacharya
Songs: 1. Tumi ni amaar bandhu—S. D. Burman
2. Bandhu banshi dao mor—S. D. Burman

Rec. No. Hindustan Records H-305
(It was a short film released along with *Prafulla*.)

1937
Rajgee
Director: Sukumar Dasgupta
Cast: Menaka Debi, Dhiraj Bhattacharya, Bhabani Das, Shanti Mukherjee
Lyrics: Ajay Bhattacharya
Jt. Music Director: Bhishmadeb Chattopadhyay
Songs: By
1. Bondhu, etodin chhile aankhijal hoye—
2. Akasher chand ogo—
3. Bhul kore chaoaya bhul kore paoaya—
4. Chokher jal ar phelbi keno –
5. Ore khyapa man-- Bhabani Charan Das
6. Bhanga nayer pale—do—
7. Akashe nibhiya gelo lakkha tarar deep—Girin Chakrabarti
8. Ore bandhu re, maner katha—S. D. Burman
9. Saaje nawal kishore chander—S. D. Burman

1939
Jakher Dhan
Director: Hari Bhanja
Cast: Jahar Ganguli, Shila Halder, Sushil Ray, Ahindra Chaudhuri, Rabi Ray
Lyrics: Hemendra Kumar Ray
Krishnadhan Dey
Jt. Music Director: Dhiren Das
Songs:
1. Dolanchampar dolnate aaj
2. Bhar piyala, bhar piyala
3. Ore man-mayuri naach dhorechhe
4. Chander meye tomar paye
5. Amra baba tanchhi ganja
6. Chalre chalre balre, jay duranta pran

7. Amader praner sukher jharnatala
8. Pulak uthale nayaner tale
9. Sakhi, tor aankhir kone
10. Bandhu amaar elo nare

1940

Amar Geeti
Director: Hiren Basu
Cast: Ahindra Chaudhuri, Pramod Ganguli, Srimati Chhaya, Sabitri
Lyrics: Hiren Basu
Jt. Music Dir.: Bhishmadeb Chattopadhyay
Songs:
1. Taba sashwata ragini bajichhe digante
2. Din chhilo go amaar
3. Jibaneri khelaghare aay sej pete
4. Katokal ar gharer konete
5. Mrityurupe eso sathi
6. Batayane elo, elo utal hawa
7. Ajike mor maner shakhe
8. Ja bhenge jay bare bare

Rajkumarer Nirbasan
Director: Shukumar Dasgupta
Cast: Dhiraj Bhattacharya, Ahindra Chaudhuri, Chandrabati, Purnima
Lyrics: Ajay Bhattacharya
Jt. Music Director: Hariprasanna Das
Songs:
1. Jaago pratham pranay laj laye—Hemanta Mukhopadhyay
2. Amare bhulbe keman kore
3. Tumi ele aaj mor aankhi dhare
4. Banshuriyare, kothay shikhechho—Sachin Dev Burman
5. Chander desher barata loye je
6. Bhramara kohilo kamal aankhi tolo
7. Phire jay morichika

List of Songs of S. D. Burman as Music Director (Bengali films) ♪ **239**

1941

Pratishod
Director: Sushil Majumdar
Cast: Naresh Mitra, Dhiren Ganguli, Chhaya Devi, Shila Halder
Lyrics: Premendra Mitra
Songs:
1. Ki maya laaglo chokhe sakalbela—S. D. Burman, Pramod Ganguli, Siddheshwar Mukhopadhyay
2. Sagar chhenche tulbi manik
3. Man kende othe sure—Chhaya Debi
4. Aste jodi jabei tabe—Chhaya Debi, Pramod Ganguli
5. Abodh neye ujaan beye—S. D. Burman
6. Fagun bay aagun taher—Shila Halder
7. Janina kothay achhi—Ramala Debi
8. Thoter kone haasi bujhi—Ramala Debi

1942

Abhayer Biye
Director: Sushil Majumdar
Cast: Chhaya Debi, Ahindra Chaudhuri, Rekha Mitra, Dhiraj Bhattacharya
Lyrics: Premendra Mitra
Jt. Music Director: Robin Chattopadhyay
Songs:
1. Adhar jale hathat keno jhikimiki
2. Kuriye mala gathbe
3. Man bale je melo melo
4. Han, ai dile betaab use
5. E kemon dola ke jaane
6. Bhulbe bhabo, bhulechho ki?

Milan
Director: Jyotish Bandyopadhyay
Cast: Chitra Debi, Suprabha Mukherjee, Renuka Ray, Chhabi Biswas, Dhiraj Bhattacharya
Lyrics: Ajay Bhattacharya

Premendra Mitra
Songs:
1. Phul kay ali tumi
2. Laho abhinandan mander malikay
3. Aaj prabhate sonar meghe
4. Jiban kire khelar putul
5. Shyama nayre bhayankari
6. Baje Krishner manjeer
7. Madir fagun dine mane ki rabe

Ashok
Director: Ajay Bhattacharya
Cast: Ahindra Chaudhuri, Chhabi Biswas, Naresh Mitra, Malina Debi, Padma Debi
Lyrics: Ajay Bhattacharya
Songs:
1. Ami noi go tomar noi kaharo
2. Prabhu anal-dahan jetha
3. Manbo na haar manbo na
4. Manik rattan chaine prabhu
5. Ajio rajani holona je geetimoy
6. Khelaghar bhange jadi besh to
7. Baisakhi purnima elo na ki
8. Chand nai akashe
9. Kon ba desher rajar Kumar

1943

Jaj Saheber Naatni
Director: Kaliprasad Ghosh
Cast: Ramala Debi, Jahar Ganguli, Manoranjan, Purnima
Lyrics: Shailen Ray
Songs:
1. Madhumalatir kunjo amar sapne manjurio
2. Baner pakhi bandhlo basa
3. Raat holo nijjhum

List of Songs of S. D. Burman as Music Director (Bengali films) ♪ **241**

4. Baro nastami dustami kare chandre—Bimal Bhushan
5. Paye chala pathkhani je digante milay
6. Tomare loye cholbo sethay he atithi
7. Biday jodi nebe bandhu nio
8. Ajke mora khelbo duti harin harini
9. Ogo chakita-gamini harini nayana
10. Ei khanetei ajke mora bandhbo moder basa
11. Jhara patay chheyechhe mor ban
12. Se je ek japani meye
13. Ami ami ami go, sei japani meye

1944

Chhadmabeshi
Director: Ajay Bhattacharya
Cast: Jahar Ganguli, Chhabi Biswas, Padma Debi, Shanti Gupta, Sandhyarani
Lyrics: Ajay Bhattacharya, Patitpaban Bandopadhyay
Songs:
1. Kon deshe chhilo chand
2. Pardeshiare tor bhanglo basa
3. Phul jodi phutlo
4. Akash keno dilo dhara nayane go
5. Ajike madhu bane
6. Bandar chharo jatrira sabe—S. D. Burman
7. Are chho chho chho keya sharam ki baat
8. Ram mile Sita sane

Pratikare
Director: Chhabi Biswas
Cast: Chhabi Biswas, Shailen Chaudhuri, Renuka Ray, Reba Debi
Lyrics: Premendra Mitra
Songs:
1. Achena ki chena kiba jaane
2. Boli, boli tobu je bala holo na
3. Jadio parira bhule kakhano raatey

4. Milana raati pohalo (Rabindra-sangeet)
(Record No. Hindustan Records H-1119G)

Matir Ghar
Director: Hari Bhanja
Cast: Ahindra Chaudhuri, Chhabi Biswas, Jahar Ganguli, Malina Debi, Padma Debi
Lyrics: Shailen Ray
Songs:
1. Shyamrup dharia esechhe maran—S. D. Burman
2. Cheye dekhi bare bare tare
3. Se je elo, se elo, elo, elo
4. Ki naame dakibo tare jar anurage
5. Man phul nahe, banaphul priyo bahire
6. Bhalobasar basa moder kothay balo—Hemant Mukhopadhyay
7. Kaal Sagarer maran dolay jethay bhange—S. D. Burman
(Record No. HMV N-27454-56. Song No. 1 and 7 Hindustan Records H-1086)

1945
Kalankini
Director: Jyotish Bandopadhyay
Cast: Ahindra Chaudhuri, Jahar Ganguli, Dhiraj Bhattacharya, Renuka Ray, Sabitri
Lyrics: Pranab Ray
Songs:
1. Kajal nayan achin meye
2. Rimjhim rimjhim—S. D. Burman
3. Amader sapner bhubane
4. Sundara he sundara
5. Tumi jabe chhile sathe
6. Dol diechhe dol
(Record No. HMV No. 27571-73)

1946
Matrihara
Director: Gunamay Bandopadhyay
Cast: Malina Debi, Purnima Debi, Jahar Ganguli, Kamal Mitra
Lyrics: Shailen Ray
Songs:
1. Toor chokkhe royechhe baan
2. Raat kata sabe char namale ki
3. Chhoto holo baro raat eki day
4. Rakhal banshari bajale bajale
5. Tomar laagi amaar gaane

1950
Samar
Director: Nitin Basu
Cast: Ashok Kumar, Sumitra Debi, Ruma, Kanu Ray
Lyrics: Sajanikanta Das, Gauriprasanna, Bratindranath Tagore, Mohini Chaudhuri
Songs:
1. Rangin hawar laglo chhoyan—Arun Kumar
2. Tarit tarangamayi kaapis bujhi sukhe
3. Gun gun sure gunjare madhukar—Gita Ray
4. Tomar dewa shikal chhilo charam shanker
5. Eki abhishape mala shukalo—Gita Ray
6. Sundari lo sundari, dal bendhe aay (Kishore Kumar, Gita Ray, Arun Kumar and others)
(Record No. HMV No. 31294-95)

1971
Chaitali
Director: Sudhir Mukhopadhyay
Cast: Biswajit, Tanuja, Basanta Chaudhuri, Manmohan
Lyrics: Chandidas, Bidyapati, Gobinda Das, Gauriprasanna Majumdar, Ananda Baksi

Songs:
1. Phulon-me shey phul chuna—Lata and Usha Mangeshkar
2. Shyam bhai bine shyam hai—Lata Mangeshkar
3. Bahudin pare bondhva milalo ghare—Dhananjay Bhattacharya
4. Janama abadhi hum o rup—Dhananjay Bhattacharya
5. Nithura he rai, tonhare dohai—Dhananjay Bhattacharya
6. Shudhai ami ei pathtake—Manna De
7. Duti Katha jeno—Manna De, Tanuja
8. Hai! Payal baaj gayi aaj meri—Lata Mangeshkar
(Record No. HMV EMOE-1009/BOE-1018)

1976

Aradhana

Director: Shakti Samanta
Cast: Rajesh Khanna, Sharmila Tagore, Pahari Sanyal, Ashok Kumar
Lyrics: Gauriprasanna Majumdar, Ananda Baksi
Songs:
1. Madhabi phutechhe oi han—Lata Mangeshkar, Rahul Dev Burman
2. Aaj hridaye bhalobeshe—Kishore Kumar, Lata Mangeshkar
3. Chandra je tui mor surya je tui—Lata Mangeshkar
4. Safal hogi teri aradhana—S. D. Burman
5. Eto kachhe dujane prem bhara—Kishore Kumar
6. Mor sapaner sathi tumi—Kishore Kumar
7. Gunjane dole je bhramer—Kishore Kumar, Asha Bhonsle
(Record No. HMV EXLP-3404)
(After S. D. Burman's death, son Rahul Dev Burman got the recordings done in the tones of the original Hindi film *Aradhana*-1969).

Gauri

Only one song for this film was recorded in Kishore Kumar's and Rahul Dev Burman's voice. No other details are available.

Courtesy: Debashish Mukhopadhyay

Appendix IV
List of Songs of S. D. Burman as Music Director (Hindi films)

1946

Eight Days (Aath Din)
Filmistan
Director: Dattaram Pai
Lyrics: Gopal Singh Nepali
Cast: Ashok Kumar, Veera, S.L.Puri, V.H.Desai

- Ummed Bhara Panchhi tha khoj raha sajni: S. D. Burman
- Banka sipaiya ghar jaye ho, barson ke baad: Kishore Kumar and Chorus
- Apni gori ki nagri me jana, o jana zara dhire dhire: Binapani, Lalita Dewalkar, Mangla & Chorus
- Babu babu re dil ko bachana, tere dil ka banega nishana: S. D. Burman, S. L. Puri
- Kisise meri preet lagi, ab kya karun: Meena Kapoor
- Pahle nasamjha pyar tha, samjha to tumhi chal diye: Ameer Bai
- Ek nayee kali sasural chali, dubli si dulhan banke: Chitalkar, Meena Kapoor

Record No.: Gramophone Co. of India Ltd. N26914-15/17.

Shikari
Filmistan
D: Savak Vachha
L: Gopal Singh Nepali
C: Ashok Kumar, Veera, Paro, Kishore Kumar, Ram Shukal
* Dol rahi hai naiya meri(two parts): Ashok Kumar, Paro
* Teri bina sooni sooni hai meri phulwari re: Paro
* Rangeela rangeela rangeela re, jawani men satake: Paro (Chorus)
* Chhupo chhupo o marne se darne walo: Paro
* Ek chhotisi pehchan kahin ban na jaye preet
* Har din hai naya har raat nirali hai: Ameer Bai, Ashok Kumar
* Duniyane hame rahne na diya milke: Ameer Bai
* Jab ghar me lagi aag, sabhi bansi bajaye: Paro (Chorus)
* Aaj punam ka chand khila: Ashok Kumar, Paro
Record No.: Gramophone Co. of India Ltd. N26721-25

1947
Chittor Vijay
Murari Pictures
D: Mohan Sinha
L: Harikrishna Premi
C: Surendra, Wasti, Rajkapoor, Madhubala, Menka Devi, Leela Pande
* Aayere aye badal
* Nainonse nainonki pyas bujhao, gori naina milao
* Kahe more mohan ne mujhko bhulayare
* Pilo piloji maharaja, pilo piloji anndata
* Mai cham cham karti bijli hoon
* Ber lelo ber, ye hai jungle ke ber
* Ho rangeela ho raseela, rakhee ka din ayare
* Har zaban par ek naara, hai hamara desh pyara

Dil Ki Rani
Amar Jyoti Pictures
D: Mohan Sinha
L: Y.N.Joshi, Harikrinshna "Premi"
C: Raj Kapoor, Madhubala, Shyam Sundar

- Duniya ke rehnewalo bolo, kahan gaya chitchor : Raj Kapoor
- Nain kati hai bain (o duniya ke rehnewalo)
- Sar phod phod kar mar jana, kisi se dil na lagana: Shyam Sundar
- Bigdee huyi taqdeer meri aake banade: Geeta Roy
- Mohobbat ka khana kabhi na mithai
- Ayenge ayenge re mere man ke basaiya aayenge re: Shyam Sundar
- Loot liya dil chitchor ne..chupke se aake: Shyam Sundar
- Kyon balam hum se rooth gaye, bedardi bedardi: Geeta Roy
- Aha more mohan ne mujhko bulaya ho

Record No.: Gramophone Co. of India Ltd. N35948-50

Do Bhai
Filmistan
D: Munshi Dil
L: Raja Mehdi Ali Khan
C: Kamini Kaushal, Ulhas, Rajen Haksar, Paro
- Mera sundar sapna beet gaya: Geeta Roy
- Yaad karoge yaad karoge, ik din humko yaad karoge: Geeta Roy
- Yaad rakhna mujhe yaad rakhna: Geeta Roy, K. S. Ragi
- Aaj preet ki naatha toot gaya: Geeta Roy, G. M. Durani
- Mera piya to basen pardes re: Geeta Roy
- Ambva ki dali pe koyal bole: Paro
- Kabhi bhoole se na poochhi man ki baat rasiya: Paro
- Duniya me meri aaj andhera hi andhera: Md. Rafi
- Hume chod piya kis des gaye: Geeta Roy

Record No.: Gramophone Co. of India Ltd. N35211-14/35259

1948
Vidya
Jeet Productions
D: Girish Trivedi
L: Y.N.Joshi, Anjum Pilibhiti, Raja Mehdi Ali Khan, Madhukar
C: Suraiya, Dev Anand, Cuckoo, Amirbai Karnatki
- Bhagwan tere sansar ke hai khel nirale: Ameer Bai
- Pyar banke mujhpe koi chha gaya re: Lalita Dewalkar
- Meri muniya ki akhiyan me tu aja nindiya: Ameer Bai

- Layi khushiki duniya, hansti huyi jawani: Mukesh, Suraiya
- Jhoom rahi jhoom rahi khushiyonki nav aaj: Suraiya
- Krishna kanhayi ...ashaonki duniya mein: Suraiya
- Kise malum tha do din mein sawan beet jayega: Suraiya
- Jeevan jyothi bujhti jaye, tujh bin kaun jagaye: Ameer Bai
- Bahe na kabhi nain se neer...yahi preet ki reet: Mukesh
- Kinare kinare chale jayenge, jeevan ki naiyako khete huwe: Suraiya
- Raaton ki neend chheen li

Record No.: Gramophone Co. of India Ltd. N35319-23

1949
Kamal
Hind Kamal Pictures
D:Surya Kumar
L: G.S.Nepali, Raja Mehdi Ali Khan, Prem Dhavan
C: Surendra, Nayan Tara, Jeevan, Mohana

- Ab raat gayee hai beet re, aya jo savera pancchi koyi: Surendra
- Bharat mata ab zanjeeron me hai bebas lachar: Geeta Roy (Chorus)
- Toote bandhan toote bandhan aj re: Geeta Roy (Chorus)
- Jhoom jhoom ke nach re manva, gaaye jaa: Surendra
- Kehne ko hai taiyar magar kaise kahe hum: Geeta Roy, Surendra
- Pyara pyara hai sama, my dear come to me: Meena Kapoor, Motilal
- Aaj kathin hai preet dagariya: Lalita Rao
- Mai to udas hoon magar woh bhi hai sogwar kyon: Surendra
- Meri kashti ko mohabbat ka kinara milgaya: Geeta Roy
- Ek roz bichadnewalonka kab tak dil milkar: Geeta Roy
- Ai dile bekarar jhoom

Record No.: Gramophone Co. of India Ltd. N36012-13/GE 8413-15

Shabnam
Filmistan
D: Mitra
L: Qamar Jalalabadi
C; Dilip Kumar, Kamini Kaushal, Paro, Cuckoo

- Ye duniya roop ki chor, bachale mujhe babu re: Samsad Begum
- Hum kisko sunaye haal, ye duniya paise ki: Lalita Dewalkar
- Mara dil tadapke kahan chala itna to batake ja (Two parts): Geeta Roy
- Ik bar tu ban ja mera o pardesi phir dekh mazaa: Samsad Begum
- Tu mehal mein rehnewali....phir tera mera pyar kya: Mukesh, Samsad Begum
- Dekho ayi pehli mohobbat ki raat: Samsad Begum (Chorus)
- Tumhare liye huye badnam tum jano ya na j: Mukesh, Samsad Begum
- Pyar me tumne dhoka seekha ye to batao kaise: Mukesh, Samsad Begum
- Kismet me bichhadnatha huyi kyon unse mulaqat re: Mukesh, Geeta Roy
- Qadar meri na jani chhodke jaanewale: Samsad Begum

Record No.: Gramophone Co. of India Ltd. N35975-78/N36005-06

1950
Afsar
Navketan
D: Chetan Anand
L: Narendra sharma, Vishvamitter Adil
C: Suraiya, Dev Anand, Ruma Devi
- Gun gun bole re bhanwar, sun sun kya laya khabar: Suraiya
- Beli le jare kaahe der lagaye
- Man mor huwa matwala, kisne jaadu dala re: Suraiya
- Nain diwane, ek nahin mane, kare manmani, mane na: Suraiya
- Ajee preet ka naata jodnewale: Geeta Roy, Suraiya
- Pardesi re , jaate jaate jiya mora liye ja: Suraiya
- Jat khol de kiwad pat khol de: Manmohan Krishna
- Saadh ke ghar chhokria: Manmohan Krisha

Record No.: Gramophone Co. of India Ltd. N36376-77/N36403-4

Mashal
Bombay Talkies
(Music done jointly with Manna Dey)
D: Nitin Bose
L: Pradeep
C: Ashok Kumar, Sumitra Devi, Ruma Devi, Cuckoo
- Upar gagan vishal, neeche gehra patal: Manna Dey (Chorus)
- Duniya ke logo, lo himmat se kaam: Manna De

- Jab tum the hamare aur hum the thumhare: Arun Kumar
- Aaj nahi to kal bikhar jayenge yeh badal: Lata Mangeshkar
- Ankhon se door door hain par dil ke pas jo: Lata Mangeshkar
- Kitni sach hai ye baat re koi maane ya na mane: Geeta Roy
- Mohe laga solva saal, hai mai to margayi: Samsad Begum, Arum Kumar (Chorus)

Record No.: Gramophone Co. of India Ltd. N36472-75

Pyar
Sunrise Pictures
D: V. M. Vyas
L: Rajendra Krishna
C: Raj Kapoor, Nargis, Shyama, Neelam, Kesari
- Kachi pakki sadkonpe meri tamtam: Kishore Kumar
- Aa gayire banke ki rani aagayi : Geeta Roy
- Yun kaho hum ek hain aur doosra koyi nahi: Kishore Kumar, Geeta Roy
- Jalti hai duniya tera mera pyar hai: Kishore Kumar, Samsad Begum
- Woh sapnewali raat, milan ki raat, kabhi to ayegi: Geeta Roy
- Bewafa yeh to bata loota chaman kyon pyarka: Kishore Kumar, Geeta Roy
- Do din hasaya pyarne, sau din rulane keliye: Geeta Roy
- Mohobbat ka chhota sa ek aashiyana, kisine banaya, kisine mitaya: Kishore Kumar

Record No.: Gramophone Co. of India Ltd. N36371-75

1951
Baazi
Navketan
D: Guru Dutt
L: Sahir Ludhianvi
C: Dev Anand, Geeta Baali, Kalpana Kartik, Roopa Varman
- Tadbeer se bigdi huyi taqdeer banale: Geeta Roy
- Suno gajar kya gaye, samay guzarta jaye: Geeta Roy (Chorus)
- Laakh zamanewale, dale dilonpe tale: Geeta Roy
- Yeh kaun aya ki mere dil ki duniya men bahar aye: Geeta Roy
- Dekh akeli mohe barkha satayere: Geeta Roy (Chorus)
- Sharmaye kahe, ghabraye kahe, sun meri raja: Samsad Begum

- Mere labon pe dekho aaj bhi tarane hai: Kishore Kumar
- Aaj ki raat piya dil na todo man ki piya manlo: Geeta Roy
- Piya mose na nain

Record No.: **Gramophone Co. of India Ltd. N36624-25/N36650/ N36743**

Bahar
A. V. M. Productions
(Music done jointly with N.Dutta)
D: M. V. Raman
L: Rajendra Krishna
C: Vyjayantimala, Karan Dewan, Pandari Bai, Om Prakash, Baby Tabassum
- Duniya ki maza lelo duniya tumhari hai: Samsad Begum
- Saiyan dil mein aana re, aake phir na jaanare: Samsad Begum
- Duniyawale kitne zalim hain teri duniya wale: Geeta Roy
- Ai zindagi ke rahi, himmat na haar jaana: Talat Mehmood
- Chhodoji chhodoji chhodoji, kanhaiya kalaiya hamar: Samsad Begum
- Kusoor apka, huzoor apka(Two parts): Kishore Kumar
- Bhagwan do ghadi zara insaan banke dekh: Geeta Roy
- Pyar ki bahar leke, dil ka quarar leke: Samsad Begum
- Saiyan dil mein aana re: Gayetri Basu
- Duniya ka maza le le: Rama Devi

No.: **Gramophone Co. of India Ltd. GE 6931-35, ECLP 5943**

Buzdil
Filmart
D: Shaheed Latif
L: Shailendra, Kaifi Azmi
C: Nimmi, Kishore Sahu, Premnath, Cuckoo, Laxmi, Asha
- Main albeli, rum jhum baje ghoongar mora: Lata Mangeshkar
- Jhan jhan jhan payal baje, kaise jaaoon pee se milan ko: Lata Mangeshkar
- Rote rote guzar gayi raat re , aayi yaad teri har baat re: Lata Mangeshkar
- Kaahe ab re balaam dhire dhire tera gham: Surinder Kaur
- Dar laage, duniya se balma ho, ulfat na bane afsana: Talat Mehmood, Lata Mangeshkar

- Jaanena haye, yeh duniya janena dil ki lagi: Lata Mangeshkar
No.: **Gramophone Co. of India Ltd. N36749-51**

Ek Nazar
Kuldeep Pictures
D: O. P. Dutta
L: Rajendra Krishna
C: Nalini Jayawant, Rehman, Gope, Karan Dewan, Kuldeep
- Mujhe preet nagariya jana hai, dil se dil kaise samjhawun: Md. Rafi, Lata Mangeshkar
- Dard lage pyara pyara pehle pehle pyarka: Lata Mangeshkar
- Yeh aasun khushi ke aasun hai: Talat Mehmood
- Dekho karte hai pyar dono aapas me: Geeta Roy (Chorus)
- Jaane wale dekho hamen bhool na jaana: Lata Mangeshkar
- Bas chupke hi chupke se pyar hogaya: Geeta Roy
- Jaa dekh liya tera pyar , o saajan bedardi: Lata Mangeshkar
- Dil kisi ki yaad mein barbad hai, sun ne wale bas yahi faryad hai: Lata Mangeshkar
- Naye zamane ki mohabbat: Kishore Kumar
No.: **Gramophone Co. of India Ltd. N 36613-N36636-39**

Naujawan
Kardar Productions
D: Mahesh Kaul
L: Sahir Ludhianvi
C: Nalini Jaywant, Premnath, Nawab, Yashodhara Katju, Cuckoo
- Thandi hawaye lehrake aye rut hai jawan: Lata Mangeshkar
- Dil ka dard na jane duniya, jaane dil tadpana: Lata Mangeshkar
- Piya piya , hum aur tum, pee pee piya: Kishore Kumar, Samsad Begum
- Pan ghat pe dekho aayee milan ki bela: Md. Rafi, Geeta Roy (chorus)
- Zara jhoomle, jawani ka zamana: Md. Rafi, Geeta Roy (chorus)
- Dekho ji, kuch bhi karlo jeet hamari hai: Kishore Kumar, Lata Mangeshkar
- Ek aag dehekta raag: Manna Dey (chorus)
No.: **Gramophone Co. of India Ltd. N36657-59**

List of Songs of S. D. Burman as Music Director (Hindi films) ♪ **253**

Sazaa
G. P. Production
D: Fali Mistry
L: Rajendra Krishna, Sahir
C: Nimmi, Dev Anand, Shyama, Gope, Mukri
- Tum na jaane kis jahaan me kho gaye: Lata Mangeshkar
- Aa gup chup gup chup pyar kare: Hemant Kumar, Sadhya Mukhopadhyay
- Ho gayire teri hogayi, pahle hi mel mein: Lata Mangeshkar
- Rup nagar ke saudagar, o rang rangeele jaadoogar: Lata Mangeshkar, Pramodini Desai
- Dhak dhak dhak, jiya kare dhak, ankhiyome akhiyaa: Lata Mangeshkar (Chorus)
- Hum pyar ki baazi haare, dil roye dard ke mare: Lata Mangeshkar
- Aaja aaja tera intezar hai: Talat Mehmood, Lata Mangeshkar
- Yeh baat koi samjhayere, kyon aaj nazar sharmayere: Sandhya Mukhopadhyay
- Chhai kari badariya

No.: **Gramophone Co. of India Ltd. N36792-95**

1952

Jaal
Filmarts
D: Guru Dutt
L: Sahir Ludhianvi
C: Geeta Bali, Dev Anand, Poornima, Krishna Kumari
- Yeh raat yeh chandni phir kahan (Two parts): Hemant Kumar
- De bhi chuke hum dil nazrana dil ka: Kishore Kumar, Geeta Roy
- Zor lagake haiya....pair jamake haiya...jaan ladake: Geeta Roy (chorus)
- Chori chori meri gali aana hai bura: Lata Mangeshkar (Chorus)
- Kaisi yeh jaagi agan, lagi hain dil mein lagan
- Pighla hai sona, door gagan par: Lata Mangeshkar
- Soch samajhkar dil ko lagana, dekho bura hai zamana: Geeta Roy
- Bachna zara yeh zamana hai bura
- Hansne wale a chand
- Yeh baharon ka samaan

No.: **Gramophone Co. of India Ltd. N50118-120/M50162**

Lal Kunwar
N. V. M. Productions
D: Ravindra Dave
L: Sahir Ludhianvi
C: Suraiya, Nasir Khan, Jairaj, Usha Kiron, Agha
- Mudkar idhar ko bhi meri sarkar dekh lo: Geeta Roy, Asha Bhonsle (chorus)
- Dil ka bhed jan lo :Asha Bhonsle
- Tum jo mile arzooko dil ki rah milgayi: Suraiya
- Rajajani laaga mohe nainwa ka baan re: Samsad Begum
- Nigahe kyon milayi thi agar yoon chhod jana tha: Suraiya
- Awaz deta hai sola ka seen: Asha Bhonsle
- Preet sataye teri, dil deke gham leliya: Suraiya
- Dekho aayi milan ki raaten

No.: **Gramophone Co. of India Ltd. N50244-47**

1953

Armaan
Film Technicians of India
D: Fali Mistry
L: Sahir Ludhianvi
C: Dev Anand, Madhubala, Shakila, Gulab
- Jab duniya badli hai , phir kyon na badle: Asha Bhonsle
- Mai pankh lagake ud jawun aur phir na palat ke aawun: Asha Bhonsle
- Jaadu bhari yeh fizaye, sochta hai: Geeta Roy
- Ye hansi yeh khushi, lakhon baras yuhi aaye: Geeta Roy
- Krodh kapat ke andhiyare mein jeevan jyot jagaye jaa: Manna Dey (chorus)
- Chahe kitna mujhe tum bulaoji, nahi bolungi: Asha Bhonsle
- Bol na bol ai jaanewale, sun to le diwanonki: Talat Mehmood, Asha Bhonsle
- Bharam teri wafaonka mita dete to kya hota: Talat Mehmood

No.: **Gramophone Co. of India Ltd. N50541-44**

List of Songs of S. D. Burman as Music Director (Hindi films) ♪ 255

Babla
M. P. Productions
D: Agra Doot
L: Sahir Ludhianvi
C: Master Niren, Sova Sen, Paresh Banerji, Manju De
- Raat ke raahi thak mat jaana, subah ki manzil door nahin (Two parts): Manna Dey (chorus)
- Hamri munder bole kaga sakhi ri: Raj Kumari
- Leheronke rele sang naiya mori khele: Hridaynath Mangeshkar
- Raat khushi ki aayee, aaj duniya nayee hai: Lata Mangeshkar
- Jag mein aye koyi, koyi jaayere: Talat Mehmood
- Raat ke raahi thak mat jana: Lata Mangeshkar
No.: **Gramophone Co. of India Ltd. N75006-08**

Jeevan Jyoti
Musical Pictures
D: Mahesh Kaul
L: Sahir Ludhianvi
C: Chand Usmani, Shammi Kapoor, Shashikala
- Chhayi kaari badariya, bairaniya ho Ram: Lata Mangeshkar
- So jaare soja meri akhiyonke taare: Lata Mangeshkar
- Lag gayi akhiyan tumse mori: Md. Rafi, Geeta Roy
- Balma ne man har leena, kaisa jaadu kiyare: Asha Bhonsle
- Saari khushiyan saath aayee, aap jab aaye: Samsad Begum
- Sakhi re darasan pyaase nain: Asha Bhonsle (Chorus)
- Tasveeren banti hain, mere khayalon mein aaj
- Chandni ki palki mein: Asha Bhonsle
- Man sheetal naina: Geeta Roy (chorus)
No.: **Gramophone Co. of India Ltd. N50466-468**

Shahenshah
G. P. Productions
D: Amiya Chakrabarty
L: Sahir ludhianvi
C: Kamini Kaushal, Ranjan, Shakila, Agha, Cuckoo, Neeru

- Koi raag chhed, dabi aag chhed: Asha Bhonsle
- Naazonke pale, katon pe chale: Talat Mehmood
- Dil deke dil ko lele, kismat ke hai yeh mele: Geeta Roy
- Jaam tham le, sochte hi sochte na beete saari raat: Samsad Begum
- Chahat ka khazana hai tere liye, thokar mein zamana hai: Lata Mangeshkar
- Aayee baharen leke raaten pyar ki: Asha Bhonsle (chorus)
- Jeenewalonko jeete ji marne ka gham kyon ho: Lata Mangeshkar
- Khaak huwa dil jalte jalte: Lata Mangeshkar
- Shahi ki zanjeere todte chalo: Manna Dey (chorus)

No.: Gramophone Co. of India Ltd. N50521-23/N 50632-33

1954

Angarey
Akash Chitra
D: K. B. Lall
L: Sahir Ludhianvi
C: Nargis, Nasir khan, Vanmala, Paro, Jeevan

- Dhum dham tum tamu, naacho gaao mil jul kar tum: Lata Mangeshkar
- Gori ki nainon mein nindiya bhari: Kishore Kumar, Samsad Begum
- Tere saath chal rahe hain, yeh zamin yeh chand taare: Talat Mehmood, Lata Mangeshkar
- Pyar bhari dhadkanonke har leke aaoongi: Lata Mangeshkar
- Doob gaye aakash mein taare, jaake tum na aaye: Talat Mehmood
- Chup chup kyon hai bol zuban se: Asha Bhonsle (chorus)
- Oos basti ko jaane wale, leta jaa paigam mera: Lata Mangeshkar
- Roop ki raani aayi, pyar ki daulat layi, aao dilwalo lelo: Samsad Begum
- Ummid ki jholi mein kyon bhar diye angaare: Lata Mangeshkar
- Unhe khokar dukhe dil ki dua se aur kya maangoon: Lata Mangeshkar

No.: Gramophone Co. of India Ltd. N50666-69/N 50771

Chalis Baba Ek Chor
Kavyarts
D: P. L. Santhoshi
L: P. L. Santhoshi

C: Kamini Kaushal, Balraj, Smriti, Jagdeep, Om Prakash, David
- Aaj nahi kal: Samsad Begum
- Yeh duniya daulat ki gulam, is par bolo Totaram
- Bisvi sadi hai yeh bisvi sadi: Samsad Begum
- Yaaron ne baahen jo daale gale to dekhne wale jale: Lata Mangeshkar
- Teriya teriya totari do jaan ausne do: Lata Mangeshkar, Chitalkar
- Piya pyare kya man mein tumhare-mai janore
- Saajanva ho to saath, to bhali lagi yeh raat
- Kismat ne baag lagaaya hai, kuch phool bhi hain: Lata Mangeshkar
- Dil mein hai baat aisi kanon mein kahi jaaye: Kishore Kumar, Lata Mangeshkar
- To duniya basi basi jaaye, kaanon mein kahi jaaye
- Humein hunsta dekh: Lata Mangeshkar
- Doodhwala bhiyya: Samsad Begum (chorus)
- Ae meri guiyyan: Lata Mangeshkar (Chorus)

No.: Gramophone Co. of India Ltd. N50890

Radha Krishna
G. P. Productions
D: Raja Nene
L: Narendra Sharma, S.Athaiya, Sahir
C: Kamini Kaushal, Ratan Kumar, Agha
- Jhoom uthe nain mere dekh tujhe sanware: Lata Mangeshkar
- Aisi bansi bajaayee main to khogayi jadoogar tohe: Lata Mangeshkar (chorus)
- Raas rachaaoji, pran bachaaoji: Asha Bhonsle (chorus)
- Tum bansi ho mai taan, hum tum do nahin: Lata Mangeshkar, Geeta Roy
- Ek to manka dheeraj loote, dooje jiya jalaye: Lata Mangeshkar
- Akhiyan karkat hai ji, kinne mara abir gulal: Lata Mangeshkar (chorus)
- Suno sakhi kal chale jaayenge, Vrindavan se Kanhai
- Neel gagan mein maandal baaje....sakhiri aali: Asha Bhonsle (chorus)
- Raas rachaaogi pran: Lata Mangeshkar (chorus)

No.: Gramophone Co. of India Ltd. N50912-15

Taxi Driver
Navketan
D: Chetan Anand
L: Sahir Ludhianvi
C: Dev Anand, Kalpana Kartik, Johnny Walker, Sheila Ramani
- Jaayen to jaayen kahan, samjhega kaun yahan(Two parts): Talat Mehmood
- Dil se milake dil pyar kijiye, koi suhana iqrar kijiye: Lata Mangeshkar
- Jeene do aur jiyo, chadthi jawani ke din hain: Asha Bhonsle
- Dil jale to jale, gham pale to pale: Lata Mangeshkar
- Chahe koi khush ho chahe gaaliyaan hazaar de: Kishore Kumar, Johny Walker (chorus)
- Dekho maane nahin ruthi hasina na jaane kya baat hai: Asha Bhonsle, Jagmohan Bakshi
- Ai meri zindagi, aaj raat jhoomle, aasmanko choomle: Lata Mangeshkar
- Jaayen to jaayen kahan: Lata Mangeshkar

No.: Gramophone Co. of India Ltd. N50736/N 50783/N50830, HELP 3625

1955
Devdas
Bimal Roy productions
D: Bimal Roy
L: Sahir
C: Dilip Kumar, Suchitra Sen, Vyjayantimala, Nana Palsikar, Baby Naaz, Motilal
- Jise tu kubul karle, woh ada kahan se laaoon: Lata Mangeshkar
- Ab aage teri marzi, o mere saiyan bedardi: Lata Mangeshkar
- Kisko khabar thi, kisko yakeen tha, aise bhi din ayenge: Talat Mehmood
- Laagi re yeh kaisi anbujh aag, mitva nahin aaye: Talat Mehmood
- Albele panchhi tera door thikana hai: Asha Bhonsle, Usha Mangeshkar
- Aan aan milo shyam sanvare: Manna De, Geeta Roy
- Sajan ki hogayi gori......ab ghar ka aangan bidesh lagere: Manna De, Geeta Roy
- Aanewaale ruk ja koyi dam, rasta ghere hai, baahar lakhon gham: Lata Mangeshkar

List of Songs of S. D. Burman as Music Director (Hindi films) ♪ 259

- Manzil ki chahme raahike vaaste: Md. Rafi (chorus)
- Woh na aayenge palatkar, unhe laakh hum bulaaye: Mubarak Begum

No.: **Gramophone Co. of India Ltd.** N51704-06/N51712/N51716

House No. 44
Navketan
D: M. K. Burman
L: Sahir
C: Dev Anand, Kalpana Kartik, Kumkum, Zamboora, Sheela Vaz
- Teri duniya mein jeene se yeh behtar hai ke mar jaayen: Hemant Kumar
- Chup hai dharti chup hai chand sitare: Hemant Kumar
- Dam hai baaki to gham nahin: Asha Bhonsle
- Phaili huyi hai sapnonke baahen, aaja chal de kahin door: Lata Mangeshkar
- Bhole piya tumhe meri kasam kariyo na gham: Asha Bhonsle
- Peechhe peechhe aake, chhulo hume paake, chhup chhup jaana ho: Hemant Kumar, Lata Mangeshkar
- Oonche sur mein gaaye jaa, masti mein lehraye jaa: Kishore Kumar
- Dekh idhar o jaadugar, hume ghayal karke chala hai kaha: Asha Bhonsle

No.: **Gramophone Co. of India Ltd.** N51277-78/N 51358/N 51381

Madh Bhare Nain
Fortune Films
D: Hem Chunder
L: Shailendra
C: Bina Rai, Kishore Kumar, David, Yashodara Katju
- Pehli na doosri teesri pasand hai: Kishore Kumar
- Man panchhi albela taaronki nagari mein jaaye: Lata Mangeshkar
- Aa palkon mein aa sapne sajaa: Lata Mangeshkar
- Dekho mose saanchi kaho banwari: Lata Mangeshkar
- Leke jiya piya kahan jaavoge: Lata Mangeshkar
- Aaj ka din hai pyarka: Lata Mangeshkar (chorus)
- Diwane armaanon ke bheed mein ho zara bachke chalo meri santari: Kishore Kumar, Asha Bhonsle (chorus)

- Naye zamaane ka naya phaigaam sunane aaye hum: Asha Bhonsle (chorus)

No.: **Gramophone Co. of India Ltd. N51410-11/N51485-86.**

Munimji
Filmistan
D: Subodh Mukherji
L: Sahir, Shailendra
C: Dev Anand, Nalini Jayawant, Nirupa Roy, Ameeta, Pran
- Jeevan ke safar mein raahi milte hai bichhad janeko(two parts): Kishore Kumar
- Shivji bihane chali paalki sajay ke(two parts): Hemant Kumar (chorus)
- Pyar yeh nahin to aur kya hai: Lata Mangeshkar
- Ghayal hiraniya mein ban ban doloon: Lata Mangeshkar
- Ek nazar bas ek nazar, jaane tamanna dekh idhar: Lata Mangeshkar
- Dilki umange hai jawaan, rang mein dooba hai samaan: Hemant Kumar, Geeta Roy, Thakur
- Tum abhi the yahaan, tum abhi the yahaan
- Sajan bin neend aawe, kaise kahun main: Lata Mangeshkar
- Zindagi hai zinda: Geeta Roy (chorus)
- De liya to le le dil: S. D. Burman, Geeta Roy
- Jeevan ke safar mein raahi: Lata Mangeshkar

No.: **Gramophone Co. of India Ltd. N51328/51364/N 51466-67**

Society
Film India Corporation
D: Shaheed Lateef
L: Sahir
C: Nimmi, Nasir Khan, Kumkum, Minoo Mamtaz, Johnny Walker
- Kahan ho tum, meri tanhaaiyaan awaz deti hai: Lata Mangeshkar
- Leharon mein jhoolun taaron ko chhoo loon: Asha Bhonsle
- Ab aa bhi jaa ki tera intezar kab se hai (two parts): Md. Rafi, S. Balbir (chorus)
- Rahem kabhi to farmaao maano meri laila: Md. Rafi, Geeta Roy
- Dil nahin to na sahi, sawan ki raat hai: Asha Bhonsle

- Samajh gaye hum to, woh kitna chhupaaye: Geeta Roy
- Sharmeeli nigaahen kehti hai, tum aaj kahin: Asha Bhonsle (chorus)
- Dil ka taraana gaale, soch na kar matwaale: Geeta Roy

No.: **Gramophone Co. of India Ltd.** N51584-87/N 51670

1956

Funtoosh
Navketan
D: Chetan Anand
L: Sahir
C: Dev Anand, Sheila Ramani, Kumkum
- Dukhi man mere, sun mere kehna: Kishore Kumar
- Phul genduva na maaro, dar jaavungi: Asha Bhonsle
- Jaani jeene mein kya hai, marne mein kya hai: Asha Bhonsle
- Woh dekhe to unki inayat, na dekhe to rona kya: Kishore Kumar, Asha Bhonsle
- Jiyo hume aaj koyi na hume chhediyo: Kishore Kumar, Asha Bhonsle
- Ai meri topi palat ke aa, na apne funtoosh ko sata: Kishore Kumar
- Pyar ne kitne sapne dekhe, aas ne kitne geet boone: Asha Bhonsle
- Dene wala jab bhi deta poora chhappad fad ke deta: Kishore Kumar

No.: **Gramophone Co. of India Ltd.** N51764-65/N 51879-51881/N 51992

1957

Miss India
Rawal Films
D: I. S. Johar
L: Rajendra Krishna
C: Nargis, Pradeep Kumar, Pran, Nishi, I.S.Johar, Minoo Mumtaz
- Gori zara mukhde se ghunghat uthaona: Asha Bhonsle (chorus)
- Mere sajna aaja re aaja, raat milan ki na jaare na ja: Lata Mangeshkar
- Thokar naseeb ki jo, khaakar bhi muskuraye: Manna Dey (chorus)
- Jaawun mai kahan, ye zamin ye jahan chhodke: Lata Mangshkar, Manna De
- Albelaa mai ek dilwala, bada hoon matwala: Asha Bhonsle

- Jaise ko taisa nehle pe dehla: Samsad Begum, Lata Mangeshkar
- Baade saba kuch to bata, kaise mera dil khogaya: Lata Mangeshkar
- Maalik ne haath kahe do do diye: Manna De, Asha Bhonsle (chorus)
- Badla zamana, babu badla zamana: Md. Rafi

No.: Gramophone Co. of India Ltd. N52114-17/ 52347

Nau Do Gyarah
Navketan
D: Vijay Anand
L: Majrooh Sultanpuri
C: Kalpana Kartik, Dev Anand, Shashikala, Helen
- Ankhon mein kya ji, rupahla badal: Kishore Kumar, Asha Bhonsle
- Hum hai raahi pyarke hum se kuch na boliye: Kishore Kumar
- Aaja panchhi akela hai, sojaa nindiya ki bela hai: Md. Rafi, Asha Bhonsle
- Seele zuban, aisa naho sub kuch kho na pade nadan: Geeta Roy
- Jaane jigar hai hai, dekho to idhar hai hai: Asha Bhonsle
- Kali ke roop mein, chali ho dhoop mein kahan: Md. Rafi, Asha Bhonsle
- Kya ho phir jo din rangeela ho: Asha Bhonsle, Geeta Roy
- Dhal ti jaaye chundariya hamaari ho raam: Asha Bhonsle

No.: Gramophone Co. of India Ltd. N52321-322/N 523571/HELP 3530 N 52410

Paying Guest
Filmistan
D: Subodh Mukherji
L: Majrooh
C: Dev Anand, Nutan, Shubha Khote, Yakub
- Mana janab ne pukara nahin: Kishore Kumar
- Chand phir nikla magar tum na aaye: Lata Mangeshkar
- A-ha-ha-ha-ha-o-ee-la: Geeta Roy
- Chhod do anchal zamana kya kahega: Kishore Kumar, Asha Bhonsle
- Chupke chupke: Lata Mangeshkar
- Hai hai hai nigahen, karde sharabi jise chaahe jise: Kishore Kumar

- Nigahen mastana, dekh sama hai suhanaa: Kishore Kumar, Asha Bhonsle

No.: Gramophone Co. of India Ltd. N52166-69, 45 NLP 1026

Pyaasa
Guru Dutt Films
D: Guru Dutt
L: Sahir
C: Guru Dutt, Mala Sinha, Waheeda Rehman, Johnny Walker, Kumkum
- Jaane woh kaise log the jinke pyar ko pyar mila: Hemant Kumar
- Jaane kya tune kahi, jaane kya maine suni: Geeta Roy
- Aaj sajan mohe ang lagalo, janam safal hojaye: Geeta Roy
- Yeh duniya agar mil bhi jaaye to kya hai(two parts): Md. Rafi
- Sar jo tera chakraaye, ya dil dooba jaaye: Md. Rafi
- Hum aapki ankhon mein, is dil ko basaa deto: Md. Rafi, Geeta Roy
- Jinhe naaz hai hind par woh kahan hai (two parts): Md. Rafi
- Rut phire par din hamare, phire na phire na phire naaa: Geeta Roy
- Peechhe peechhe duniya hai

No.: Gramophone Co. of India Ltd. N52206-10/N 52255 MOCE 4010

1958
Chalti Ka Naam Gaadi
K. S. Films
D: Satyen Bose
L: Majrooh
C: Ashok Kumar, Kishore Kumar, Madhubala, Anoop Kumar, Cuckoo, Helen
- Bajoo....baboo samjho ishare, horn pukaare, pum pum pum: Kishore Kumar, Manna Dey
- Ek ladki bheegi bhaagisi, soti raaton mein jaagi si: Kishore Kumar
- Haal kaisa hai janab ka, kya khayal hai apka: Kishore Kumar, Asha Bhonsle\
- Main sitaron ka tarana, mai baharon ka fasana: Kishore Kumar, Asha Bhonsle

- Hum tumhare hain zara ghar se nikal kar dekhlo: Asha Bhonsle, Sudha Malhotra
- In haathonse sab ki gaadi chal rahi hai , wah wah (not in movie): Kishore (chorus)
- Arre arre ruk jaavona ji , aisi kya jaldi: Asha Bhonsle
- Yaane yaane yaane pyar hogaya: Kishore (chorus)

No.: Gramophone Co. of India Ltd. N52763- 65/72

Kala Pani
Navketan
D: Raj Khosla
L: Majrooh
C: Dev Anand , Madhubala, Nalini Jayawant, Agha
- Nazar laagi raja tore bangle par: Asha Bhonsle
- Hum bekhudi mein tumko pukare chale gaye: Md. Rafi
- Dil lagake kadar gayi pyare, poochho na koyi: S.D.B., Asha Bhonsle
- Achchha ji mai haari chalo maan jaao na: Md.Rafi, Asha Bhonsle
- Dilwaale ab teri gali tak aa pahunchhe: Md. Rafi, Asha Bhonsle
- Jab naam-e-mohabbat: Asha Bhonsle

No.: Gramophone Co. of India Ltd. N52722- 23/89

Lajwanti
Deluxe Films
D: Narendra Suri
L: Majrooh
C: Nargis, Balraj Sahni, Baby Naaz, Sheela Kashmiri
- Koi aaya dhadkan kehti hai: Asha Bhonsle
- Gaa mere man gaa: Asha Bhonsle (chorus)
- Aaja chhaaye kaale badra: Geeta Dutt (Chorus)
- Chandaare chandaare chhupe rehna(two parts): Asha Bhonsle
- Kuchh din pehle ek taal mein kamal kunj ke andar: Asha Bhonsle (chorus)
- Chanda mama mere dwaar: Manna Dey, Asha Bhonsle (chorus)

No.: Gramophone Co. of India Ltd. N52748-49/86-87

Sitaron Se Aage
Narasu Studio
D: Satyen Bose
L: Majrooh
C: Ashok Kumar, Vyjayantimala, Johnny Walker, Shammi
- Sambhalke sambhalke yeh duniya hai nagar hoshiyaronka: Md. Rafi (chorus)
- Dil legaya gham de gaya.ek tuih sa sanam: Geeta Dutt (chorus)
- Aaj kal parson......bidesi piya aa jaana: Asha Bhonsle (chorus)
- Chanda ki chandni ka jaadoo, yeh raat yeh samaa: Asha Bhonsle
- Mehfil mein aaye woh aaj dheere se: Lata Mangeshkar
- Pag thumak chalat balkhaye, haye saiyyan kaise dharoon dheer: Lata Mangeshkar (chorus)
- Roye jiya, aan milo more piya (Two parts): Asha Bhonsle
- Aa khilte hai gul o mere bulbul: Lata Mangeshkar (chorus)
- Ho zara ruk jaa....aas lagaye baithe hai raahon mein kab se hum: Md. Rafi

No.: Gramophone Co. of India Ltd. N 74568-72

Solva Saal
Chandra Films
D: Raj Khosla
L: Majrooh
C: Dev Anand, Waheeda Rehman, Sheela Vaz, Kammo
- Yeh bhi koi ruthne ka mausam hai diwaane: Asha Bhonsle
- Hai apna dil to awaara, na jaane kis pe aayega(Two parts): Hemant Kumar
- Dekhoji mera haal, badal gayi chaal: Md. Rafi, Asha Bhonsle, Sudha Malhotra
- Nazar ki katari yeh kaisi chali: Asha Bhonsle
- Yehi to hai woh yehi to hai: Md. Rafi

No.: Gramophone Co. of India Ltd. N 52586/N 52573/ N 52704

1959

Insaan Jaag Utha
Shakti Films
D: Shakti Samanta
L: Shailendra
C: Madhubala, Sunil Dutt, Minoo Mamtaz, Nishi, Nazir Hussain
* Mehnatkash insaan jaag utha lo dharti ke bhag jage: Md. Rafi, Asha Bhonsle (chorus)
* Jaanu jaanure kahe khan ke hai tora kangna: Asha Bhonsle, Geeta Dutt
* Chand sa mukhda kyon sharmaaya: Md. Rafi, Asha Bhonsle
* Yeh chanda russka na yeh japaan ka: Md. Rafi (chorus)
* Baat bhadti gayee khel khel mein: Asha Bhonsle
* Bahaaronse nazaaronse, yeh dekho kya ishaaren hain: Asha Bhonsle (chorus)
* Ankhen chaar hote hote, hogaya pyar hote hote: Asha Bhonsle

No.: Gramophone Co. of India Ltd. N 52966-7, N 52997, N 53013

Kaagaz Ke Phool
Guru Dutt Films
D: Guru Dutt
L: Kaifi Azmi
C: Guru Dutt, Waheeda Rehman, Baby Naaz, Johnny Walker, Minoo Mumtaz
* Waqt ne kiya kya haseen sitam, tum rahe na tum: Geeta Dutt
* Ek do teen char aur paanch, chhe aur sath aath aur nau: Geeta Dutt (chorus)
* Dekhi zamaane ki yaari, bichhde sabhi baari baari (Two parts): Md. Rafi (chorus)
* San san san woh chali hawa: Md. Rafi, Asha Bhonsle (chorus)
* Haar kabhi jeet kabhi kahe ka rona re: Md. Rafi, Asha Bhonsle
* Hum tum jise kehte hain shaadi: Md. Rafi

No.: Gramophone Co. of India Ltd. N 52970-71/53116/53179.

Sujata
Bimal Roy Productions
D: Bimal Roy
L: Majrooh
C: Nutan, Sunil Dutt, Shashikala, Sulochana

- Sun mere bandhu re, sun mere mitwa: Sachin Dev Burman
- Jalte hain jiskeliye, teri ankhon ke diye: Talat Mehmood
- Bachpan ke din bhi kya din the: Asha Bhonsle, Geeta Dutt
- Kaali ghata chhaye mora jiya tarsaye: Asha Bhonsle
- Tum jiyo hazaron saal, saal ke din ho pachas hazaar: Asha Bhonsle (chorus)
- Nanhi kali sone chali hawa dhire aana: Geeta Dutt
- Andhe ne bhi sapne dekha kya hai zamana: Md. Rafi

No.: Gramophone Co. of India Ltd. N 52981-84.

1960
Apna Haath Jagannath
Deluxe Films
D: Mohan Sehgal
L: Kaifi Azmi
C: Kishore Kumar, Sayeeda Khan, Jagdev, Sabeeta Chatterjee, Nazeer Hussain, Leela Chitnis

- Permit permit permit, permit ke liye mar mit: Kishore Kumar
- Ghan shyam ghan shyam shyam shyam re (two parts): Asha Bhonsle (chorus)
- Chhayee ghata bijli kadki, chhalki sharab aag badhki: Asha Bhonsle, Kishore Kumar
- Apne haathon ko pehchan: Md. Rafi
- Dhole tu aaj apne dil ki sab daag dhole: Kishore Kumar (chorus)
- Tum jahan jahan hum wahan wahan: Kishore Kumar, Asha Bhonsle
- Zindagi useeki hai jo zindagi se khele: Kishore Kumar (chorus)
- Tujhe mili roshni mujhko andhera: Asha Bhonsle

No.: Gramophone Co. of India Ltd. N 53301-03/53354.

Bombai Ka Babu
Naya Films
D: Raj Khosla
L: Majrooh
C: Dev Anand, Suchitra Sen, Dhumal, Manohar Deepak, Nazeer Hussain, Rashid Khan
* Chal ri sajni ab kya soche: Mukesh (chorus)
* Tak dhum tak dhum baaje duniya tera dhol re: Manna Dey
* Dekh ne mein bhola hai dil ka salona: Asha Bhonsle (chorus)
* Deewana mastana huwa dil: Md. Rafi, Asha Bhonsle
* Aise mein kachhu kaha nahi jaaye: Asha Bhonsle (chorus)
* Saathi na koyi manzil: Md. Rafi
* Kaise man mein lehar uthe: Md. Rafi, Asha Bhonsle (chorus)

No.: Gramophone Co. of India Ltd. N 53181-82/53267/69/89

Bewaqoof
Johar Films
D: I. S. Johar
L: Majrooh
C: Kishore Kumar, Mala Sinha, Pran, Sabita Chatterjee, I.S.Johar, Helen
* Mubaarak ho mubaarak ho, kushiyonka yeh zamana: Asha Bhonsle (chorus)
* Zulfonki saaye mein aaram liye jaa: Kishore Kumar, Manna Dey (chorus)
* Dhadka dil dhak se, dekha hai jabse: Manna De, Asha Bhonsle (chorus)
* Sach sach sach, o dear sach, I love you very much: Kishore Kumar
* Tumhi piya chikaara hoon hoon hoon garsiya: Kishore Kumar, Asha Bhonsle
* Dekh idhar dekh tera dhyan kahan hai: Asha Bhonsle, Manna Dey
* Michael hai to cycle hai: Kishore Kumar, Asha Bhonsle, Manna Dey
* Dildaar ghamando waalon ka har teer: Manna De, Samsad Begum,
* Hum to hai tum par: Md. Rafi

No.: Gramophone Co. of India Ltd. N 53469-72/53695

Ek Ke Baad Ek
Raj Kala
D: Raj Rishi
L: Kaifi Azmi
C: Dev Anand, Sharda, Tarla, Prabhu
- Thumak thumak thumak hai chali hai tu kidhar: Md.Rafi
- Nazar milaayi to duniya se darna kyaa: Md. Rafi, Asha Bhonsle
- Na tel aur na baati na kaabu hawa par: Manna Dey (chorus)
- Chithi ladayi bhari re chhal chhallam chhal chhallam chhal: Md. Rafi
- Haath pasaare raste raste, sab ko sadaaye dete hain: Geeta Dutt, Sudha Malhotra
- Bataao kya karoongi main, jo gham ki raat aayegi: Md. Rafi, Geeta Dutt
- Pagli hawa dil ki lage: Asha Bhonsle

No.: Gramophone Co. of India Ltd. N 53208-9/53269/53406

Kala Bazar
Navketan
D: Vijay Anand
L: Shailendra
C: Dev Anand, Waheeda Rehman, Nanda, Leela Chitnis, Vijay Anand, Helen
- Teri dhoom har kahin, tujha yaar koyi nahin: Md. Rafi
- Khoya khoya chand khula aasman: Md. Rafi
- Rim jhim tarane leke aayi barsaat: Md. Rafi, Geeta Dutt
- Sach huye sapne tere, jhoom le o man mere: Asha Bhonsle
- Apni to har aah ek toofan hai: Md. Rafi
- Na mai dhan chaahoon na ratan chaahoon: Geeta Dutt, Sudha Malhotra
- Sanjhi dhali dil ki lagi thak chali pukaar ke: Manna De, Asha Bhonsle
- Sambhalo sambhalo apna dil dilwaalo: Asha Bhonsle

No.: Gramophone Co. of India Ltd. N 53190-91/53271-72/53405

Manzil
Kalpana Pictures
D: Mandi Burman

L: Majrooh
C: Dev Anand, Nutan, Mehmood, David, Sheela Vaz
* Yaad aa gayee woh nasheeli nigaahen (Two parts): Hemant Kumar
* Dil to hai deewana na, maanega bahaana na: Md. Rafi, Asha Bhonsle
* Ab kise pata kal ho kya, dil hi diya to chahe jo ho: Manna Dey (chorus)
* Chupke se mile pyaase pyaase kuchh hum kuchh tum: Md. Rafi, Geeta Dutt
* Ai kaash chalte chalte, rangeen raahe milte: Manna De, Asha Bhonsle
* Hum dam se gaye, hum dam keliye, hum dam ki kasam, humdam na mila: Manna Dey
* Banao batiyan hato kaahe ko jhooti: Manna De
No.: Gramophone Co. of India Ltd. N 53223-24/53299-300

Miya Bibi Razi
Anupam Chitra
D: Jyoti Swaroop
L: Shailendra
C: Kamini kadam, Shrikant Gaurab, Seema, Mehmood
* Tune leliya hai dil ab kya hoga: Md. Rafi, Geeta Dutt
* Khuli ankh magar khwaab hai wohi ka wohi: Suman Kalyanpur
* Chhodo chhodo mori baiyyan sanvare: Suman Kalyanpur
* Mai hoon bhola byopari, laaya hoon cheeze pyari: Md. Rafi
* Sun meri sajni re: Md. Rafi, Mehmood, Suman Kalyanpur
* Piya bin nahi: Mahendra Kapoor, Asha Bhonsle
* Paani hote doob ... ho raja: Md. Rafi, Kamala Sista (chorus)
No.: Gramophone Co. of India Ltd. N 53448-450/53463

1962

Baat Ek Raat Ki
Alankar Chitra
D: Shankar Mukherji
L: Majrooh
C: Dev Anand, Waheeda Rehman, Chandra Shekhar, Sabita Chatterjee, Johnny Walker

- Akela hun mai is duniyaa mein: Md. Rafi
- Na tum hume jaano na hum tumhe jaane (Two parts): Hemant Kumar, Suman Kalyanpur
- Jo hai diwaane pyar ke re, sada chale talwaar pe re: Md. Rafi, Asha Bhonsle (chorus)
- Sheeshe ka ho ya pathhar ka dil: Suman Kalyanpur
- Aaj ka din bhi pheeka pheeka: Md. Rafi, Asha Bhonsle
- Jo ijaazat ho to ek baat kahoon, suno suno jaaneman: Md. Rafi, Asha Bhonsle
- Kisne chilmanse maara: Manna De

No.: Gramophone Co. of India Ltd. N 54055-56/54133

Dr Vidya

Deluxe Films
D: Rajendra Bhatia
L: Majrooh
C: Vyjayantimala, Manoj Kumar, Helen, Mumtaz

- Pawan diwani na maani, udave mora ghunghta: Lata Mangeshkar
- Yahi din hain bhanwre man arre tum nahi samajhte: Lata Mangeshkar
- Khanke kangna bindiya hanse, aayenge sajna: Lata Mangeshkar
- Pappa jamarillo, papa: Asha Bhonsle, Geeta Dutt (chorus)
- Jaani tum to dole daga daike: Lata Mangeshkar
- Ai dile awaara chal, phir wohi dubaara chal: Mukesh
- Maine kya kya na kiya, bewafa tereliye: Md. Rafi, Asha Bhonsle
- Bhigi bhigi aankh pe: Mukesh
- Hum ko hai yeh darr…ghabra tumse: Md. Rafi, Lata Mangeshkar
- Main kal phir miloongi: Lata Mangeshkar

No.: Gramophone Co. of India Ltd. N 54057-58

Naughty Boy

Shakti Films
D: Shakti Samanta
L: Shailendra
C: Kishore Kumar, Kalpana, Om prakash

- Hai hai woh matwaali adaa, mera dil fisalgaya: Kishore Kumar

- Nazren milake jo duniyan ki nazronse dare: Kishore Kumar
- Sa sa sa sare, ga ga ga re, taar dilonki ab jod do: Kishore Kumar, Asha Bhonsle
- Jahan bhi gaye hum, o mere humdam: Kishore Kumar, Asha Bhonsle
- Ab to batla arre zalim meri kismat mein kya hai: Kishore Kumar, Asha Bhonsle
- Rang yeh duniya badalti hai badal ja pyaare: Kishore Kumar (chorus)
- Tum mere pehchane phir bhi ho anjaane: Asha Bhonsle
- Ho gayee sham dil badnaam, leta jai tera naam: Manna De, Asha Bhonsle

No.: **Gramophone Co. of India Ltd. N 53784-85**

1963
Bandini
Bimal Roy productions
D: Bimal Roy
L: Shailendra, Gulzar
C: Ashok Kumar, Nutan, Dharmendra, Bela Bose
- Ore majhi.....mere sajan hai us paar: Sachin Dev Burman
- Mat ro maata lal tere bahu tere: Manna De
- Ab ke baras bhej bhaiyya ko babul: Asha Bhonsle
- Jogi jab se tu aaya mere dwaare, mere rang gaye: Lata Mangeshkar
- Mora gora ang laile, mohe sham rang daide: Lata Mangeshkar
- Jaanewaale ho sake to laut ke aana: Mukesh
- Panchi pyaare , sanjh sakaare bole tu kaun si boli: Asha Bhonsle

No.: **Gramophone Co. of India Ltd. N 54136-38/54232**

Meri Surat Teri Ankhen
Gee Pee Films
D: R. K. Rakhan
L: Shailendra
C: Ashok Kumar, Asha Parekh, Pradeep Kumar, Paro
- Poochho na kaise maine rain bitaayee (two parts): Manna De
- Ye kisne geet cheda, dil mera nache thirak thirak: Mukesh, Suman Kalyanpur

- Tere bin soone nayan hamaare: Md. Rafi, Lata Mangeshkar
- Tere khayalon mein, tere hi khwabon mein: Lata Mangeshkar
- Tujhse nazar malaane mein: Asha Bhonsle
- Nache man mora magan dhik ta dheegi dheegi: Md. Rafi

No.: Gramophone Co. of India Ltd. N 54130-32

Tere Ghar Ke Samne
Navketan
D: Vijay Anand
L: Hazrat Jaipuri
C: Dev Anand, Nutan, Rashid Khan, Nazir Hussain, Harindranath Chattopadhyay
- Dil ka bhanwar kare pukar, pyar ka raag suno: Md. Rafi
- Tere ghar ke samne, ik ghar banaawunga: Md. Rafi, Lata Mangeshkar
- Dekho rootha na karo, baat nazronki suno: Md. Rafi, Lata Mangeshkar
- Tu kahan yeh bataa is nashili raat mein: Md. Rafi
- Yeh tanhai hai re hai jaane phir aaye na aaye: Lata Mangeshkar
- Dil ki manzil kuch aisi hi manzil: Asha Bhonsle (chorus)
- Sun le tu dil ki sadaa, pyar se pyar sajaa(two parts): Md. Rafi

No.: Gramophone Co. of India Ltd. N 54147-50

1964
Benazir
Bimal Roy Productions
D: S. Khalil
L: Shakeel Badayuni
C: Ashok Kumar, Meena Kumari, Shashi Kapoor, Tanuja
- Alvida jaane wafa, meri manzil aagayi: Lata Mangeshkar
- Baharon ki mehfil suhani rahegi: Lata Mangeshkar
- Dil mein ik jane tamanna ne jagah paayi hai: Md. Rafi
- Husn ki bahaare liye aaye the sanam: Lata Mangeshkar
- Mil jaare jaane jaana, mil jaa: Lata Mangeshkar
- Matwala hai woh dil, isko kisike pyar hogaye: Lata Mangeshkar
- Ya gafoorahim ya allah, ek paresan dilki: Lata Mangeshkar, Asha Bhonsle, Usha Mangeshkar

- Gham nahin gar zindagi veeran hai: Asha Bhonsle
- Mubarak ho......taiyyar ho jaaye: Lata Mangeshkar
No.: Gramophone Co. of India Ltd. N 54571-73

Kaise Kahun
Brindavan Pictures
D: Atmaram
L: Shakeel Badayuni
C: Nanda, Biswajeet, Rehman, Naaz, Om Prakash
- Man mohan man mein ho tumhi: Md. Rafi, Suman Kalyanpur, Batish
- Kaise kahun kaise kahun, tose jiyaki mein batiyan: Lata Mangeshkar
- Zindagi tu jhum le zara: Md. Rafi
- Hole hole jiya dole sapnonki ban mein papiha: Lata Mangeshkar
- Kisiki mohabbat mein sab kuch bhulake: Md. Rafi, Asha Bhonsle
- Tum hame pyar karo ya na karo, hum tumhe pyar: Lata Mangeshkar
- Dil ka dard nirala, kisko sunavun koyi nahi hai: Md. Rafi
No.: Gramophone Co. of India Ltd. N 54465-67/54496

Ziddi
Pramod films
D: Pramod Chakravarty
L: Hazrat Jaipuri
C: Joy Mukhrjee, Asha Parekh, Nazima, Mehmood, Shubha Khote
- Teri surat se nahin milti kisiki surat: Md. Rafi
- Jaanu kya mera dil ab kahan khogaya: Md. Rafi
- Pyar ki aag mein tan badan jalgaya: Manna De
- Raat ka sama jhoome chandrama, tan mora naachere: Lata Mangeshkar
- Ai meri zindagi ek pagal hawa, aaj idhar kal udhar: Lata Mangeshkar
- Mai tere pyar mein kya kya bana dilbar: Manna De, Geeta Dutt
- Pyar ki manzil mast safar tum ho hasin hum hain jawan (two parts): Md. Rafi
- Champakali dekho jhuk hi gayeere: Md. Rafi, Asha Bhonsle
No.: Gramophone Co. of India Ltd. N 54342-45

1965

Guide
Navketan International
D: Vijay Anand
L: Shailendra
C: Dev Anand, Waheeda Rehman, Kishore Sahu, Anwar Hussain, Leela Chitnis
- Wahan kaun hai tera musafir jayega kahan: Sachin Dev Burman
- Megh de paani de chhaya de tu rama megh de: Sachin Dev Burman
- Kya se kya hogaya bewafa tere pyar mein: Md. Rafi
- Din dhal jaaye haaye raat na jaaye: Md. Rafi
- Piya tose naina laagere (two parts): Lata Mangeshkar
- Jai rama jai radhe shyam: Manna De
- Gaata rahe mera dil tu hi meri manzil: Kishore Kumar, Lata Mangeshkar
- Aaj phir jeene ki tamanna hai: Lata Mangeshkar
- Tere mere sapne ab ek rang hai: Md. Rafi
- Mose chhal kiye jaaye, saiyyan beiman: Lata Mangeshkar

No.: Gramophone Co. of India Ltd. N 54948-51/55304

Teen Deviyan
Nalanda
D: Amarjeet
L: Majrooh
C: Dev Anand, Nanda, Kalpana, Simi, I. S.Johar
- Arre yaar meri tum bhi ho gazab: Kishore Kumar, Asha Bhonsle
- Likha hai teri ankhon mein kiska afsana: Kishore Kumar, Lata Mangeshkar
- Uf kitni thandi hai yeh raat: Kishore Kumar, Lata Mangeshkar
- Khwab ho tum ya koyi haqeeqat, kaun ho yum batlaao: Kishore Kumar (chorus)
- Aise to na dekho, ki humko nasha ho jaaye: Md. Rafi
- Kahin bekhayal hokar, yoohin chhuliya kisine: Md. Rafi

No.: Gramophone Co. of India Ltd. N 54851-54

1967
Jewel Thief
Navketan
D: Vijay Anand
L: Majrooh, Shailendra
C: Dev Anand, Ashok Kumar, Vyjayantimala, Tanuja, Helen, Fariyal, Anju Mahendru
* Yeh dil na hota bechara, kadam na hote aawara: Kishore Kumar
* Dil pukaare aare aare aare, abhi na ja mere saathi: Md. Rafi, Lata Mangeshkar
* Raat akeli hai, bujh gaye diye: Asha Bhonsle
* Rulake gaya sapna mera, baithi hun kab ho savera: Lata Mangeshkar
* Hothon mein aisi baat main dabake chali aayee: Lata Mangeshkar, Bhupinder (chorus)
* Baithe hai kya uske paas: Asha Bhonsle
* Aasman ke neeche, hum aaj apne peechhe: Kishore Kumar, Lata Mangeshkar

No.: Gramophone Co. of India Ltd. N 55529-32

1969
Aradhana
Shakti Films
D: Shakti Samanta
L: Anand Bakshi
C: Rajesh Khanna, Sharmila Tagore, Ashok Kumar, Farida Jalal, PahariSanyal, Suraj Kumar, Master Puran
* Kaahe ko roye, chahe jo hoye, safal hogi teri aradhana: Sachin Dev Burman
* Mere sapnonki rani kab ayegi tu: Kishore Kumar
* Gun gunarahe hai bhaware khil rahi hai kali kali: Md. Rafi, Asha Bhonsle
* Roop tera mastana pyar mera deewana: Kishore Kumar
* Kora kagaz tha yeh man mera: Kishore Kumar, Lata Mangeshkar
* Bagon mein bahar hai, kaliyon pe nikhar hai: Md. Rafi, Lata Mangeshkar

- Chanda hai tu mera suraj hai tu: Lata Mangeshkar
No.: Gramophone Co. of India Ltd. LP 3AEX5248

Jyoti
Chitramitra
D: Dulal Guha
L: Anand Bakshi
C: Sanjeev Kumar, Nivedita, Master Suraj, Aruna Irani
- Soch ke ye gagan jhume, abhi chand nikal ayega: Manna De, Lata Mangeshkar
- Pag mein ghungru chhanke main naachu meera banke: Hemlata
- Mere shyam mere nandlala saare jagat ka rakhwala: Lata Mangeshkar, Usha Mangeshkar
- Munne mere aa main tujhe pariyonki baaten sunaawun: Lata Mangeshkar
- Ankh mere galti se lad gayi: Kishore Kumar

No.: Gramophone Co. of India Ltd. EP-TAE 1547

Talash
Ralhan Productions
D: O. P. Ralhan
L: Majrooh
C: Rajendra Kumar, Sharmila Tagore, Balraj Sahni, O.P.Ralhan, Helen, Shahu Modak
- Meri duniya hai maa tere anchal mein: Sachin Dev Burman
- Palkonki peechhe se kya tumne kehdala: Md. Rafi, Lata Mangeshkar
- Khayi hai re humne kasam sang rehne ki: Lata Mangeshkar
- Aaj ko jhunli raatma dharti par hai aasman: Md. Rafi, Lata Mangeshkar, Rahul Dev Burman (chorus)
- Karle pyar karle ke din hai yehi: Asha Bhonsle
- Kitni akeli kitni tanha si lagi unse milke main aaj: Lata Mangeshkar
- Tere naina talash karen jise woh hai tujhi mein kahin: Manna De
- Mera kya sanam meri khushi hai tumhari: Asha Bhonsle, Mahendra Kapoor

No.: Gramophone Co. of India Ltd. LP 3 AEX 5235

1970

Ishq Par Zor Nahin
Twinkle Star Productions
D: Ramesh Saigal
L: Anand Bakshi
C: Sadhana, Dharmendra, Biswajeet, Madhumati, Uday Chandrika
- Mehbooba teri tasweer kis tarah mai banawun: Md. Rafi
- Yeh dil deewana hai, dil to deewana hai: Md. Rafi, Lata Mangeshkar
- Maane koyi chaahe na maane, jaane koi chaahe na jaane: Manna Dey
- Sach kehti hai duniya ishaq pe zor nahin: Lata Mangeshkar
- Mere bairagi bhanwara mujhe tadpaona: Lata Mangeshkar
- Main to tere rangrati mere mitwa mere saathi: Lata Mangeshkar
- Tum mujhse dur chale janana, mai tumse dur chali jaawungi: Lata Mangeshkar
- Pyar bhari ek baat chali armanonki barat chali: Asha Bhonsle

No.: Gramophone Co. of India Ltd. LP 3 AEX 5254

Prem Pujari
Navketan International
D: Dev Anand
L: Neeraj
C: Dev Anand, Waheeda Rehman, Zaheeda
- Prem ke pujari hum hain ras ke bhikari: Sachin Dev Burman
- Shokhiyon mein ghola jaye phoolon ka shabab: Kishore Kumar, Lata Mangeshkar
- Taqat watan ki tumse hai himmat watan ki tumse hai: Md. Rafi, Manna Dey (chorus)
- Doongi tenu reshmi rumal o banke zara dere aana: Lata Mangeshkar (chorus)
- Phoolon ki rang se dil ki kalam se: Kishore Kumar
- Rangeela re tere rang mein yun ranga hai: Lata Mangeshkar
- Gham pe dhool dalo: Kishore Kumar, Bhupinder

No.: Gramophone Co. of India Ltd. LP 3 AEX 5244

1971

Gambler
Amarjeet
D: Amarjeet
L: Neeraj
C: Dev Anand, Zaheeda, Zahirra, Jeevan, Shatrughan Sinha
* Mera man tera pyaasa, poori kab hogi asha: Md. Rafi
* Apni hotonki bansi banale mujhe: Kishore Kumar, Lata Mangeshkar
* Choodi nahi mera dil hai dekho dekho tutena: Kishore Kumar
* Kaisa hai mera dil tu khiladi: Kishore Kumar
* Dil aaj shayar hai gham tera nagma hai: Kishore Kumar
No.: **Polydor /LP 2392008**

Naya Zamana
Pramod films
D: Pramod Chakravarty
L: Anand Bakshi
C: Dharmendra, Hema Malini, Aruna Irani, Mehmood, Pran
* Koi ilzam lagaye, apne to ilzam lagaye kahiye kuchh aur: Lata Mangeshkar
* Wahre naujawan aaj kal ke: Kishore Kumar
* Kitne din ankhen tarsenge ik din to badal barsenge: Lata Mangeshkar
* Aya mai laya chalta phirta hotel: Manna De, Mehmood
* Rama rama gazab huyi gaware: Lata Mangeshkar
* Duniya O duniya tera jawab nahin: Kishore Kumar
* Das gayi .....rain kajarari.....main haari: Lata Mangeshkar
No.: **Gramophone Co. of India Ltd. LP MOCE 4028**

Sharmeelee
Subodh Mukherjee Productions
D: Samir Ganguly
L: Neeraj
C: Shashi Kapoor, Rakhee, Jayashree T., Narendranath
* Khilte hain gul yahan, khilke bikharne ko (Two parts): Kishore Kumar
* Meri o meri o meri sharmilee, ao na tarasao na: Kishore Kumar

- Megha chhaye aadhi raat, bairan ban gayi nindiya: Lata Mangeshkar
- Aaj madhosh huwa jaayere, mera man, mera man, mera man: Kishore Kumar, Lata Mangeshkar
- Kaise kahe hum pyarne humko kya kya khel dikhaye: Kishore Kumar
- Reshmi ujala hai, makhmali andhera: Asha Bhonsle
- Khilte hain gul yahan, khilke bikharne ko: Lata Mangeshkar

No.: Gramophone Co. of India Ltd. LP MOCE 4041

Tere Mere Sapne
Navketan Enterprises
D: Vijay Anand
L: Neeraj
C: Dev Anand, Mumtaz, Vijay Anand, Hema Malini, Jayashree T

- Ud chala hawavonke sang sang dil jaane kidhar: Asha Bhonsle
- Mera sajan phool kamalka, kali main raat raniki: Asha Bhonsle
- Jaise raadha ne maala japi shyam ki maine odhi chunariya tere naam ki: Lata Mangeshkar
- Hey maine kasam lee, hai tune kasam lee nahi honge juda hum: Kishore Kumar, Lata Mangeshkar
- Jeevanki bagiyan mehkegi, lehkegi chehkegi: Kishore Kumar, Lata Mangeshkar
- Ta thai tatathai atathai thai thak, thirke pag jiya gaaye jaaye hai: Asha Bhonsle
- Mera antar ek mandir hai tera hai tera: Lata Mangeshkar
- Andhi praja andha raja.....zamana dhat tere ki (Two parts): Manna Dey (chorus)

No.: Polydor /LP 2392009

1972

Anuraag
Shakti Films
D: Shakti Samanta
L: Anand Bakshi
C: Ashok Kumar, Vinod Mehra, Moushumi Chatterjee, Nutan, Rajesh Khanna, Master Satyajeet

List of Songs of S. D. Burman as Music Director (Hindi films) ♪ **281**

- Mera raja beta boojhe ek paheli: Lata Mangeshkar
- Sunri pawan pawan puruvaiyya: Lata Mangeshkar
- Neend churaye, chain churaye, daaka daale, teri bansi: Lata Mangeshkar
- Tere nainonke main deep jalaawunga: Md. Rafi, Lata Mangeshkar
- Raam kare, babuwa hamaar, phulwako hamri umar lag jaaye: Kishore Kumar

Yeh Gulistan Hamara
Guru Dutt Films Combines
D: Atmaram
L: Anand Bakshi
C: Dev Anand, Sharmila Tagore, Jayashree T., Johnny Walker, Pran
- Kya yeh zindagi hai, kaisi bebasi hai: Lata Mangeshkar (chorus)
- Suno meri baat, chalo mere saath: Kishore Kumar (chorus)
- Mera naam aao, mere paas aao: Lata Mangeshkar, Danny
- Gori gori gaav ki gorire: Kishore Kumar, Lata Mangeshkar
- Raina soyi soyi naina jaage jaage: Lata Mangeshkar, Sachin Dev Burman, Rahul Dev Burman (chorus)
- Tushima re tushima: Lata Mangeshkar
- Saare jahan se achha: Sushma Sreshtha (chorus)

Zindagi Zindagi
Jan Pictures
D: Tapan Sinha
L: Anand Bakshi
C: Ashok Kumar, Sunil Dutt, Waheeda Rehman, Deb Mukhrjee, Farida Jalal
- Zindagi ai zindagi, tere hai do roop: Sachin Dev Burman
- Mera sub kuchh mere geet re, geet bina kaun mera meet re: Manna De
- Khush raho saathiyon, tumhe chhodkar hum chale: Kishore Kumar
- Kaun sachcha hai aur kaun jhoota hai.....phir apna vote do: Manna De
- Teri jaat kya hai, O meri jaat kya hai: Kishore Kumar
- Piya tune kya kiyare.....tere bin laage na jiya: Sachin Dev Burman

- Tune hume kya diyaare zindagi: Kishore Kumar
No.: Gramophone Co. of India Ltd. LP MOCE 4134

1973
Abhimaan
Amiya
D: Hrishikesh Mukherjee
L: Majrooh
C: Amitabh Bachchan, Jaya Bhaduri, Asrani, Bindu
- Meet na milare manka: Kishore Kumar
- Nadiya kinare herai aayi kangna: Lata Mangeshkar
- Teri bindiyare hai hai teri bindiyare: Md. Rafi, Lata Mangeshkar
- Lute koi man ka nagar, ban ke mera aa saathi: Kishore Kumar, Lata Mangeshkar
- Ab to hai tumse har khushi apni: Lata Mangeshkar
- Piya bina, piya bina piya bina basiya: Lata Mangeshkar
- Tere mere milan ki yeh raina: Kishore Kumar, Lata Mangeshkar
No.: Gramophone Co. of India Ltd. LPD MOCE 4183

Chhupa Rustam
Navketan Enterprises
D: Vijay Anand
L: Neeraj, Vijay Anand
C: Dev Anand, Hema Malini, Vijay Anand, Bindu, PremNath
- Hum chhupe rustam hai (two parts): Manna Dey (chorus)
- Dheere se jaana khatiyan mein o khatmal: Kishore Kumar
- Jo mai hota ek toota tara teri raatonka ...to kya hota: Kishore Kumar, Asha Bhonsle
- Bolo kya hum ko doge: Kishore Kumar, Asha Bhonsle
- Mar jaawun sharmaake ooyi, main hoon chuee- muee: Asha Bhonsle
- Jala mera aashiyan, hai mai kya karoon: Lata Mangeshkar
- Jaanu mai jale mera dil ....dikhe na dhuwan dikhe na agan: Asha Bhonsle
No.: Gramophone Co. of India Ltd. LPD MOCE 4175

Jugnu
Pramod Films
D: Pramod Chakravarty
L: Anand Bakshi
C: Dharmendra, Hema Malini, Jayashree T., Mehmood
- Chhote chhote nanhe munhe pyare pyare re: Kishore Kumar, Sushma Shreshta (chorus)
- Tera peechha na main chhodunga soniye: Kishore Kumar
- Jaane kya pilaya tune bada maza aaya: Lata Mangeshkar
- Meri payaliya geet tere gaaye: Lata Mangeshkar
- Gir gaya jhumka girne do: Kishore Kumar, Lata Mangeshkar
- Jab baagon mein jugnu chamke aadhi raatko: Lata Mangeshkar

No.: **Gramophone Co. of India Ltd. LPD MOCE 4179**

Phagun
Dachi films
D: Rajendar Singh Bedi
L: Majrooh
C: Waheeda Rehman, Dharmendra, Jaya Bhaduri, Vijay Arora
- Piya sang khelo holi phagun aayore: Lata Mangeshkar (chorus)
- Kab maane o dil ke mastane, samjhane ko aaye: Kishore Kumar, Asha Bhonsle
- Sandhya jo aaye, man ud jaaye: Lata Mangeshkar
- Mero to giridhar gopal doosro na koyi: Lata Mangeshkar, Usha Mangeshkar
- Phir raat huyi ek baat huyi chori chori mulaqat huyi: Kishore Kumar, R. S. Bedi, Pankaj Mitra, Sunil Kumar
- Bedardi ban gaya koyi jaavo manaavo more saiyyan: Sobha Gurtu

No.: **Gramophone Co. of India Ltd. LPD 33 ESX 4191**

1974

Prem Nagar
Vijaya & Suresh Combines
D: K. S. Prakash Rao
L: Anand Bakshi, Fani Badayuni

C: Rajesh Khanna, Hema Malini, Asrani, Aruna Irani, Prem Chopra, Meena T., Kamini Kaushal
- Hun, ek muamma hai, samjhneka: Kishore Kumar
- Bye bye Miss goodnight, kal phir milenge: Kishore Kumar (chorus)
- Pyaase do badan, pyaasi raat mein: Asha Bhonsle
- Yeh kaisa sur mandir hai, jis mein sangeet nahin: Lata Mangeshkar
- Thandi hawavone gori ka ghunghat uthadiya: Kishore Kumar, Asha Bhonsle (chorus)
- Kiska mehal hai kiska yeh ghar hai: Kishore Kumar, Lata Mangeshkar
- Yeh lal rang kab mujhe chhodega: Kishore Kumar
- Ja...ja ..ja mujhe na ab yaad aa: Kishore Kumar

No.: **Gramophone Co. of India Ltd. LPD MOCE 14004**

Sagina
Rupa-Sree International
D: Tapan Sinha
L: Majrooh
C: Dilip Kumar, Saira Banu, Om Prakash, Aparna Sen, Anil Chatterjee
- Aag lagi hamri jopadiyaamein hum gawen malhar: Kishore Kumar, Dilip Kumar
- Tumhare sangto rain bitaayi kahan bitaawun din: Kishore Kumar, Lata Mangeshkar
- Gazab chamkai bindiya tori aadhi raat: Kishore Kumar, Asha Bhonsle (chorus)
- Sala mai to sahab bangaya: Kishore Kumar, Pankaj Mitra
- Chhote chhote sapne hamaar, chhoti asha chhota pyar: Sachin Dev Burman

No.: **Gramophone Co. of India Ltd. EP 7EPE 7052**

Us Paar
Cineye Films
D: Basu Chatterjee
L: Yogesh
C: Vinod Mehra, Moushumi Chatterjee, Padma Khanna
- Pyara hindola mera, udan khatola mera: Asha Bhonsle

List of Songs of S. D. Burman as Music Director (Hindi films) ♪ **285**

- Yeh jabse huyi jiyaki chori, patang sa ude: Lata Mangeshkar
- Tumne piya diya sub kucch mujhko apni preet daike: Lata Mangeshkar
- Ai mere man main hoon magan, unse milan ki shyam: Md. Rafi
- Piya maine kya kiya mujhe chhod ke jaiyonaa: Manna De

No.: Gramophone Co. of India Ltd. LPD EALP 4014

1975

Chupke Chupke
N. C. Sippy
D: Hrishikesh Mukherjee
L: Anand Bakshi
C: Dharmendra, Sharmila Tagore, Amitabh Bachchan, Jaya Bhaduri, Om Prakash

- Chupke chupke chalre purvaiya: Lata Mangeshkar
- Ab ke sajan sawan mein: Lata Mangeshkar
- Sa re ga ma, ma sa re ga: Kishore Kumar, Md. Rafi
- Baagonmein, kaise, yeh phool, khilte hain: Lata Mangeshkar, Mukesh

No.: Gramophone Co. of India Ltd. 7EPE 7152

Mili
N. C. Sippy
D: Hrishikesh Mukherjee
L: Yogesh
C: Amitabh Bachchan, Jaya Bhaduri, Ashok Kumar, Shobha Khote, Aruna Irani

- Badi sooni sooni hai zindagi ye zindagi: Kishore Kumar
- Maine kaha phoolonse haso to woh khil khilakar hasdiye: Lata Mangeshkar (chorus)
- Aye tum yaad mujhe gaane lagi har dhadkan: Kishore Kumar

No.: Gramophone Co. of India Ltd. 7EPE 7180

1976

Arjun Pandit
L. B. Films
D: Hrishikesh Mukherjee

L: Majrooh
C: Ashok Kumar, Sanjeev Kumar, Vinod Mehra, Srividya
* Dil mera uda jaaye, chalre hawa chal dhire: Kishore Kumar
* Bolo preetam kya boli thi main aage re: Lata Mangeshkar
* Baadalon mein vaadiyon mein: Lata Mangeshkar
No record was released.

Barood
Jugnu Enterprises
D: Pramod Chakravarty
L: Anand Bakshi
C: Ashok Kumar, Rishi Kapoor, Shoma Anand, Reena Roy, Shreeram Lagu, Master Rajoo
* I love you, you love me, lo mohobbat hogayee: Asha Bhonsle
* Matlab jo samjhe mere sandeshka: Kishore Kumar
* Samundar samundar yahan se wahan tak: Lata Mangeshkar
* Dil kaaton mein uljhaya hai: Lata Mangeshkar
* Tu shaitanonka sardar hai: Mukesh, Shivange Kolhapuri
No.: Polydor /LP 23920077

Deewangee
(One song was composed by S. D. Burman)
Subodh Mukherjee Productions
D: Samir Ganguly
L: Anand Bakshi
C: Shashi Kapoor, Zeenat Aman, Jr. Mehmood, Helen
* Chal sapnonke shahar mein tujhe le jaata hoon: Kishore Kumar
(The other five songs are set to music by Ravindra Jain)
Record No.: Gramophone Co. of India Ltd LP-ECLP 5452)

1977

Tyaag
Producer: Films and Films International
Director: Deendayal Sharma
Cast: Rajesh Khanna, Sharmila Tagore

Lyrics: Anand Bakshi
* Hum tum hai tum: Kishore Kumar, Lata Mangeshkar
* Man pukare din tere: Kishore Kumar, Lata Mangeshkar
* Kore Kagazpe likhwale: Kishore Kumar, Asha Bhonsle
* Tujhe pyas hai mere pas: Asha Bhonsle
* Sun pappu tujhe: Kishore Kumar, Sushma Shreshtha

No.: Polydor /LP 6405023.

1950-60

Saaz

Producer: Shaheen Pictures
Director: S. M. Nawab
Cast: Nasir Khan, Nigar, Arti Kamath, Yakub
Lyrics: Jan Nisa Akhtar
* Bole nau lakh meri juwani:
* Tarap rahe armaan:
* Mera ji ji aaji: Lata Mangeshkar (chorus)
* Jaagi dil me muhabbat: Md Rafi, Shamshad Begum
* Chali jaogi de kar:
* Bade majeki baat: Kishore Kumar, Geeta Roy
* O ho nadiya:

(The film was never released.)

This list has been prepared with details from 'S. D. Burman's Hindi film output', published in *Screen* dated 4 August 1978. I am grateful to Debashish Mukhopadhayay and Sanjoy Sengupta for providing me year-wise list of Hindi film songs where S. D. Burman acted as music director. This very list has given me an opportunity to make suitable corrections to the data submitted.

Acknowledgements

The author gratefully acknowledges the following for permission to reprint copyright material:

- *Abarjaner Jhuri*, Nabadwip Chandra Dev Burman (Tribal Cultural Research Institute and Collection Cell, Government of Tripura)
- 'A Case for Folk Music' S. D. Burman interviewed by Sankarlal Bhattacharya (Circa 19 March, 1972, Hindustan Standard magazine)
- *Amar Jeevan*, Madhu Bose.
- 'Ananya' by Shakti Samanta (*Aajkal*, Sunday, 25 September. 2005)
- Articles on S. D. Burman
  - Rajyashwar Mitra (Shrangadev)
  - Heeralal Sengupta
  - Narayan Chowdhuri
  - Rabin Sengupta
- 'Bachche To Bachche Baap Re Baap' by Anindya Chattopadhyay (*Anandalok*, 22 May, 2001)
- *Bhati Gung Baiya*, Shyamal Chakraborty (Akshar Publication, Tripura)
- 'Bhishan Ashambhabey' by Kabir Suman (*Aajkal*, Sunday, 25 September 2005)
- 'Dakhina Pawan' by Nabendu Ghosh (*Prantik Shahitya Patra*, July-August, 2006)

- 'Dev Anand on S. D. Burman' by Rajiv Vijayakar (November 2002, *Screen*, India)
- 'Ganer Goopan Putra' by Anindya Chattopadhyay (*Sananda*: Parbani yearly issue, 2006)
- *Gomati* (Cultural and Tourism Department, Government of Tripura, 1998, 2005)
- *Jeebaner Jalsaghare,* Manna Dey (Ananda Publishers, Kolkata)
- *Kathay Kathay Raat Hoye Jay*, Pulak Bandopadhyay (Ananda Publishers, Kolkata)
- Kumar Sachin Dev Burman Centenary Issue (*Prantik Sahitya Patra*, Jan-Feb, 2006)
- 'Maestro Who Was A Misfit' by Ajit Merchant (http://www.sdburman.net/website/Articles/Article_aMaestroWhoWasAMisfit.htm)
- 'My Days with Sachinda' Manna Dey interviewed by Satish Kalra (http://www.sdburman.net/mannadeys_interview.html)
- 'My God, That's My Tune' R. D. Burman interviewed by V. S. Gopalakrishnan and Meera Pandya. (*Filmfare*, June 16-30, 1984)
- *Ogo Mor Geetimoy,* Geetasri Sandhya Mukhopadhyay (Sahityam, Kolkata)
- Rahul Dev Burman: Prince of Music by Khagesh Dev Burman (Unpublished).
- *Rajmala Ba Tripurar Ithihas*, Kailash Chandra Singha (Akshar Publications, Tripura)
- 'Sachin Kantha' by Kalyanbandhu Bhattacharya (*Desh*, Binodan, 1385 issue)
- 'Sachin Kartar Sangsaare, Shwabhabe, Sangeete' by Sachin Bhowmick (*Anandalok*, Puja Issue, 1977)
- *Sachin Karta,* Pannalal Roy (Srimati Ratna Saha, Akhaura Road, Agartala, Tripura)
- *Sargamer Nikhad*, S. D. Burman (Published serially in Bengali weekly magazine *Desh* in 1970)
- *Shatabarsher Aalokey Sachin Karta* edited by Rabindra Debnath, Pratima Debnath, (Dharmanagar, Tripura)

Acknowledgements ♪ 291

- Sudha Sagar Teerey, Suresh Chakraborty (Ananda Publishers, Kolkata)
- 'Sachin Kartar Shangey' by Brajen Biswas (*Anandalok* 12 October, 2005)
- 'Some Choicest Flowers' by Raju Bharatan (http://www.sdburman.net/website/Articles/Article_SDBNavketanLPReview.htm)
- 'Ten of My Favourite S. D. Burman Songs' by Dusted Off (http://dustedoff.wordpress.com/2009/10/01/ten-of-my-favourite-s-d-burman-songs/)
- 'The Lata–S. D. Tuning—Meetha Paan' by Dr. Arunabha Roy (http://www.sdburman.net/LataSDB_MeethaPaan.html)
- 'The Soulful Burman' by Shubha Mudgal (http://www.livemint.com/Leisure/RhpK1XxKnZE7GMY0l5edbN/The-soulful-Burman.html) May 13, 2010.
- 'The Veteran Composer With a Magic Melody' by Dr S. C. Srinivasan (http://www.sdburman.net/website/Articles/Article Remembering SDBDr Channiga.htm)
- 'Tripurar Bharatbhukti O Chakla Roshanabad', Pannalal Roy (*Tripura Darpan*, Agartala, Tripura)
- 'Tumi je Giyachho Bakul Bichhano Pathe' by Manna Dey (*Anandalok*, 12 October, 2005)

While every effort has been made to trace copyright holders and obtain permission, this has not been possible in all cases; any omissions brought to our attention will be remedied in future editions.

Made in the USA
Monee, IL
03 May 2026